CASINO WOMEN

CASINO WOMEN

Courage in Unexpected Places

**Susan Chandler
and Jill B. Jones**

ILR PRESS, AN IMPRINT OF

CORNELL UNIVERSITY PRESS   ITHACA AND LONDON

First published 2011 by Cornell University Press
Printed in the United States of America

Library of Congress Cataloging-in-Publication Data

Chandler, Susan Kerr.
   Casino women : courage in unexpected places / Susan Chandler and Jill B. Jones.
     p. cm.
   Includes bibliographical references and index.
   ISBN 978-0-8014-5014-3 (cloth : alk. paper)
  1. Casinos—Nevada—Employees. 2. Gambling industry—Nevada—
Employees. 3. Women service industries workers—Nevada. 4. Employee rights—Nevada. I. Jones, Jill B. II. Title.

   HV6721.N45C43   2011
   331.4'8179509793—dc22   2011009589

Cornell University Press strives to use environmentally responsible suppliers and materials to the fullest extent possible in the publishing of its books. Such materials include vegetable-based, low-VOC inks and acid-free papers that are recycled, totally chlorine-free, or partly composed of nonwood fibers. For further information, visit our website at www.cornellpress.cornell.edu.

Cloth printing   10 9 8 7 6 5 4 3 2 1

*For Nevada's women casino workers
and their dreams of a better world*

Sólo le pido a Dios
Que el dolor no me sea indiferente,
Que la reseca muerte no me encuentre
Vacío y solo sin haber hecho lo suficiente.

I only ask of God
That he not let me be indifferent to the suffering,
And when death, that dusty time, comes
That I not be alone and empty, having not given my everything.

—León Gieco

Contents

Acknowledgments   xi

1. "You Have to Do It for the People Coming"   1

Part I   **BACK OF THE HOUSE, FRONT OF THE HOUSE**

2. "They're Treating Us Like Donkeys, Really":
Housekeeping and Other Back of the House Work   15

3. "Kiss My Foot": Cocktail Waitressing   29

Part II   **UNION WOMEN**

4. "I'll Always Love the Union"   47

5. "Here's My Heart"   61

Part III   **NONUNION WOMEN STAND UP**

6. Darlene *Jespersen v. Harrah's Entertainment, Inc.*   79

7. Liberation Theology, Pit Boss Style   97

Part IV   **DEALERS: THE ILLUSION OF POWER**

8. Dealing: The View from Dead Center   109

9. Stuck   125

10. Big Tobacco Rides the Strip   137

Part V   **WOMEN IN MANAGEMENT**

11. Crossing Over to the Other Side   157

12. Conclusion: "A Marvelous Victory"   170

Notes   179

Bibliography   201

Index   219

Acknowledgments

Casino Women has been a long time in the making and in consequence we have many thanks to extend. The first go out to the women casino workers themselves who with enormous grace let us into their worlds and in the process changed our lives. It is why we dedicated the book to them. We hope they are pleased with it. We want to mention in particular Tahis Castro and Ellie Hays, whose names do not appear anywhere in the book but whose examples of love and spirit stand at the very center of it. Thank you for believing in us and putting us in contact with so many casino women. (Because of Institutional Review Board constraints and sometimes a genuine threat to the women's livelihoods, we have not in most cases been able to use our informants' real names. Some will be relieved that their names are not in print; but many others, justly proud of their work on behalf of casino workers, would be proud to have been named.)

At the Culinary Union and Culinary Training Academy thanks particularly to present and former members and staff: Courtney Alexander, Bobbette Bonds, Mary Burns, Hattie Canty, Tahis Castro, Nicolasa de la Puente, Margarita Farmer, Grace Gatti, Carmen Hamilton, Wanda Henry, Jeanette Hill, Steven Horsford, Geoconda Arguello Kline, Scott McKenzie, Peggy Pierce, Mirna Preciado, D Taylor, and Pilar Weiss. At the Alliance for Workers Rights, thanks to Tom Stoneburner—much-loved and too-early-departed—and Kricket Martinez. At the Progressive Leadership Alliance of Nevada, we thank Bob Fulkerson, Jan Gilbert, Joe Edson, and Rosa Molina for their work on behalf of Nevada's low-income families and for their support of Susan's early work, *Working Hard, Living Poor: A Living Wage Study for Nevada,* which provided so much helpful context.

A long list of colleagues, scholars, activists, officials, students and others stepped in with valuable support during the years *Casino Women* was in the making. They include Rukaiyah Adams, Tony Badillo, Andrew Barbano, Dan Cook, Judy Cornelius, John Dobra, Ruby Duncan, Irene Fisher, Joanne Goodwin, Chuck Holt, Jim Kiernan, Cecilia Khan, Cassandra Little, Kit Miller, Marianne Miller, Maya Miller, Diane Nassir, Ruth Needleman, Cornelia Pillard, Richard Pillard, Tony Platt, Kate Price, Chris Pritsos, Paulina Raento, Katharine Robinson, Ann Stromquist, Shelton Stromquist, and Claytee White. Thanks, too, to Valerie Corson Rios for sharing a set of interviews she conducted with cocktail waitresses. A special thank you to Annelise Orleck, who models engaged narrative history in her wonderful book, *Storming Caesar's Palace,* and provided helpful commentary in *Casino Women's* last stages. Forgive us if we have forgotten anyone. Of course, any errors are our own.

At the University of Nevada, Reno, thank you to colleagues who no doubt wondered if "the book" would ever appear, and in particular to Denise Montcalm, director of the School of Social Work; Charlie Bullock, former dean of the College of Human and Community Sciences; Candace Bortolin and Kim Truesdell; and our graduate assistants including Angela Bai, Elizabeth Dorway, Cecilia Khan, Heather Cabral, Matt Lauzon and Wendy Miley. To our many students, thanks for inspiring us. The university provided each of us with well-used sabbatical leaves and a Junior Faculty Development Grant. Thank you, too, to the Lois and Samuel J. Silberman Fund for early support of our research.

The idea for this book originated in a Nevada hot springs, and we especially want to thank the five faculty women who gathered there. Sustaining us over the years, they have been wonderful friends and capable desert campers. They include Catherine Smith and Alicia Smalley, who were so important at the beginning of *Casino Women* and sadly did not live to see its completion, Ellen Pillard, Valerie Cohen, and Deborah Achtenberg. Women friends have supported us throughout, no surprise given the nature of *Casino Women,* and in addition to the hot springs group, we thank Marie Boutte, Christiana Bratiotis, the early Thanksgiving crowd, Mary Hylton, Ann Stromquist, Stephanie Pace, and the Tecopah Obies (Susan's classmates from Oberlin's Class of '65).

A heartfelt thanks to Fran Benson, our editor at Cornell University Press, who took a chance on us and, with Kitty Liu, Candace Akins, and others, guided neophytes through the publication process.

Finally and most important, our families.

Jill B. Jones

Thanks to my parents, Grace and Ralph Backman. They would have liked *Casino Women.* Their own immigrant histories echo some of its stories: My father's father left his family in Gothenburg, Sweden, and traveled alone to Utah when he was barely thirteen years old. My mother's Welsh grandmother was only twenty-one when she emigrated from St. Brides Major in Wales, a small coastal village I have had the pleasure of visiting. Thanks to Earl Jones, my artist husband. For more than fifty-one years he has been both ballast and source of inspiration. The depth and integrity of his own creative work have always served as a model. Thanks to my children, Nathan, Sarah, and Sam, all artists—painters, photographers, and poets. Their unending love, insight, and creativity have not only sustained and supported me but also have been a constant source of delight and amazement. Finally, I only have to look into the faces of my three beautiful granddaughters—Chloe, Sophie, and Grace—to be reminded of how important it is to work toward a more just and humane future. It is mainly to them—and to the other young people in our increasingly fragile world—that my hopes in the creation of this book have been directed. Finally to Stephanie, a friend through the ages and almost like family, thank you for believing in me and in the casino women.

Susan Chandler

My mother died during the writing of *Casino Women*, and while many of my interests remained a mystery to her, she loved me unconditionally and surely would have been pleased to see her daughter's name in print. Thank you, Mom. Thanks, too, to Aunt Ruthie Pinkson, who stood up for women throughout her life. She claimed the first copy of *Casino Women*, but died before it could be delivered. My love to Kevin and Cindi Kerr and to the extended Pillard family who year after year provided Cedar Beach and its delights. Thanks, too, to all the Chandlers, especially Kelly, Dan, Kaitlyn, and TJ, and for memories of hundreds of labor songs sung. And at the center of it all, from the beginning and always, the next generation: Joey Chandler and Sue King; Katy and Kyle Chandler-Isacksen; and Gary Chandler and Liza Prado. My life! I doubt they knew how much a part of *Casino Women* they would become. A crowd of little ones joined us during the writing of the book and successfully put it and all other efforts in perspective: Liam Bun, Lucius King, Eva Quetzal, Wylie Bee, and Leo Isaiah. Welcome to the world, all. And finally, my beloved partner, Ellen Pillard, who was there for all of *Casino Women*'s ups and downs, provided counsel again and again, and thankfully kept on with her own engaged life.

CASINO WOMEN

"YOU HAVE TO DO IT FOR THE PEOPLE COMING"

Our system is one of detachment: to keep silenced people from asking questions, to keep the judged from judging, to keep solitary people from joining together, and the soul from putting together its pieces.

—Eduardo Galeano, *The Book of Embraces*

We met Geoconda Arguello Kline and Mirna Preciado in their tiny office at Culinary Union headquarters in downtown Las Vegas. The Culinary Union, which represents casino workers throughout Nevada, is at 60,000 members one of the largest union locals in the United States.[1] The aging, low-slung, blue-and-white building with CULINARY painted across it in huge letters has an energy that is palpable. It is as international as the Miami airport, and workers from dozens of countries go in and out the doors on union business.

Geoconda, president of the union since 2005, and Mirna, a staff organizer, came to Las Vegas in the early 1980s. Originally from Nicaragua, Geoconda, her parents, and daughter had settled first in Miami. At home, before the war, they had been moderately well-off, but in 1979 Miami the best job Geoconda could find paid $5.00 an hour, no benefits. For four years she struggled. "It was very, very difficult," she remembered, "because you can't really live on $5.00 an hour. If your kid gets sick, you have to go to the Jackson Memorial [Public Hospital] and stand in the line because you don't have the money." Mirna, on the other hand, had come to Las Vegas straight from Mexico, eager to try life in the United States—"in Mexico, you know how it is," she said. "You work for a week and you get paid like $24."[2] Both women, in a strange coincidence, had brothers with union jobs on the Strip, and it was their brothers who insisted they try Las Vegas.

Neither Geo nor Mirna was sympathetic to unions or even familiar with them when she arrived. Mirna, a divorced mother of two, used to hide from union organizers in the parking lot of the Frontier Casino where she had found work as a waitress. "I was the last one who signed the card to become union," she said. "I was really scared. Really, really scared. Me by myself and my kids—how am I going to do it? I didn't know nothing about that I have rights." Geoconda, a single mother, too, worked as a maid at Fitzgerald's Casino in downtown Las Vegas. She also resisted the union organizers when they pressed her to become active. "It was hard," she said. "I never worked as a maid before....My little girl, she was born with a disease. She had five surgeries. I didn't really want to be involved in the beginning, be part of the union. I just bought my house....It was, 'No, I don't want to be involved because I have my kid sick and I know I can't do much.'" But the organizers kept talking, explaining that the company was threatening to take away the health benefits. "Now that was something that really affect[ed] me," Geoconda said. "Because if I don't have the union, I can't take care of my kids....I would pick the best specialist for [my daughter], the best places to take her....And then I was thinking what would happen [if I didn't have union benefits]...and I start getting involved." A union all of a sudden made sense: "You compare," she said, "I was making almost double what I was making in Miami....And I saw the difference. I saw completely the difference. I saw what I could offer to my kids, the benefits, and I saw I could save money and buy my first house."

Geoconda spoke of her growing experience as a union member with collective power and her realization that workers, even immigrant workers, have rights: "When I start to organize at Fitzgerald's," she said, "it was an incredible experience for me because I start to really believe in the power. When I organize the coworkers and people are ready to leave, it was like for me this fist. We got the power. The companies can't have everything....And it was like I really found this is the truth. You never knew your power and the power your coworkers can have together. If we get together, we can move companies." When the strike deadline came, the Fitzgerald workers were ready—but at 4:00 a.m. the company folded. "We signed the contract," Geo said. "Came back to work. After the negotiations we feel great." Geoconda worked at Fitzgerald's for another year and then was hired by the union as an organizer. "And from that time to now," she said, "I'm involved in union fights."

Geo's and Mirna's lives intersected in 1991 on the picket line of the Frontier Casino. Five hundred fifty workers, Mirna included, had walked out of the Frontier in protest against the draconian wage and benefit cuts exacted by owner Margaret Elardi. The longest work stoppage in U.S. history (from September 1991 to January 1998), the Frontier strike solidified the Culinary Union's identity and strength in Las Vegas, and for strikers provided years of education in power and rights, grassroots organizing, national and international solidarity, and "keeping on keeping on" when strikers' spirits flagged and desert temperatures soared. (We shall learn considerably more about the Frontier Strike in chapter 5). In this strike, where Geoconda was a lead organizer and Mirna a picket captain, the two women developed their friendship, the kind of abiding friendship that comes from long struggle together.

A decade later, Mirna and Geoconda talked about their experience. "I changed totally," Mirna said. "I was happy, because for the first time in many years—you know—I feel strong. I could do something on my own. I'm a woman from Mexico. I don't even speak good English, but I could fight for my rights. That's the beauty of when you learn about what the union is, because the person that I am right now, the woman that I am right now, it's what I learned in the union."

We asked Mirna if she had ever had doubts as months turned into years on the picket line. She replied, "This is hard to believe [for] people who haven't been in a strike—but the longer the strike was going, the more years, the stronger you get as a union member.... Yes, sometimes I cry. Sometimes I argue with Geoconda. 'I can't stand it no more. I wish I could go home. How long is this going to take?' Yes, many times. But I never thought to say, 'I'm going back to work to the Frontier.' Geoconda always used to tell me, 'Mirna, we're going to win. We're going to win. Let's stick together.' We keep fighting. So we won."

Discipline, too, was part of building power. Mirna and Geoconda exchanged memories about how Mirna changed and what Geoconda learned working with her. "I was one of the bad girls probably of the strike," Mirna began. "Geoconda knows. The first years in the strike, I'd say, 'Geoconda, we're going to buy a lemonade.' We used to leave the line once in a while. [But Geoconda] was always there. 'Come on, let's go, Geoconda. You need a break.' 'No, [she would say].' We didn't understand. Later, I didn't leave the line like at the beginning. I knew the responsibility. That's what I mean, the changes—you grow."

Geoconda reflected on her own growth as an organizer and how she came to see beneath the surface of workers' complaints. "It's tough," she said. "The strikers walk four or five hours. Some, they have to go to other jobs to support their families. Some days was great. Some days was not that great. But people worked through the struggles and know they're going to have their victory one day." She continued, "The struggle makes you see a lot of things you not see before in human beings. It's a process. Summer here is pretty hot. That's when they come to us and say, 'it's so hot.' We know that they aren't talking only about the weather. They're talking about, 'I can't take it.' That's what they really wanted to submit to you. And that's why we always say, 'It's not that bad.' We try to [find] something.... You know, really pay attention to how [they] feel that day. 'My family,' [they say], 'got a lot of pressure.' [You talk, and then] they start feeling better. After awhile—it's hot, but we're okay. Keeping going, be another day."

Paolo Freire in *Pedagogy of the Oppressed* speaks of *conscientization,* the growth in adult learners of an awareness of their place in history.[3] In a final exchange, Mirna and Geoconda spoke about their own historical consciousness. "That's the thing about the union," Mirna began. "It's the workers who are here [at the union hall]. Just like me. Geoconda used to be a maid. Me, somebody from Mexico who didn't speak English, who didn't know nothing. We're just workers.... We're just workers organizing workers from our experience."

And Geoconda, always eloquent, replied:

> What makes a good organizer [is someone who] understands what [the change] is going to be. That's your goal, that change. And you speak it every day when you talk to your committee.[4] You talk to them about rights and [the] future. And when they say it's too difficult, [you say] yes, but somebody did a more difficult thing [to get us] where we are. We're lucky. Some people got killed. Some people got tear gas for where we are right now. And you have to do it not only for you, you have to do it for the people coming. I think if you're an organizer, you understand that part. It's not only you who's doing it. Somebody did it before, and you're doing it for somebody in the future. That's the beauty of being an organizer—when you understand the movement. It's a change for the families, a change for better. It is great. It is great for me.

For the past decade, we have been asking women, Geoconda Kline and Mirna Preciado among them, to talk with us about their lives and experience as Nevada casino workers.[5] Most of these women worked on the lowest rungs of the casino hierarchy as maids, waitresses, laundry workers, janitors, bartenders, and cocktail waitresses. Others—dealers, pit bosses, supervisors, and vice presidents— were higher placed. In long (two- to four-hour), semistructured, confidential interviews, we asked about the women's backgrounds, their families, their experience at work, and their opinions about the casinos' relationships with workers, families, and the community. In addition to these interviews we spoke at length (and nonconfidentially) with Culinary Union activists and staff as well as former and current women casino workers who had publicly taken on Nevada's gaming industry.[6] The individual interviews, supplemented by focus groups of former casino workers, Latino leaders, educators, and health and social service professionals who worked with casino families, set in motion numerous other inquiries. We talked with over seventy key informants—labor leaders, demographers, economists, lawyers, researchers, legislators, advocates, community activists, etc.—and visited research centers, archives, libraries, federal courts, the legislature, union halls, demonstrations, bars, and coffee shops in Las Vegas and Reno, all in an effort to assemble the context of the women's lives and become familiar with the industry that dominates Nevada.

William Blake writes of "see[ing] a world in a grain of sand," and that fairly well captures the challenge (and opportunity) of understanding and appreciating these remarkable women's lives in the context of the history, economy, and forward motion of the state and nation.[7] The entire process, and in particular the women's stories, opened worlds we did not know existed and, it is fair to say, changed our lives.

Las Vegas and Reno, its considerably less glamorous sister 450 miles to the north, are arguably the most gendered cities in the nation, and for years the enormous profitability of the gaming industry there has ridden on the backs of women assigned classic female occupations—making beds and serving food, on the one hand, and providing sexual allure on the other. It is a world that feminists routinely scorn, but to their loss, for in this world women like Geoconda Kline—maid, immigrant, and now president of one of the most powerful union locals in the country—consistently emerge.

The stories of Nevada gaming are legion and peopled almost exclusively by the men, historic and contemporary, who have extracted the state's considerable wealth, Benny Binion, Bugsy Siegel, Howard Hughes, Sheldon Adelson, and Steve Wynn among them. Women, when present in the literature, which is nearly never, serve as objects of heterosexual men's desire, occasionally as molls (think Julia Roberts in *Ocean's Eleven*) and sometimes as birds with broken wings (Sera in *Leaving Las Vegas* as an example). The absence of women in this geography extends to more serious and scholarly works as well—in Marc Cooper's 2001 *The Last Honest Place in America*, a study we like very much, the only woman consulted at length was a lap dancer, herself recently a man.

There is, however, another geography, almost completely invisible, and it constitutes the ground of this book.[8] This alternative world is characterized by a deeply caring culture quite different from the fabulous, profit-driven world of global gaming, and in it women like Geoconda Kline and Mirna Preciado predominate. Its population is of all colors and many nations; native and immigrant; straight, gay, lesbian, and transgendered. It possesses graduate degrees and sixth-grade educations. It is highly skilled, able to turn over thousands of hotel rooms a day, pour $500 bottles of wine, and sweep millions of dollars in chips off gaming tables. When organized as it is on the Las Vegas Strip, it has incomparable staying power and organizing skills that match any political campaign in sophistication.

Casino Women is an inside, women-focused look into the world of corporate gaming, on the one hand, and the alternative culture of the workers who make it run, on the other. It is necessarily a complex study for it explores the gaming industry in two distinct locales (largely unorganized Reno, where workers' low wages and meager benefits mirror those of hospitality workers generally, and highly organized Las Vegas, where well-compensated union families play a major role in city life) and over a sixty-year sweep of time, during which gaming moved from Mafia domination to global empire. The subjects discussed in *Casino Women* work in a wide range of jobs, some unionized (maids, cooks, janitors, waitresses, and cocktail waitresses)—that is, where there are unions—and others not (dealers, middle management, vice presidents).

In this exploration of places unseen, three themes repeatedly asserted themselves.

Transformation was the first. "I changed totally," Mirna Preciado said, summing up her experience as a Frontier striker and union activist, "and...for the first time in many years I [felt] strong." We heard this story of transformation again and again from women activists we interviewed. How and why did that sea change occur? How was it, for example, that a young African American woman—Hattie Canty, whom we meet in chapter 4—moved west from Louisiana in a major social migration, found work as a maid in a Mafia-run Las Vegas hotel, and despite being assigned a role at the bottom of the economy, joined with others to create the preeminent grassroots organizing union in the nation and in time became its president? Or that a white, Nevada-born, working-class woman—Edna Harman in chapter 7—a Navy veteran, moved from alcohol, tranquilizers, and dealing cards to a lifelong connection with liberation theology and Maryknoll missioners that landed her in Bolivia and speaking to rallies of immigrants in Reno? Much divided these activist women—some organized within the casinos, others outside. Some were deeply religious; others had no religion at all. They varied widely in their countries of origin, family composition, race, and class background. What united them was their compassion for others and their willingness to take on commitments larger than their own and their families' lives.

The union activists were not the only women who experienced this transformation. Unorganized women also stood up to gaming corporations and reported, like Mirna, changing "totally." Dealer Teresa Price (see chapter 10, "Big Tobacco Rides the Strip") who like all dealers was forced by virtue of her job on the gaming floor to eat smoke, hour after hour, year after year, was one. "Who made the rule that gambling and smoking go together?" Teresa asked. "And why do dealers have to die?" Teresa's question in time opened a religiously kept secret world of collusion between Big Gaming and Big Tobacco designed to keep casinos full-smoking environments. Another nonunion woman, bartender Darlene Jespersen—in chapter 6—said "no" to her casino and its requirement that female food and beverage employees wear a heavily made-up, stereotypical "Barbie" face to work. Darlene was terminated and eventually brought suit against the company in a case that made her a *cause célèbre* in law schools across the country.

But the women's narratives unfold a story much larger than individual transformation. The collective actions of union activists like Geoconda and Mirna changed the lives of tens of thousands of working Nevadans significantly for the better. In Las Vegas, "the hottest union city in America,"[9] those changes included winning wages on the Strip that enable a maid to buy a house; "Rolls-Royce" health coverage free to members and their families (to use the *New York Times'* designation[10]); the opportunity to win a better-paying job through free classes at the Culinary Training Academy; the chance to take a leave from work and participate in the Union's powerful grassroots political machine; and most important, dignity. These are enormous contributions that make life for union families quite different from that of hospitality workers generally. Furthermore, these changes were accomplished not by governors, legislators, agency leaders, or university personnel (including faculty), but rather, as Mirna said, "just workers organizing workers." How and why that was possible is a second theme the book explores.

But not all women acted. Many were fearful and remained silent. Why that was—and the consequences of silence—is a third theme that emerged from the women's stories. Casinos have an enormous impact on women workers, and often for the worse. Dealers in particular—in chapters 8 and 9—reported being miserable at work but afraid to speak out—"one word and out you go," they said. All too often their fear was accompanied by self-loathing and despair. Middle managers—in chapter 11—rarely acknowledged despair, but their dreams of what a management job and "crossing over to the other side" might bring were seldom realized.

It was only relatively late in the book's process that we became aware of the contrast between the two groups of women, one at the bottom of the casino hierarchy that stood up against enormous odds, and the other, in more privileged positions, that feared resistance and/or took on corporate goals as their own. It was one of the most fascinating—and ultimately, most illuminating—of the book's findings.

We must begin, however, with the story of corporate gaming and its rule in Nevada.

Las Vegas is the only city you can see from space. Home to international gaming—a trillion-dollar industry with legendary profit-making capabilities and a dominance in the state that extends far beyond casino walls—Las Vegas for the last two decades has grown faster than any other major U.S. city. For the over fifty million people who annually visit Nevada, spending over six times more on gaming than is spent on all other forms of sport and entertainment combined,[11] Las Vegas and the state's 260-plus gaming locations provide a wonderfully illicit air, a mix, in poker enthusiast Ben Affleck's words, of "glamour and seediness that appeals to something fundamental in the American psyche"—and possibly makes less traumatic the transfer of over $25 billion annually from gamblers' pockets to gaming's coffers.[12] Separated from the main by neon, a Mafia history, and tens of thousands of acres of desert, Las Vegas and gambling feel like anomalies. In reality they are pure capitalism.

Mario Puzo, author of *The Godfather* and a Las Vegas regular, wrote with enthusiasm in 1976, "Las Vegas is the product of men reputed to have the most cunning criminal minds that America or the world has ever produced. And it is no small tribute to the dazzling alchemy of American democratic capitalism that the whole operation has turned out to be one of the most creditable achievements of our society. Decadent society though it may be."[13] Twenty-five years later, historians Sally Denton and Roger Morris, assessing a vastly changed, now corporate, Las Vegas, seconded Puzo's assessment. "Nevada's gaming industry sits squarely in the mainstream of U.S. power," they wrote. "[Las Vegas is a city in the] unbroken grip of a criminal and then corporate tyranny…a fount of cash, legal and illegal, for criminals, businessmen, and politicians from every continent…[and] a reflection of the near-complete rule of money in American life."[14]

Gaming's size is measured principally by its income, and the numbers are stunning. In 2008, the total annual revenue from gaming and the hotel rooms, food, and beverages associated with it stood at $25.3 billion; gross gaming revenue alone was $11.6 billion.[15] Frank "Lefty" Rosenthal, the former casino mogul made famous by Robert DeNiro's portrayal of him in the movie *Casino*, commented on casinos' profit-generating capabilities. "I don't agree with the premise or the concept that it's entertainment," he said.

> I know of no industry in our country that can equal the amount of interest and volume, and handle what legalized gambling is doing throughout this country today.…The general public doesn't understand the strength of gambling…it just has such enormous potential, the number is sky high.…It's the only industry that I'm aware of in the world where the player really has virtually no chance, and the only industry in the world where the pre-requisite need not be knowledge or competency; the only pre-requisite is the license.[16]

The arrival of Howard Hughes in the 1960s, along with the passage of the 1967 Corporate Gaming Act, opened gaming to Wall Street and an access to capital that quickly outstripped any resources the mob could muster.[17] With gaming no longer tainted by Mafia rule, banking and investment interest soared, and brokers advised investors that "well-run gaming operations" were "extremely profitable and exhibited an excellent record of economic growth and resilience even in times of national economic recession."[18] Evolving business and market-ing strategies—"scientific management" in the 1980s and "global distribution systems," "branding," and the addition of shopping malls, players clubs, high-tech planning and management support systems in the 1990s—all brought sig-nificant financial gains. Total gaming revenues between 1983 and 1993 increased by 183 percent, and net operating income by 554 percent; absolute return on average assets rose 11 percent, return on invested capital 14 percent, and return on stock equity 17 percent.[19] It was a bonanza.

The top gaming corporations steadily became global empires. Studies of eco-nomic globalization have most often focused on portable high-tech industries such as electronics and production sites such as Saipan and the U.S.-Mexico border.[20] But globalization also drives the fabulously capital-rich tourist and en-tertainment industry in global destinations such as Las Vegas and Los Angeles, cities who deal in tourists and capital from all over the world and whose work-forces epitomize the transmigration of labor.[21] Recently, expansion into Macau, led by billionaires Sheldon Adelson and Steve Wynn, has been especially profit-able for global gaming. In 2008 Macau generated $13.5 billion of gross gaming revenue, nearly double the amount generated by the Las Vegas Strip during the same period.[22]

If Las Vegas is Nevada's global city, Reno is its peripheral one, and like other peripheral cities, struggles to maintain itself, often seeing state resources sucked away from it and into the orb of Las Vegas's larger sun. Working conditions in the two cities are vastly different (although casinos in both cities share the same corporate lineage). Largely un-unionized (Reno owners decided in 1975 when multiple contracts simultaneously expired to break the back of organized labor, and they very nearly succeeded), Reno casinos offer minimum wage to start and the stingy benefit packages characteristic of the hospitality sector generally.

In a pattern familiar to neoliberalism and globalization, a few giants have come to dominate the gaming industry, relations among them continually changing as their owners consolidate, merge, buy, and sell. They include the following:

- Harrah's Entertainment, the world's largest provider of branded casino entertainment and the most geographically diversified gaming corporation (Harrah's owns or manages over fifty casinos on four continents);
- Wynn Resorts, owner of high-end casinos in the United States and Macau, headed by Steve Wynn who, more than anyone else, conceived and devel-oped today's Las Vegas;
- MGM Mirage, owner of seventeen gaming properties in Nevada, Missis-sippi, and Michigan and dominant on the Las Vegas Strip where it controls half of the city's hotel rooms and a third of its slot machines; and

• Las Vegas Sands, located in Las Vegas and Macau, but in recent years more and more identified with its highly profitable Asian base.

The coming of global giants in historian Eugene Moehring's words also "enthroned [in Nevada] a powerful elite of casino executives," such as Steve Wynn, whose net worth in 2009 was $1.5 billion, and Sheldon Adelson, who in the same year was worth $3.4 billion.[23] Both men easily made Forbes 2009 list of billionaires, even in an economic downturn.[24] These men wield enormous influence not only in the industry but in the state as well. "When Steve Wynn picks up the telephone, most politicians jump," Don Williams, Las Vegas political consultant, said, commenting on the intersection of economic and political power. "He doesn't get everything he wants, but he rarely loses."[25] In an ominous turn, the world at the top increasingly distanced itself from ordinary citizens, and in a trend seen internationally, the gap between rich and poor in Nevada continued to widen, with gaming CEOs earning more before lunch than casino janitors could make in a year.[26]

Complete control is gaming's watchword, both on the casino floor and off. Eye-in-the-sky cameras, a collection of thousands of ceiling-mounted cameras so effective that they can read the serial numbers on a dollar bill, monitor the behavior of players and employees. Outside the casino, control is even stronger. "By [the gaming industry's] contributions to politicians," Sally Denton and Roger Morris write in *The Money and the Power*, "its tax revenue to reliant public treasuries, its hold over collateral enterprise, and not least its millions spent for ceaseless lobbying that leaves nothing to chance, the industry gains and wields unique influence throughout the nation and world. No political act is accomplished without their express approval."[27] In the legislature, gaming's influence is nearly total and over the years has produced tax policies that have created in Nevada an "all-purpose shelter for private wealth."[28] The state has no personal income tax (a policy it shares with only seven other states); no franchise tax; no inheritance or gift tax; and no corporate income tax (forty-seven of fifty states tax corporate income).[29] The boon for corporations, including developers and corporate mining, is monumental.

Nevada's tax on gaming—6.75 percent of gross gaming revenues, by far the lowest in the nation—is also an artifact of the industry's legislative control. Gaming corporations in other states pay taxes of 15 to 35 percent, and in Macau the rate stands at an amazing 39 percent, an amount gaming moguls are evidently willing to pay.[30] Nevada's sacred cow, the gaming tax rate is something few politicians dare challenge. Nevada State Senator Joe Neal in 2001 attempted to raise the top tier of the tax to 10.25 percent, a rate he later reduced to 8.25 percent, but was unable at either level to convince a single legislator to sign on to the bill. Las Vegas columnist Steve Sibelius labeled it the "silence of the lambs."[31]

Nevada's general fund, in consequence of these policies, is frequently strapped even in boom years and subject to enormous volatility. In the most recent downturn, when for the first time gaming stock, by conventional wisdom recession proof, tumbled, Nevada found its state budget the fifth hardest hit in the nation.[32] The state's infrastructure, education system, health care, social services, and general quality of life languish at the bottom of nearly every register, a "disastrous" case of "public sector poverty and private sector affluence."[33] It prompts a familiar response among Nevadans, "Thank god for Mississippi," which occasionally edges the state out of its place at the bottom.

But of course not everything is controlled, and that is the story of this book. Although Las Vegas is a preeminent global city, it is certainly an unusual one, for within it live 60,000 union members whose ability to fight together for their futures, as the Elardis learned at the Frontier, should not be underestimated. Global corporations may appear to hold all the cards (an impression they are eager for us to have), but that is not the case. Power invariably is laced with weakness. Gaming, for example, is uniquely labor intensive, dependent on an hourly basis upon thousands of workers to turn over rooms, pour drinks, deal cards, and serve meals. That dependency provides a space within which workers can move. And while corporate gaming has brought untold riches to its corporate owners, it has bequeathed them with weaknesses as well. Modern stockholders are notoriously fickle, and a negative quarterly profit report can profoundly affect investment. Extended strikes are anathema in that situation. Nor can casinos, dependent upon the cash of the thousands of visitors who daily pour into them, risk sullying the Strip's image with picket lines and labor-management conflict.

Casino Women is the story of women moving, and sometimes not moving, in the context of enormous corporate power. It begins with an overview of women's work in the back and front of the house in which maids, the most invisible workers in gaming's highly gendered universe, and cocktail waitresses, the most visible, tell their stories.

Part I

BACK OF THE HOUSE, FRONT OF THE HOUSE

"THEY'RE TREATING US LIKE DONKEYS, REALLY"

Housekeeping and Other Back of the House Work

You're nothing, you're a bus person. You're just here.

—Reno casino worker

What does a casino offer? It doesn't offer much, does it? Because I don't think being a dishwasher, you're going to end up being a supervisor or being one of the top.... They want you as a dishwasher. They're not going to say, well, this person has been here for many years, let's give [her] a chance doing this and doing that.

—Former Reno casino hostess

Alicia Bermudez, a dark-haired, energetic woman in her forties, works in the laundry of a high-end Reno casino. At the time we interviewed her, she had been employed there for ten years. She was making $9.53 an hour and took home about $550 every two weeks. Her annual raises, like those of every Reno worker we interviewed, had been miniscule—"18 cents, 15 cents, the most high, 23 cents—and nobody can survive with that sum," Bermudez said emphatically.[1] "I'm a mother and when I'm going to the grocery store I fill up my purse with coupons. I just see how much money [is] in my budget...pay your energy [bill], pay your telephone bill, and you know, the kind of things we need....I have a lot of fellow workers, and we really have a struggle with how we're going to spend our money. We have to count every cent."

Working in a casino laundry, Bermudez said, is "like you work in a concentration camp." Workers at her laundry wash, dry, and fold towels, sheets, and uniforms for three casinos. The work is heavy and "fast, fast, fast, like a machine." Supervisors hang over employees: "Always they're looking at you. Somebody go to the bathroom [and] spend like five or six minutes, and they're asking, 'Are you sick? Did you have some kidney problem?' or 'You should go see your doctor and bring us excuse, because we cannot tolerate to see you in the bathroom too many times.' Yes! We've been told that."

Alicia's main concern, however, was with fire. The dryers and ironers were packed into a tightly crowded space, and "when something catch here on fire," she said, "we're going to die like roast chicken because we don't have any way to go through fire. If they have an accident, someone—maybe more than one or five—they're going to be dead right away."

Alicia generally was disgusted with management and especially with the famous corporation that had recently acquired her casino. "They're very tight," she said, "and very cheap. They don't care about how you feel. They don't care about employees like a human being. They think we're robots.... And the managers and supervisors, most of time [they] walk on your rights. In my department, they prohibit us to talk when we work. Why? I'm just working with my hands. They say, 'No. Because we lose production.'... They're treating us like donkeys really. They don't care if [the employees] are sweating blood. They're happy with that. I'm very disappointed with them. And I'm very angry."

Injustice directed at new immigrant workers especially angered Bermudez. "I see my coworkers treated like nothing," she said, "and they don't talk back. Like now in my department, they just hire a lot of new Chinese people...and also some from India, from Mexico. The ones that can hardly say in English, 'yes' or 'no'." She went on, "I want to be treated the way you expect me to treat you. I want everybody can respect us. I'm just lousy employee here, but I'm human, you're human. You have a heart, you have same thing I have. Same thing I do, you do. I don't see the difference to treat us like nothing."

Alicia's concern for justice drew her to unions, which she had first become aware of in Mexico. Growing up, she lived across the street from the headquarters of a large union and on Saturdays and Sundays she liked to sit on the curb and listen to the organizers. She learned, she said, "how unions protect workers' rights" and "how we can make more money being union." Alicia continued, "The [corporations] want to abuse us because we're the minority. Even in casinos, even in big corporations in Mexico. They really like to make you feel like a little worm and just step on you. It's what I learned a long time ago. That's why I keep on fighting now."

When the Carpenters Union began an organizing drive at her casino in the 1990s, a fellow worker invited Alicia to a union meeting, and remembering the labor organizers in Mexico, she thought this was her opportunity to make a contribution. "Now I have a chance to work and to help me, to help some of my coworkers—to help this town," she thought. "This town is a bad town. It's like nobody care about this town. When they have this power here in the hand, they want to manipulate the minority. [That's] my own thinking. I can be wrong."

That organizing drive and the next went down to defeat, but two years later when the Culinary Union came to town, many employees joined up. Organizers came from across the United States, and Alicia got "a good lady from California." The two women organized day and night, talking with employees about the union. "Every day we work very hard," Mrs. Bermudez said. "I wasn't expecting nothing. Just having hope in my heart [that] one day I would have my contract, one day I want to win that union election."

Culinary Union organizing campaigns in Nevada are won carefully and systematically, one worker at a time, generally through off-hours home visits and lunch-break conversations.[2] "Many nights, many days, I didn't have dinner," Alicia remembered. "I just have a cup of coffee and water. Just sit down around the cafeteria, finding this table, finding another table, until my forty minutes was over. And I did that for months, for years." Eventually, she said, "I enrolled those people in the union, yes. But I was fighting very hard for that. It's not easy. And to beat a big corporation, wasn't easy. Was very hard."

Bermudez carefully learned her rights, and although she was harassed almost every day, she was never fired. Once the company called a meeting to announce the results of an employee survey in which they had asked workers, according to Bermudez, "What we can do to make the customer happy? What we can do to make this job better? and blah, blah, blah." She described the meeting: "All was fellow workers there, and [the vice president] was giving his nice speech about how they progress, all the money coming in, all the money they're going to spend here, and the last thing he said—he mention about the survey, you know—'We're very happy because every employee was happy to work here.' I just stand up and I said, 'Excuse me, sir. You're wrong! I'm working and I'm not happy. And you know when I'm going to be happy? When my union contract be signed.' "

Taken aback, the vice president exclaimed, "You're too emotional!"

"No," Alicia replied. "When I'm talking about money, I'm not emotional. You just talking about your goals, about how much money you have…but you don't care. You care less about the employees. We can hardly make money to eat and pay our house rent.…We need more money. We make just nothing. You would be happy to get raise every year 13 cents or 10 cents? [If] your supervisor hate you?"

Alicia Bermudez's casino became the second of only two casinos in northern Nevada to go union. "Tears was coming from my eyes that night," she said. "I was very, very happy. It's like I have my hand full of gold—that's how I feel—because my salary is going up. I'm going to make more. I don't want to spend eighteen years and get ten cent raise every year or three cents."

Alicia Bermudez talked to her young daughter about everything that was going on with the union. Sometimes her daughter would say, "Why you do that, Mama? Because days you disappear." Taking her child in her arms, Bermudez replied: "I'm not disappeared. I disappear from the house, but I'm attending something very important. Maybe for you, because I don't know that you want to go to college. I don't want you to start like a cook over there making $5.50 or

$5.25 or $6.25 how they pay the cooks now. That's a lousy salary." Alicia continued, "So I told her this is why I fighting. Because I don't know if I can be alive
tonight. I can die tomorrow, but at least when I gone I'm going to be very happy
wherever I go because I see the people be protected by the union. They can have
not the best salary, but they can have something decent at least."

Back of the house workers like Alicia Bermudez—maids, laundry workers,
porters, janitors, cooks, dishwashers—constitute the vast majority of casino and
hotel workers, with maids alone accounting for between 25 and 30 percent of
employees.[3] Nearly always female and, in Nevada, predominantly immigrant
and Latina, these women serve as the base of gaming's enormous global empire,
working—if they are employed in non-union casinos—long hours at low pay
and in jobs characterized by hard labor, high rates of injury, and few if any ladders to advancement. Unseen and unheralded, back of the house workers appear
to work without voice in a geography in which they are present, but like ants,
silent, as—one imagines their employers thinking—befits their lack of education
and inability to contribute anything of consequence to the larger culture.

In our experience, however, back of the house workers are neither silent nor
invisible. Repeatedly, we discovered women like Alicia who speak out, form
family-like ties with other workers, and defend each other. Critically, they build
within the context of daily interactions a culture quite at odds with that of the casino and its drive to maximize profits. They often, like Alicia, possess a keen sense
of both power and injustice and a sophisticated understanding of themselves as
a group with interests utterly distinct from those of corporate management. Not
satisfied with the rank to which they were assigned, back of the house workers
often have the improbable notion that they are more than arms that work and
that together with their fellow workers they can actually change the world. They
possess as well a sense of history and a vision for the future, like the one Alicia
shared with her daughter. Somehow they find ways to educate themselves, perhaps sitting on a curb listening to Mexican organizers or absorbing lessons from
union activists. In time they may become activists themselves.

This leads us to a central question of this book. How is it that these employees, who are overwhelmingly women, immigrants, and workers of color, by all
estimates invisible, and who have fled from poverty or economic and political
upheaval in their countries of origin and arrived in Nevada with basic English,
little money, and sometimes no papers—how is it that out of their ranks women
like Alicia Bermudez arise? How is it that two of the last three presidents of the
Culinary Union have come from housekeeping? That they have built one of the
strongest unions in the country? That the Culinary Union focuses its organizing
efforts on them?

In this chapter back of the house women tell their stories. They are all from Reno, a useful place to begin, for it reflects much more than Las Vegas the realities faced by nonunionized service workers in the United States and around the globe. The women describe their initiation into maid work, the nature of that work, the injuries they suffer, the abuse that daily accompanies their efforts, and then remarkably take us into a world whose hopefulness we did not anticipate encountering.

Who applies for back of the house work in northern Nevada casinos? The conventional wisdom is that the women who seek out these quintessential jobs of globalization are disregarded workers, non-English speakers, simple and easily manipulated—and happy enough for maid work because they qualify for few other positions.

The portrait contains a grain of truth. For nearly all the women, many of whom were the sole reliable source of income in their families, applying to be a casino maid was not a difficult decision; it was a matter of survival. Because of this most women assessed casino work from two sides, and though critical of conditions they encountered, they were well aware that many families' livelihoods depended on it. "I think casinos—well, they provide, and they do that on a quick basis," is how one Latino focus group member summed it up. "[You can get a job fast] and no education required. It's just physical labor. We know what we came to do: we came to work. And that's what we're doing."[4]

"If you're Latino," a social worker in a Reno family resource center serving Latino families told us, "you can apply for maid, you can apply for dishwasher, those are the main jobs that you find. You can find [them] quickly. And if you speak some English, you can [be]...a change person, but that's not frequent." Nearly everyone commented on this universal tracking of Latinas into back of the house work. It was discriminatory, but as a maid from El Salvador said, "One has to take it because we need the job."

There was an interesting and important turn to this opinion, however. In the view of many Reno housekeepers, tracking Latinas into housekeeping jobs, though discriminatory, said something as well about the value employers placed on their skills and work ethic, a source of power that did not elude the women's notice. One Salvadoran woman said with feeling, "They know the Latina women they work hard," and backed up her observation with the story of how she secured her first job. "I was going to watch the river," she said, "and this guy was in the door [of his casino], and he started speaking to us and he offered me the job. And over there, 100 percent of the people working in the housekeeping department were Hispanic, and he loved them very much. That guy was very nice. He loved Hispanic people."

Regardless of who was hired, it was the estimate of most that it was Latinas who stayed. One maid laughed, "The Americans sometimes would come a day and leave. The Spanish people stayed longer." It was her opinion that "the Americans" weren't pushed as hard to finish and that often Latinas were left to complete the work: "So we have the case in the casino where if you were Latino you had to clean fifteen rooms. But if you were African American, maybe you can clean thirteen, because you say, maybe, 'oh, I cannot handle it.' And if you were white, the same thing. But Latinos, after they finish, because they're hard-working people, they have to do the work that's been left by the other people."

Many immigrant workers come to Nevada with an education and professional experience, but lacking English and the opportunity to use their degrees in this country, they find themselves cleaning toilets. About this there was a good deal of sadness. Raquel Marquez was an example of such a woman. A teacher, graduate student, and political activist, Mrs. Marquez fled El Salvador in 1980. "I was a member of the Human Rights Commission," she said, "and also I was a member of the teachers and students union. I participated in the Commission of Truth they were having because too many people were disappearing and we have to find out who was doing that. Of course it was the military…and because of that, I got in a controversy with the government." One day a man from the government came to her and said, "If you want to leave, you have twenty-four hours or else." Raquel, whose daughters were eight and nine, was devastated. "I thought that [he was] kidding," she said, "but then I went to talk to some of my friends, and they said, 'you have to leave.' And that was that. My heart, I left behind."[5]

Raquel knew a couple in Reno who was willing to take her and her daughters into their small apartment. "I have to sleep on the floor," she said, tears rolling down her face. She hoped to return to El Salvador, "but," she cried, the memory still fresh twenty years later, "the next year some of my colleagues were killed. Monsignor Romero got killed so I knew I couldn't go back." After a couple of months, Raquel applied for a maid job in a casino. "It was very traumatic," she said. "Like I told you [my family] we don't have anything fancy—but my father was kind of a landlord.…We had cows, we had chickens. We had land." In contrast, the casino, Raquel said, "well, that [was] horrible.…I had to work for money for food, it's not like I enjoy it. I wouldn't [be] cleaning rooms in my country. I was a teacher."

Reno housekeepers spoke at length about the nature of maid work and what they had learned from their experience on the job. Housekeeping is essentially a collective undertaking, one that provides many opportunities to reach out to each other and share opinions about what is happening. The women rapidly gained confidence in their ability to take on this hard work and among themselves drew conclusions about the relations of power within the casino.

Valerie Miller was an anomaly—a white housekeeper, born and raised in Nevada. When we first met Valerie, she had worked nineteen years as a housekeeper. The work paid poorly and taxed her body, but it had also provided warm and lasting friendships. She especially enjoyed a group of Vietnamese coworkers, who, she said, were "like brothers to me.... I just grew up with those guys. Some people [would] talk to them and [then say], 'I didn't understand a word they said!' I understood them perfectly because I worked with them so long."[6]

Her closest relationship, though, was with Hannah Gertz. "[In housekeeping] you always work with a partner," Valerie explained. "So I got Hannah, and we had floors twenty-four to twenty-seven. Those rooms were our responsibility...and her and I did them together. [When] they raised the rooms to fifteen, we'd have thirty rooms we'd do.... It was fun. It was horrible. We'd have to hurry so fast.... Our faces would be all red. But gosh, I've worked there so long I feel like the people there are my family."

Miller was proud that she and Gertz had been assigned the top floor executive suites. "They thought we were the best," she said, "so they put us together up there." The two women worked hard to clean the rooms perfectly—"because it's like your home," Valerie said. "You want it to look good, too. Well, that's how I've always been anyway. My mom taught us that—do a job good."

After almost two decades as a housekeeper, Valerie Miller's knees were failing. They hurt so badly she had applied for and gotten a job supervising other housekeepers. "I have bursitis, and it's from being on my knees," she explained. "That's why I changed to this job—to get off my knees. Sometimes I couldn't walk, my knees [were] so bad.... [They offered me] light duty, but I never took it. You lose pay and I'm a single parent, so I couldn't do that.... I tried not to limp and [to] not think about it, but they were [getting] worse and worse.... Gosh, I didn't want to be crippled—that's what I was worried about... I'm going to end up in a wheelchair."

For many years, Valerie Miller, although painfully shy, had stood up for housekeepers. She and Hannah had fought to require the casino to provide workers with anti-hepatitis shots. "We have to clean throw-up sometimes, you know," she explained. "We do that a lot. And blood. We felt that we should have the hepatitis B shot...because, gosh, it's so easy to get something.... Hannah and I, we just kept bugging them. We fought for that shot, and they're going to give them to us now.... Me, I'm a fighter. I like to stand up for what's right."

When the Culinary Union began organizing in her casino, a friend who had become an organizer asked Valerie for her support. "Okay," she responded, "Sure, I'm there." Eventually, Miller herself became a leader, "because," she said, "when [the present owners] took over it was terrible.... They were slave drivers. They wanted one person to do several people's jobs.... Yeah, they're really cheap. They're really bad. That's why we wanted the union."

It had been a real struggle, she said, getting people to stand up for themselves. "You know, [the workers] are the ones with the power, [but] they're different races, and they're so scared. They're afraid of the boss. They're afraid of losing their job. Just couldn't get it through their heads, you know." Of course, the company did everything possible to fan workers' fears. "They were very angry," Valerie said. "They were retaliating against us. They were threatening people that they're going to get fired if they keep being involved with the union. But, you know, I kept staying involved. I was scared, too, because I didn't want to lose my job. But, you know, I just did it because I felt that that was what was right. You know, somebody needed to do something about the company. They were something else."

Valerie was appointed spokesperson for one of the early visits to the bosses. "I was shaking," she laughed. "I was literally scared to death, but I did it anyway. It was really hard, but it was really worth it." And it wasn't only at work where things had improved. "It has made me stronger in my whole life," she said. "I stood up to my husband.... I took steps to get him out of our lives where I couldn't before.... It took me a long time to get there, but I finally did it. I'm getting off my knees. I'm doing something for myself."

Valerie Miller's narrative, to which we shall return, captures well the nature of maid work—heavy, fast-paced, and injurious. Back of the house work is hard physical labor, and body stories, that is, stories of injured knees, raw hands, sore backs, marked the women's narratives. Valerie described as well the critical themes that emerged from housekeepers' description of their work, one of the most important being its collective nature and the close ties that developed among workers. These included friendships like those between Valerie and her Vietnamese "brothers" that defy the conventions of separation so dominant in our society, a kind of anticolonial imperative, as it were, that emerged from daily life on the job. Pride in work well done, often handed down through generations, and the women's effort to present the casino in the best possible light also appeared frequently in women's stories, something rarely remarked upon in conventional assessments of maids and their work. And finally, the great contradiction that corporate management—who benefits enormously from the work of these employees, to all appearances exemplary (Valerie was once named Employee of the Month)—seemed entirely willing to enforce work regulations that used up women's bodies with disastrous effect, not only on the women and the families who love them and depend upon their income, but also on society as a whole. We all must work, but few among us are faced with the reality of ending up in a wheelchair as a result of our labor.

And maid work was getting harder. Maids surveyed in a number of studies report a significant increase in work burden and a higher number of work-related injuries.[7] The number of rooms maids are assigned to clean (fourteen to eighteen in an eight-hour day) generally has not increased, but "amenities creep" makes each room more difficult to clean. Rooms that in the 1980s had two single beds, now have two queen beds or a double and a queen. Mattresses are stiff, good for guests, but hard on the maid lifting them. Instead of one or two pillows, maids now strip and stuff four to six pillows per bed. Sheets and duvets are notably heavier. Most rooms now have irons, ironing boards, coffee pots, and hairdryers, all requiring extra maid service, heavier carts, and more trips to the linen closets. Despite the extra work, hotels generally have not increased staff; in fact, they often have reduced it, eliminating the teams of porters who help maids with heavy lifting.[8]

The rates of injury are stunning as growing numbers of studies document. An early New Zealand ergonomic study found that twenty "loaded forward flexion movements"—such as lifting a mattress to tuck in the sheets—are required to make a bed, and that the "low lifting" required to make large, close-to-the-floor beds (the current trend) is especially associated with back pain.[9] In a 2002 study conducted in Las Vegas and San Francisco, researchers concluded that workload change over the previous five years had greatly increased maids' odds of pain. The weight and awkwardness of linen carts and the weight and size of bedspreads were all potential sources for ergonomic stress, as were cleaning products that did not work effectively and required repeated scrubbing.[10] Seventy-seven percent of room cleaners in that study experienced work-related bodily pain, but they very often—like Valerie—declined to report it for fear of losing income or their jobs. Rather, they worked with the pain and self-medicated by taking aspirin and personal days off. The study concluded that room cleaners are a high-risk group for painful and disabling work-related muscular skeletal injuries and that maids' rates of occupational injury far exceed national rates for workers in general. There is a pressing need for worksite injury prevention, the study went on, noting that hotels could easily prevent many common ergonomic problems with interventions such as electrical carts or by retrofitting carts with bigger wheels to reduce pushing forces.[11]

Chronic exhaustion, even more than injuries, marked back of the house workers' lives. Both women and focus group members in our study commented repeatedly that mothers with families "stay exhausted all the time." As one worker described it, "After they get out [of work], they clean the house, they make the dinner for the husband and the kids, they take care of the kids, and after that they go into the laundry, they iron the clothes, and you can find this woman is still taking care of the house around 11 p.m. I don't know what time they get to sleep. It's very amazing. These people are so strong. I feel very sorry for them, because…god!"

For this heavy work, Reno housekeepers repeatedly reported that they started at $6.00 or $6.50 an hour and that tips were rarely more than $10.00 a week. Annual pay increases, as Alicia Bermudez experienced, were more an insult than a raise, and ten years of service could easily be measured by less than a $2.00 or $3.00 per hour wage increase. These are wages that punish families and punish the communities where they are the norm. To make matters worse, casino hours are notoriously irregular in Reno. During down seasons, such as the cold, snowy months after Christmas when gamblers from California hesitate to travel over the Sierras, women said they saw their hours reduced by ten to twenty hours. A steady job with overtime suddenly becomes a sinkhole.

As hours disappear, so do benefits, if they existed in the first place. Nonunionized casinos, in a trend seen generally in the nation, employ multiple strategies—such as keeping workers part-time and cutting back hours—to ensure that employees do not qualify for benefits. Even when they qualify, health insurance, which in nonunionized Reno properties may cost $40 a month for an individual and $150 for a family, is often too costly for many back of the house workers. Diana Saren, a housekeeper, in a comment heard repeatedly, said, "When you're making $6.50 an hour and you've got a family of five—you're not getting [insurance]…. It's just too expensive. [You] don't make enough money to pay rent and electric and food and gas and pay for child care and then have to pay insurance on top of that."[12]

Reno social workers in a study focus group, several of whom had worked in casinos themselves and all of whom regularly served casino families, spoke with passion about the insecurity casino families face. "They really have trouble making ends meet," said one, "because they're never sure what hours they're going to work or how many hours they're going to get during a week, so they can't actually budget and plan." The social worker assured us, "These are not people who have just started. These are people who've been working there a long time." Another added, "[Workers] can't get [health] coverage. The hours are forty, and then cut down to seventeen—very, very arbitrary. An employee does not know when they will be cut. [So] the rent doesn't get paid that month. It sets off a whole chain. If the rent doesn't get paid, then you can be evicted. The eviction laws in Nevada are five days, and you can be out for no reason. That is pretty scary for a family that is struggling to make it. People have to choose between do I buy food for my family or do I spend $150 a month getting insurance for my child. It's absolutely amazing. [I] know families of five or six that live on $700 a month."[13]

Especially painful is the fact that back of the house jobs in nonunionized casinos with rare exception go nowhere. A dedicated social worker added that in all of her years of working with casino families, most of them Latino, she had "met only one mother who got to work beyond housekeeping. She worked [as a change person]....I have not met fathers that have made it beyond busboy or the very, very low jobs in restaurants."

What is the remedy if wages are low, benefits uncertain, annual raises minute, and ladders to better jobs nonexistent? For many workers it is to seek second and third jobs. Ana Ramirez chose that path. Mrs. Ramirez came to Reno from California, fleeing poverty and an abusive husband. She had heard there was plentiful work in Reno and quickly secured a job as a porterette (janitor) at one of city's finest corporate casinos. Ramirez worked every day cleaning bathrooms and banquet rooms from 6:00 p.m. until 2:00 a.m. It was hard work, and recently she had seriously injured her knee when she fell carrying a load of towels up a short flight of stairs. She was generally exhausted when she got off work at 2:00 a.m., but instead of going home, she walked to her second job, cleaning a fast-food restaurant. When she finally returned to her apartment at 10:30 in the morning, she slept for a few hours, but by 2:00 p.m. was up cooking her grandchildren's dinners and helping them with homework. Then it was back to the casino at 6:00 for another night of work. Ana Ramirez had worked two full-time jobs for most of the last eight years.[14]

Working two jobs is a critically important reality and one insufficiently noted in the literature on global labor. We asked maids, cooks, janitors, and kitchen workers in northern Nevada casinos how many people in their departments work more than one job. "Oh, half, at least," "maybe 60 percent," "I think three-quarters," were answers we consistently received.

"Two full-time jobs?" we asked, somewhat in disbelief.

"Yes, most of them," workers replied.

The toll that working two jobs takes on children, on couples trying to maintain a relationship, and on workers' physical and mental health is enormous—as is the toll on the community. Exhaustion, compromised immune systems, marital issues, worry about children, especially teenagers, and depression were all regularly reported. "I could tell you about the physical pain," a cook said, touching knees and shoulders. "But the mental cost is even greater. I love books and used to read a lot. Now I am too tired—and depressed, too. What is there to look forward to?"

What made hard work devastating was the disrespect that accompanied it. Dignity was nearly impossible to come by, as was appreciation for a job well done. "[It's the] the way they treat you," Alicia Bermudez said. "They just think you're a workhorse and they kick your butt and send you out there, and then they don't even give you a thank you. It's not right. You have to treat people how you want to be treated." Another young maid added, "Well, it's like you would do something nice or you're always on the ball, working hard, not even a thank you. I guess money for me is not a lot, but a thank you is a lot, because I know they're seeing my work....I know I'm being appreciated."[15]

Rudeness was a daily accompaniment to the job, especially for immigrants and women of color. Worse, maids said, customers repeatedly accused house-keepers of dishonesty. Raquel Marquez, the former teacher from El Salvador, remembered, "You get some kind of people, very demanding, and they think because you are Hispanic, and because you are cleaning rooms, you are the worst." She went on, "Most of the [housekeepers] are very humble people. They came from Mexico, from faraway places. And the customer was always making remarks. I heard many times when people have been accused of stealing things out of the rooms.... They were [brought] down, they were searched for jewels, for money. And when people get frustrated, when they get drunk, when they lose money, they take it out on the poor employees.... They're so demanding. They want extra towels, extra cleaning. They slip on the floor, and they say it's because the maid left some water over there. Well, it's horrible how they accuse the poor Hispanics, especially the Hispanics. And they know these people can't communicate. It's horrible. So for me that was like a trauma."

A member of the study's Latino focus group had worked in the tourist industry in Mexico where her experience was vastly different from workers' experience in Reno. "What happens [here] is a lot of times these tourists don't want Mexicans around them," she said. "It's like everywhere you go, racial remarks are really there. You're not treated with a lot of respect. People say, 'Agua!' or 'Hurry up!' They're not polite. [I]n Hispanic culture... we treat other people with a lot of respect.... You're taught since you are born how to talk to other people, always have good manners. It makes it really hard for people working for the casinos. They really don't feel comfortable.... Kind of, you're nothing, you're a bus person. You're just here. And that makes a big difference."

That message—"you're nothing, you're a bus person, you're just here"—stood at the heart of back of the house workers' experience in Reno. It appeared in nearly every woman's narrative as a trauma and shock to the system. Set along-side inadequate wages and the enormous wear on women's bodies, the disrespect was soul breaking.

At the same time and in ways we did not anticipate, the abuse provided the material from which women learned about power. For although the women were worn down by the disregard, in time most women we interviewed came to understand that they and their group had dignity—as Alicia Bermudez put it, "I'm human, you're human"—and that their interests were different from those of the corporations. In short, they began to dissect the relationships of power, something that we shall see later that not every group of workers could do. This is the root of class and race consciousness and very significant when it begins to appear.

The women's emerging consciousness both drew from and contributed to the construction of a powerful workplace culture alternative to the one that labeled them as "nothing," a culture that would provide a strong foundation for the collective resistance that came later.[16] At the heart of the culture was the women's hard work—which guaranteed their own and others' continued employment. Housekeepers appreciated working as a team and repeatedly spoke with warmth and concern about their fellow workers. "I was with a group of women," said one, "who really helped each other, and it was really hard work and there was no way anybody would have been able to do it [alone]." They shared their knowledge freely. As one worker, Estela Contreras, described it: "My rule is this. Whatever I know, everybody has to know. If I have a chance, I teach everybody to do what I do. . . . Every time they need some help, I don't care if I have things to do, I can do it later, but I help them. I do those things for anybody in my work area, and I've done it everywhere I work."

Outside of work the women were resourceful as they struggled to find solutions to problems congruent with their values. They shared child care when possible and introduced new workers to resources such as the flea market. Women spoke with pride about how the immigrant community maintained its cohesiveness. "Hispanics [may] live ten or twelve in the same house, but they have a house," Raquel Marquez said. "They have a refrigerator. They have a stove. They cook. They buy their food together. They have a barbecue. They have fun— listen to music. They live like a family even if they're not family."

Resistance was a critical part of the culture. While many women were fearful and kept their heads down, most felt keeping quiet was not always a good strategy. "I never felt intimidated by the supervisors," one young housekeeper commented. "I never let them know I was afraid of them. Most of them like to know that they're in charge, and I never let any of them know that. Yes, they were my supervisors, but they were not going to make me feel less." Raquel Marquez talked passionately about the abuse of immigrant workers, but then added: "Lately," she said, "I think Hispanics are getting more power. For some reason we always talk back. I mean from El Salvador we always talk back."

This is the crucial point. Quite remarkably, women like Raquel Marquez, Valerie Miller, and Alicia Bermudez stood up for themselves and others. It is a rule we learned again and again: despite the magnitude of the power differential, there were always women who found an opportunity to deepen their own and others' humanity, women who worked for a better world, who learned that collectively they could build power. When that idea took root and especially when it became action, we began to see a tremendous transformation, the transformation that stands at the center of this book.

But it is very difficult. It is difficult individually, and it is even more difficult to change the culture of a workplace so that it is not one or two or twenty people acting in defense of one another, it is a hundred, two hundred, a thousand. Paulo Freire writes that that the impulse for a deeper humanity can only come from the oppressed, but in responding to that impulse the oppressed come up against not only the oppressor but also against the ideas and spirit of the oppressor within themselves—and the fear that their own action will bring an even greater oppression down upon themselves. They become resigned, inhibited from waging struggle for freedom, incapable of running the risks. They "desire authentic existence (freedom), yet they fear it," Freire concludes.[17]

This is an essentially hopeful book, but we end this chapter with a story of discouragement because it is important to record the depths of desolation, especially in communities such as Reno where union density is low and losses far more common than victories.

The winter afternoon had drawn down, and Valerie Miller began to speak even more frankly of her discouragement and depression. She was disgusted beyond measure at fellow workers' failure to join in the struggle—and their quickness to blame leaders when the union contract failed to live up to expectations. "Shoot," she said, "sometimes I feel like hitting them. 'Shut up. Leave me alone. Drop dead.'"

> Really, these last few months, [I'm] just tired of fighting with the people, and tired of fighting for everyone. I'm tired.... Because I'm getting so disgusted with the people. Shoot, just fight so hard for them, and they still don't want to stand up. That's what I was thinking. And now they're talking about after this contract is over, they want to vote the union out—I thought, "God, you're idiots!"—because they didn't get everything they wanted. And I said, "Well, if everyone had stood up, [you] would have got what you wanted."

The stress had taken a significant toll on Valerie's health. "I have to take Prozac," she said, "which I'm not real happy about taking, but I have to. I try and get off of it, and I can't. I just feel like crying all the time. And I'm not really like that. I try to be happy all the time. But, yeah, I just got to a point where, God, everything was really depressing me really bad."

In the next chapter, we talk with cocktail waitresses, whose jobs, unlike those of back of the house workers, require them to be highly, even painfully visible. Following that, we move our inquiry to Las Vegas, where despair and depression have a considerably smaller foothold.

"KISS MY FOOT"

Cocktail Waitressing

I'm gonna have to give a shout out to Wynn's cocktail waitresses. It's quite rare that you get served by hotties that aren't bitches. Speaking of cocktail waitresses, has anyone seen the one at Paris with the booty the size of large Coleman cooler, all thong'd up?

—"Chuck," posting on "The Board" at Lasvegastripping.com

We fought hard to get the respect we deserve in this town. We're here to work, we're not here to show off our bodies for any man who comes in the door. We're here to make a living and that's the way it's going to be. The ladies that taught me the business are the ones that have the stories to tell. How they fought to get what they had, how they fought to get the stations, how they had to go out with someone to keep their jobs. They're the ones.

—Wanda Henry, former Las Vegas cocktail waitress, Culinary Union staff

Heidi Abrahamson had only been cocktailing for eighteen months at the time of our interview. Young, beautiful, and a U.S. Air Force veteran, she was steadily making her way through an undergraduate degree at the University of Nevada, Reno. Her student job was fine, but, she laughed, she was "tired of eating Top Ramen." Although Heidi disliked both casinos and casino employees—"the whole aura promotes alcoholism and gambling," she thought—she decided to apply for a job as a cocktail waitress. She figured she could tolerate it, at least until she caught up on the bills (a story we heard often). "I'm still there," she sighed, a year and a half later. "It's quick and easy cash. [Now] I feel bad that I kind of had this attitude about casinos. I went in there [feeling] like I was above the people there. I remember the lady that interviewed me—she looked like she'd been through the wringer. Like she'd been in casinos for all her life—the smoke skin from smoking and alcoholism and so forth. I thought, 'oh, my gosh. I don't fit in. This is not me.'"[1]

Heidi's first day on the job in her nonunion Reno casino nearly broke her. "Training!" she said. "They throw you to the wolves." The "seasoned girl" she was instructed to follow was "kind of pissy...she [didn't] want to be bothered with the new one that's never cocktailed. They're like, okay, now you're on your own. So you're fumbling around, and you can't remember where the people are at…and you're just freaking out."

Casino cocktail waitresses walk the gaming floor, offering free drinks to anyone gambling. Heidi was assigned sections on the main floor and the mezzanine. "The worst sections in the casino," she groaned. "It's all nickels and quarters…basically people that aren't going to tip you but maybe 25 cents." From the beginning the work was intense: "When it's really busy you're slammed," she said. "You have people yelling at you in all directions. 'I want a drink! Come here, waitress!'…It's tiring. Your arms are aching. Your body's aching. I'd have to run down [to the casino floor], do that whole full section. Then run up the escalator, do a quick round, get orders, take the order back to them. I mean, I'm carrying trays of drinks."

For Heidi cocktailing was both good and bad. It paid the bills, and to Heidi's surprise she grew fond of the people she worked with. "Before," she said, "I had kind of a snooty attitude about casino workers. Now I've met some really interesting people from all walks of life. I'm so amazed at how many educated people work in a casino that have masters' degrees or doctorates." She added, "There are those few, though, those girls that just graduated from high school—that's their career. They don't want to do anything except save up to get their boob jobs…and move to Vegas for the money."

As for the bad, the cigarette smoke and the smells nearly undid her. "I can't handle [them]," she said. "You can smell the alcohol and the coffee and the people's body odor, and it's like the smoke just has a stagnated, profuse [air]—I go home, and I'm just like, ooohhh. The first thing I do is take a shower and throw my clothes in the wash. Every day. Every time I work." Heidi's health had deteriorated dramatically. "I'm always sick," she said. "The cigarette smoke is just unbelievable in the casinos. I just feel like it's lowered my immune system. When I go home my eyes are burning. I have a lot of sore throats."[2]

Heidi regularly had to fend off sexual advances, another thing she hated. Recently, she had had an experience with an inebriated guest. "Oh, baby, I'm going to tip you so well tonight!" he called out.

"That's good, thanks," Heidi replied.

"Do you like cigars?"

"No, I don't smoke cigars."

"I didn't even know what he was talking about," Heidi said. "So I was serving a drink, and he threw a $20 bill at me. He goes, 'Here you go. This will help prepare you for me for the rest of the evening.' And I think, great, I've got some freak in my section.…Ten minutes later, he goes, 'Monica. Monica.' I'm like, so that's what he meant by the cigar. Lovely.…I was just so upset. I went and told my boss, and they escorted him out. He was pretty toasted."

More difficult to handle were advances from management. "It's wise just to play along," Heidi said. "Kind of flirt back and go, 'oh.' If you get in their face and you say, 'Excuse me? I'm going to file a harassment on you,' they'll make your life rough, give you rotten shifts, sections. Oh, yes."

Learning the "tricks of the trade," like how to ply customers with drinks in order to secure more tips, particularly bothered Heidi. "You learn who the alcoholics are," she said. "Like this one lady was drinking vodka tonics. God, she probably had over twenty of them. She was there all day…and she was smashed. But she won a royal flush, and it got to the point where I knew what she was drinking, so every time I came out and did a round, I just bought her a drink.…I wanted to cut her off, but they tell you not to do that. She gave me like $50."

Heidi had no intention of staying in the casino. "I just don't like wearing sexy little outfits," she said, "and being a piece of meat running around for people to gawk at or to make their one-liners—'hey, baby, you have beautiful eyes.' I just don't feel like it's intellectually stimulating. It's very boring." Heidi avoided telling people she worked in a casino. "It's embarrassing," she said. "I don't really tell people what I do unless they specifically ask. 'You work in a casino? Why do you do that? You're smart. You should be doing something more significant with your life.'"

Heidi also worried that she was contributing, she said, "to the demise of the community." She told us, "I don't feel good about what I do." She continued, "We have a lot of regulars, a lot of them are homeless. They'll come plunking in nickels or whatever money that they get from the state, and it's sad. Their hygiene is really poor, and I'm thinking, God, I should be giving them my tips. Shouldn't be serving them drinks." She described a couple who "were pretty drunk, but they were the sweetest couple. They were really, really poor. I was talking to them…they don't have much to eat, and I felt sick. I don't get out and do stuff because I'm so tired I don't want to deal with people after work, but when I see people come in…I brought them a whole big thing of meat that I had in my freezer. And she came in the next day and picked it up."

Cocktail waitresses' bodies sell casinos. In their tiny tailored uniforms and high heels, "libidinous beauties" excite the gamblers and deliver the drinks that water the action.[3] In contrast to housekeepers who are essentially invisible, cocktail waitresses like Heidi walk the casino floor fully and painfully apparent, breasts, shoulders, thighs, and buttocks displayed for the pleasure of gamblers and the profitability of the corporate enterprise.

In 1975, Gabriel Vogliotti wrote *The Girls of Nevada* (a book that our university library, whether protecting it from theft or students from its influence, keeps out of circulation). Vogliotti was a journalist who in reporting the gambling scene became so closely tied with its rarified world at the top that he himself became a power within gaming and was eventually appointed director of the Nevada Resort Association (the "super secret club of Nevada gambling tycoons," the book's jacket confides).[4] Vogliotti wrote in loving detail of gambling's "girls," and his observations provide a useful entrée to owners' conception of the lucrative marriage of gaming and sexual stimulation. Casino executives, Vogliotti wrote,

> seemed to have anticipated the Yale University researchers [who found] that the American male has some form of sex thought, conventional to orgiastic, about once every four hours each day. Without benefit of Yale, the owners seemed to know that the throb of reverie grows when the male enters their lobbies and sees more bosoms, groins, and sex suggestions than Paris ever dreamed up. As they built the Las Vegas skyline, the owners adapted, amiable about taking man as he is.[5]

Benjamin "Bugsy" Siegel ranked first among owners in his whole-hearted embrace of "the girls" and male gamblers' attraction to them, according to Vogliotti.[6] There are many legends about Siegel, but the one true one in Vogliotti's measure was that he "pioneered the great sex exchange of Las Vegas.... [Siegel] was ahead of his time," Vogliotti wrote, "in believing that every man should have as much coitus as he can stand...and it was his grand design that has made Las Vegas the most acutely pelvis-conscious city on earth."[7] In Siegel's conception there should be "girls, girls everywhere." This was only natural, "an age-old part of inn-keeping," Vogliotti continued. The hotel owner "has what men need for intercourse, rooms and beds...and since the age of Dickens...half-naked wenches...pouring customers' drinks have inquired if the gentlemen would like 'anything more' upstairs." "Girls" would be a part of Las Vegas, owners like Siegel determined early on—but a closely regulated one. "Don't forget Kefauver...don't forget Kennedy," Vogliotti imagines Siegel saying. "You can't be so vulgar that you offend middle-class America which fills your hotels.... but the town, the state itself, must accept the fact that it is in the sex business, and that all must push the sex image."[8]

A year after Vogliotti published *Girls of Nevada*, Mario Puzo, author of *The Godfather* and himself a committed gambler, composed a striking photo essay, *Inside Las Vegas*. Puzo wrote, echoing Vogliotti, "Las Vegas has more beautiful women than any town its size in the world. The reason for this is quite simple and only superficially cynical: MONEY and beautiful women zing together like two magnets."[9]

Cocktail waitresses, in Vogliotti's and Puzo's conception, were not showgirls; neither were they "professional whores." Cocktail waitresses were their own stratum, "the girl[s] who, in fact, [are] the biggest earners of all the girls of Nevada," Vogliotti wrote.

Legend says that most of them double as whores, which is non-
sense.... [Cocktail waitresses] come in grades. There are the leggy kids
who serve the swimming pools.... A little better off [are] ... the girls who
serve the coffee shops and restaurants ... and a notch higher [are] ... those
who serve the lounges. But the girl of legend is the one they all envy, the
"pit girl," the one who is allowed behind the tables, the girl who gets as
close to players as a nurse taking a pulse. She serves men who taunt fate,
who equate money with courage, who go into the gambling trance; that
ecstasy in which a man believes that his wisdom is greater than that of
the house.... She is an accessory to the world's most sophisticated, most
flattering larceny.... She has top clearance and is, without question, the
most informed of all the girls of Nevada. She has an inside view envied
even by the FBI. In her eight hours she is elbow-to-elbow with the dealers
and bosses ... she sees the ... whispered conference that decides whether
the pit will agree to a player's demand for another $20,000 or cut him
off.... She senses the unspoken order of a pit boss to bring more scotch
to a frenzied player, just as she catches his invisible "no" when a drunken
player demands the drink that will make him a stretcher case.... She is
there, smiling, when a disheveled player decides to quit, looks at her, and
says, "Honey, I'm dead beat and lonesome." Players confide in her ... she
sees players who are being clutched by gorgeous showgirls, the elite of
prostitution, and players who picked up a street tramp.... She sees all
this while holding the tray that gives her invisibility. Players get so used
to the pretty, pleasant girl and her sympathetic sounds that they find her
presence essential to the environment. When such a girl decides that she
herself wants to dip into it she needs no broker to pick her man.[10]

Vogliotti's is a man's view, full of hype and his own excitement at being close to
the action and the "girls." More important, it is the owners' view, and in that way
a measure of the dominant ideology, the ideology created by those in power that
quickly passes into and defines the popular imagery. It is scarcely accurate—to
get the real story one would have to talk with the women themselves—but it is a
deadly serious representation of the culture that owners wished to create, their
idea of how best to construct the scene in which money and beautiful women
could "zing together like magnets."

Today much has changed, and casinos' association with the sale of sex, many
contend, is more illusion than reality (although there is still plenty of reality).
Bugsy Siegel would be pleased that groins still throb and "girls" still titillate, but
today it is the *promise* not the reality of sexual fulfillment that makes cash registers
ring. Kate Hausbeck, Las Vegas feminist and scholar, argues this view: "[It is] all

about selling the image of endless potential, the seductive myth that everyone can be beautiful, glamorous, and have their deepest desires fulfilled.... The very presence of the female form is sufficient to connote vice, intrigue, glamour and sex.... It's the sin of Sin City, the magnet: gluttony, excess, rabid commodification, and most important, a belief that you can be anyone and can have anything."[11]

Cocktail waitresses still function as magnets, of that there is little doubt. Visitors to Las Vegas websites and message boards regularly exchange information on which casinos have the best-looking cocktail waitresses. "We were at the Wynn yesterday, playing a little 4–8 poker," wrote "Mikey" in one post. "One of the cocktail waitresses in the poker room was DROP DEAD gorgeous.... Every time she came in the room with a tray of drinks our game came to a stop while everyone, dealer included, got in some quality ogling time."[12] "Chuck" offered a more raw assessment: "I'm gonna have to give a shout out to Wynn's cocktail waitresses. It's rare that you get served by hotties that aren't bitches. Speaking of cocktail waitresses, has anyone ever seen the one at Paris with the booty the size of a large Coleman cooler, all thong'd up?"[13]

Although today cocktail waitresses may deliver only the illusion of sex, they deliver another commodity—alcohol—in actuality and great quantity. Slipping among the guests, waitresses offer free drinks to anyone who is actively gambling, gathering, if they are fortunate, a dollar for each drink—or a nickel or quarter if they are stuck like Heidi in a lousy section in Reno. Free alcohol is a boon to the tip-earning women and a virtual gold mine for the casino. The casinos' rationale is straightforward: free drinks attract customers; keep them at the gaming tables (gamblers need not interrupt play to satisfy their thirst); and provide that measure of bravado that encourages guests to take more chances and make higher bets.[14] Gamblers, their minds loosened by alcohol, loosen their wallets as well.[15]

In this regard, cocktail waitresses' most important function is delivering the bottom line in the form of a steady stream of happy gamblers who hour after hour lay their money down. For minimum wage and tips from guests, an incredible bargain, the casino buys a team of women who with considerable strength and skill accurately delivers tens of thousands of drinks, handles with precision widely divergent guest expectations, and provides for men like Chuck and Mikey a frisson of danger—who knows what else besides alcohol your smiling cocktail waitress might deliver?

In this chapter we examine the world of cocktail waitresses. It is a collection of body stories—revealed breasts, protruding bunions, trashed wrists, and smoke-blackened lungs—of sexual come-ons and closely regulated weight requirements—of exhaustion and drugs that make smiles brighter and wearing high heels easier. We pay close attention to what those breasts, bunions, wrists, and lungs tell us about who has power and who does not, bearing in mind Michel

Foucault's idea that the body is a primary locus of power and bio-politics a principal means by which power is exercised. We note as well the tight control casino executives exercise over cocktail waitresses and their bodies in this world where ostensibly "anything goes."

But control, it turns out, is never total. Cocktail waitresses are rarely docile; guests may consider them babes, but most are working-class women with strong ethics of care for each other and their families. And because they are regularly exposed to the raw side of both management and guests, they have few illusions, something that generally serves women and workers well. Cocktail waitresses, who feminists worry might be the least likely to come back at men in power, actually can do it with gusto. In the end, we realized, there was a great deal about both kindness and toughness that we could learn from them.

Kathleen Ramige, when she took part in one of the study's focus groups, directed an important Reno social service agency, but she remembered her poverty days well. She waited tables then, and to save money lived in her car. From that perspective cocktailing looked good. "They squeezed my size 6 body into a size 4 uniform—I was falling out of it," she said, remembering the application process. "They interviewed me by asking me to turn around, looked at my butt, and hired me."[16]

Stories of similar "interviews" were common. "I had to try on a uniform," another cocktail waitress said, "and you went into a 'management office' and I think there were two guys, the manager and his assistant, and you had to wear your uniform and then kind of walk around so they could look at you. I did that and they said, 'well, I'm sorry,' because I was thin, I was skinny, and I'm sure I didn't look like too much. This was the first time that I had ever done [something like] this. It was like I'd really asserted myself. I started crying…and they said, 'Okay! Can you start tomorrow?'"

Like housekeeping, cocktailing is at heart hard labor. Genette Louis, a long-time cocktail waitress who was completing a graduate thesis on postmodern theory at the time we interviewed her, had worked in Oregon in forestry and trucking, often as a laborer. She had come to Reno seeking to distance herself from a drug addiction and the friends associated with it. "I had done lots of physical work," Genette said, "but I was surprised by how taxing [cocktailing] was on my body."[17] She got up to demonstrate how to carry a tray: "I'm taking out about 25 pounds of drinks at the end of my arm all the time and then bending around with the tray and setting it down.…It's very crowded and I am squeezing into little tight places and trying not to spill my drinks and move my tray around and set them down and trying to do it as fast as possible." Volume was critical, Genette said: "The more drinks you get out the more money you're going to make." Keep up the pace, "as quick as [you] get done, go back out"—every waitress agreed that was how to make a living.

Pain was omnipresent. "You know there's pain," Genette said, "when you see waitresses taking valium to get their muscles relaxed so they can get through a shift." Most of the tray's weight is "centered right on your wrist," explained another Reno cocktailer. "You can't keep yourself straight, because you're constantly carrying that weight on one side of your body.... [I] come back with the empty tray in my non-tray arm to try and alleviate some of the pain, [but] there's only so much you can do. My chiropractor just told me, you're squishing the left side of your body. I know I can't hold this hand up for very long anymore."[18] Another woman added, "It's very physical and very mental. My right hand, my neck sometimes, my lower back.... It's a known fact, you do this job, you're eventually going to have tendinitis, carpal tunnel, neck aches, backaches, and feet problems."

Casinos occasionally instituted safety guidelines, for example, ones limiting the number of drinks waitresses could carry per tray, but like so many regulations, they were not enforced and tended to go by the boards in the press to serve guests and secure tips. Besides, there was sometimes a certain amount of pride in being able to handle the volume. "I still like to see if I can still carry 20 drinks, you know," one cocktail waitress said. "God, in the 80s that's the way everyone worked. Double-stacked trays. Condos we called them. And you did it in high heels!"[19]

The cocktail waitresses considered making workers' compensation claims, but nearly always rejected the idea. "I tried to do a claim on my knee," Genette said, "because I was just getting terrific pain, which now looks like it's pretty much related to my back twisting through the slots." She continued, "[If you file a workers' comp claim] the first thing they do is take you off work for five days and run you through their doctors. It's a hell of an incentive. [You] heal up real fast." In the end, Genette, who later underwent multiple surgeries and now lives with chronic pain, went to her own doctor, paid for physical therapy herself, and continued to work.[20]

Cocktail waitresses, who not only hike many miles per shift carrying heavy loads but also do it in the roar and clang of smoke-filled casino floors, uniformly reported being utterly spent at the end of a shift, a well-documented characteristic of waitresses' lives and one that historically has limited their participation in community and reform activities.[21] "How do I feel at the end of the day?" said Heidi Abrahamsen. "Tired. I don't want to deal with people. I just want to go home and isolate...and I'm a really outgoing person. Before working in the casino, I was always on the go, working out every single day, visiting friends. Not anymore. I just go home."

Cocktailing demands much more than strength and endurance, however. A cocktail waitress, who may deliver several hundred drinks on a single shift, must keep an enormous number of orders in mind, call them into the bartender in prescribed order, humor him along if he's in a bad mood, and quickly return drinks to customers who invariably have moved around in her absence. Equally important, successful cocktail waitresses must accurately read customers' needs; handle the aggressive moods of inebriated and/or losing players; cool down men excited by her all-too-exposed body—firmly enough to thwart unwanted advances, but friendly enough to win a tip; and whenever possible have a genuine moment with guests. It is a highly skilled job—and in that there is considerable irony for many imagine cocktail waitresses as bimbos, capable of doing little more than looking fine.

Cocktail waitresses, in order to do their job successfully, learn quickly to rely on other waitresses. Kris Marroquin, whose story ends this chapter, spoke eloquently of the relationships that developed at her unionized casino: "It's kind of like a big family," she said. "We have our squabbles just like your family. [But] I probably am closer to the people I work with than my own family because I don't have any family down here....With the girls at work—I mean, we've been through childbirth. We've been through divorces. We've been through marriages....A lot of times, that's the only people you have to turn to, the people that you have here. So it's really an extended family." This "rich group life"—built on hard work, pride in a collective ability to serve many well, shared survival strategies, and standing up for each other—has consistently characterized waitresses' work lives, labor studies scholar Dorothy Cobble argues. These informal practices in time construct a culture that facilitates the development of union consciousness, she writes—and we shall see that among casino cocktail waitresses as well.[22]

Cocktailing pays poorly but is tipped well, and cocktail waitresses nearly always reported "the money" as the best part of the job. This was critical, for most cocktail waitresses took seriously their responsibility to earn a livelihood for themselves and their families. Lacking capital, degrees, and/or family resources to fall back on, most cocktail waitresses, despite sometimes ample earnings, were thoroughly working class in orientation; mostly they were in the work world for the long haul and in this way were significantly different from middle class women. "[We] generally make more than anybody else on the casino floor," one waitress reported. "More than dealers, more than pit bosses. Definitely more than any of the slot department people unless they're upper management." In high-end Las Vegas casinos, where cocktail waitresses are members of the Culinary Union, women reported earning over $60,000 a year and sometimes as high as $100,000. "If you are in your twenties and have the looks, you can make a lot of money," a Las Vegas waitress reported. "The waitresses working the table games and pit make the most; $50K a year and higher would be easily attainable if you get the hours."[23] In Reno, waitresses work hard for every tip and are proud of annual incomes of $35,000.

Hazards abound, however, in these well-tipped jobs. Cocktail waitresses, if they are looking to have a good time, don't need to look far, and in that there is considerable danger. Most steered clear of drugs, alcohol, and gambling, but everyone had seen women sink into the mire—and sometimes had done so themselves. The physical demands of the job can lead to addiction: "Drugs help you wear heels, drinking helps you wear heels, anything that takes your mind off the pain. Heels help you make tips," Genette said, drawing a connection we had not considered. Difficult periods in their home lives sent Sally and Jerrie down that road. "I didn't want to be home, and it was really easy to find where the party was from the casino floor where I was working," Sally said. Jerrie, too, hated going home where she fought nearly constantly with her drug-addicted husband: "So I would stay at the casino.... The first time I sat down and played a machine, I won. Second time, I won. Third time, I won. This went on for a long time before I really, really started losing money. I kept it a secret." She added, "You're spending your tips every day. You're scrounging around for money to pay your rent, pay your bills. You're not spending time with your family because you're at the machines, or you're after-work drinking. Gambling's a lot like a drug and alcohol problem. You relapse and you relapse and you relapse and you relapse. You basically have to hit bottom before you stop."[24]

Heidi herself had stopped staying after work in order to avoid those dangers. "Ohhhh, yes, that's a problem," she said, nodding her head vigorously. "My girl-friend…, she's been drinking more than normal, and she's just stressed after work. She'll sit at the bar by herself, have a few drinks, and then she'll gamble. And now she's started gambling just to kind of go into la-la land."

Relationships with guests were another area frequently commented on by the women, and a very telling one. While waitresses, like those at diners, for the most part treasure connection with "regulars," cocktail waitresses reported much more ambivalent relationships with them.[25] On the one hand, after the money, relationships were the best part of the job. "You meet people from everywhere," one young waitress told us. "Hawaii, Alaska, you know, places that I normally would not go. All walks of life." Gloria Hansen, a cocktail waitress who was celebrating her sixty-fifth birthday—yes, sixty-five—the week we interviewed her, was one of our favorites in this regard, and confounded every expectation we or casino owners might have had about cocktailing. Gloria worked in one of only two union houses in Reno and was retiring after thirty-one years cocktailing, twenty-two of them at her current casino. She liked customers and they liked her. She attributed her relationships with guests to her longevity at the casino—and her longevity at the casino she attributed to the Culinary Union, in which she had been consistently active.[26] "It's a friendly place," Gloria said, sizing up her casino. "I mean, because so many of us have worked there for a long time. [You get to know] your customers real well. I have customers that live away that I have visited, spent the night in their home.... And they have visited me. We've just become friends over the years. And people will die, and somebody will call me and tell me so-and-so died today."

Tom Stoneburner—"Stoney"—director of the Alliance for Workers Rights, talked to us about Gloria Hansen, whom he knew well. "I really admired that lady," he said. "She [has] this certain grace about her and an elegant air in the way that she carried herself. But, come on, she's sixty-five years old, and she's not going to make anybody's centerfold. Nor am I. The funny thing is all the other cocktail waitresses respected her and looked up to her, and the truth of the matter is she made as many tips as anybody out there. She went out, and she was who she was—and the guests loved her. They still ask for her in there."[27] And while the conventional wisdom among cocktail waitresses was that sex earns tips, Gloria had a completely different idea. She had long ago decided, she said, that it wasn't the heels or sexy uniforms that earned waitresses tips. "No," she said. "They don't pay any attention to what you look like. Most of them don't. They're too involved with their game ... they're looking for service." At a time when many waitresses were complaining that their tips were getting "worse, worse, worse," her own, she smiled, were getting better.

But for every genuine connection with guests, like those Gloria reported, there were many disheartening ones. Cocktail waitresses *hated* how guests considered them "trash." "It's degrading," said Heidi Abrahamson. "It's really degrading. You just feel like a piece of crap." Said another waitress, "[They think] we're all hotties," which Bugsy Siegel and owners who followed him would confirm was integral to profit generation. "Guys just think they could hit on you and you would be taking them up on it left and right. They don't realize that you have a ring on your finger underneath that tray and it does mean something."[28]

Also it was hard to love guests and have a great relationship with them when they were acting badly. Cocktail waitresses observe guests as much as guests observe them, and the women often despaired at the "humanity" they saw arrayed around them. Sally, an outdoor enthusiast, when asked her impression of gamblers and the casino atmosphere, replied: "Worthless. Totally, utterly worthless. I see people lose days upon days in the casino when it's beautiful outside. And they lose their families. They lose their homes. I think there is nothing more pathetic than seeing our regulars come back in every other day, people who have pawned everything they own so they can gamble.... It makes me sick."[29] Another waitress thought the casino atmosphere was "disgusting": "You're dealing with people that are in there drinking and throwing their money away.... I don't agree with it being okay for people to throw their money away. Especially when we have people in our local community that are starving."[30]

Because from the beginning cocktail waitresses have been central to the operation of casinos, management has always tightly controlled them. The monitoring of cocktail waitresses' weight particularly draws managers' attention. Steve Wynn, by the report of several cocktail waitresses, threatened to transfer them to another job if they did not slim down. The waitresses claimed that Wynn told them they were "too fat to serve drinks, and that they had 'fat asses' and he was hiring a personal trainer to help them slim down."[31] In Atlantic City the Borgata Casino informed its cocktail waitresses—the Borgata Babes—that if they gained more than 10 percent of their current body weight, they would be suspended without pay for ninety days, and those who didn't shed the extra pounds would be fired.[32] The story made *The New York Times* and papers throughout the country; ironically, the exposure did not embarrass the company but only increased tourists' interest in seeing the Borgata Babes.

Bartenders particularly wield a great deal of power. By filling drink orders slowly or ignoring the orders of a waitress out of favor, they can hugely impact a cocktail waitresses' daily take. Here, again, gender asserts itself. Cocktail waitresses, the women said, are supposed to give a bartender 20 percent of their tips, and if he is fair he will give the barback 20 percent of his. Nonunionized Reno cocktail servers minced no words expressing their frustration with bartenders and the systems that channel a sizeable portion of cocktailers' tips into their pockets. "It's stupid and ridiculous," said Jerrie. "The cocktail waitress is the one that's doing all the work. Bartenders make a lot more money hourly than cocktail waitress do. And to tip them 20 percent of my hard work, I didn't feel was fair." Bartenders have always made more money, Sally, like Jerrie a waitress in a nonunion casino, added, "because mostly they're men, and the men behind the bars are usually friends of management. I think it's just been a long line of men being back there and they just demand better wages. [There's a woman] on day shift that's had to struggle for every kibble and bit that she's gotten because they just don't want the women behind the bars. They want us out looking like hussies serving cocktails."[33]

Corporate managers may imagine and feminists may worry that everything is under control, but of course it is not. Women sent into these conditions minimally can be expected to emerge as strong, competent actors. Cocktail waitresses often surprised us by being much more. Like housekeepers, they were capable of transformation. And while their work is more individual than that of maids and their tip income sufficient to lure some into consumerism, still we can safely say that not only are cocktail waitresses much stronger than the "girls, girls, girls!"

owners build their profit-generating schemes on, they are also fully able to unite for a better world. Their working-class sensibilities; their traditions of shared pride, strong relationships, and standing up for each other in the most sexist and exploitative of environments; their lack of illusion; and their concern for the welfare of their communities, all led cocktail waitresses, especially in union casinos, to a fairly high degree of solidarity and working-class consciousness. "It's about dignity on the job," Wanda Henry, a former cocktail waitress currently on staff at the Culinary Union, said explaining her commitment to the union: "We...fought hard to get the respect we deserve in this town; we're here to work. We're not here to show off our bodies for any man who comes in the door. We're here to make a living, and that's the way it's going to be....the ladies that taught me the business are the ones that have the stories to tell. How they fought to get what they had, how they fought to get the stations, how they had to go out with someone to keep their jobs. They're the ones. Today there shouldn't be any favoritism or sexual harassment."[34] Kris Marroquin was part of this tradition.

Kris Marroquin was twenty-two and the mother of two small children when she arrived in Reno. She had left a bar job in rural Montana hoping to reunite with her errant husband, but when it became evident that nothing would save the marriage, Kris started looking for work. She didn't want to be a cocktail waitress—"How can they run around like that half-naked?!" she wondered—but finding that cocktail waitresses could make it on their own, she reconsidered. "It was basically for the money," she said adhering to a pattern we heard again and again. "I just wanted a job to where I could get enough money to go home. And here I am. Still here."[35] She had been cocktailing for fifteen years when we talked with her.

Kris, like every cocktail waitress we interviewed, had multiple body stories. She remembered that in the nonunion house where she'd first worked she was called to the office about her weight. "I'd lost my baby," she said, "and my supervisor called me in and goes, 'Well, I realize that you've miscarried...but you really need to drop a few pounds.' And I just sat there looking at him...like he's got a lot of room...big old, fat belly sitting there behind his desk."

Kris had not liked working in the nonunion casino. "There was one gal [there]," she said, "[the boss] told her he didn't like her hairstyle. And she goes, 'I always wear it this way.' And she had. And he says, 'Go fix it.' And she said, 'I always wear it this way.' And he goes, 'Well, just go home and don't come back.' And that was all over hair. I mean, he was just in a bad mood, and she got fired for it. And there was no recourse."

After that, Kris found a union house and applied for a cocktail position. "The place I work now," she said, "if he yells at my hair, tough. I think employees have a little bit more of a backbone in a union place. They're protected by the contract and...management has to go through procedures to fire them. They can't just walk out and say, 'You're fired.' You know, 'I just don't like the way you look today,' or, 'You've put on too much weight.'"

At the time of the interview Kris had been a union activist and shop steward for twelve years. She enjoyed it "because you can make changes, you know. You can protect people. You can speak for people who can't speak for themselves. It's more just like helping, you know?" Twelve years of dealing with customers and management had served her well—she had few illusions now about casino management and no trouble standing up to abuse. She understood the nature of power and how collectively to secure some of it. Laughing, she told us of "a supervisor that we had to retrain a little bit. He came from a nonunion house, and as a friend of mine at work likes to put it, 'We had to knock his dick in the dirt a few times.' But he got the point. By the time it came down to it, he ended up being the one to leave." Kris continued, "A lot of times [supervisors] try and pull stuff. They'll say, 'I'm going to write you up for that.' And [you] say, 'No, you can't...in accordance to the union contract, I'm allowed to blaa, blaa-blaa and blaa-blaa-blaa.' And eventually they have to give in."

Kris and the union spent a lot of time "educating" supervisors, many of whom were used to disrespecting employees. "I had one supervisor," she said, "that came up and started yelling at me in the break room, and I just turned around and told him, 'I'm on break. If you have anything to say to me, you can take me to your office and say it in a professional manner or else quit wasting my time.' And I walked out and left him standing there.... He can't do anything about it. Actually he came up and apologized to me later. They can't get away with treating me like crap like they can at other places because you have a recourse."

At one point another cocktail waitress approached Kris—she had overheard the bar manager commenting to a male employee that "the only thing a cocktail waitress is good for is getting on her hands and knees and barking like a dog."

"I was flying across the casino," Kris laughed. "I mean, I was going to nail him on it. And he was, 'Oh, it was just a joke. It was just a joke.'...We brought him up on sexual harassment charges because we felt that given his position as a food and beverage manager, comments like that were totally uncalled for."

"That's what you can do in a union house," Kris said. "We will not put up with [those comments.] 'We're supposed to be respecting you and working for you, and these are the kind of comments you make?'...You have to bring them down to being more human, you know? And a lot of them fight. They want to be 'I'm king up here,' you know.... They end up having to give up a lot of power. They don't like it, but they do it."

In 2001, Kris helped found Kiss My Foot, a movement of cocktail waitresses to protest casinos' high heel requirement. The Kiss My Foot women started by sending out questionnaires to podiatrists asking if they thought high heel requirements of two inches caused damage to the body. "[T]here was a doctor in Vegas," Kris said, "that had just done a two and a half hour surgery on a cocktail waitress for bunions. I mean the stuff that (I) read in the [doctors' reports]—it's just amazing. The women are being crippled for life.... Once you hurt yourself, you don't heal, especially when you're constantly forced to do it over and over eight hours a day without any recourse.... And with the weight of the tray, your whole balance is off, everything is right on the ball of your foot. I've talked to women where the balls are actually coming through their feet—it's done that much damage." Wanda Henry of the Culinary Union seconded Kris's observation. "[Waitresses] sometimes go home with blood in their shoes," she said. "You can hardly walk to the parking lot at the end of the day sometimes."[36] The women just "take pain pills...and live with the pain," Kris said, "I had a friend that slipped and hurt herself in heels. She never came back to work—she did so much damage to her body."

The cocktail waitresses supported by the Nevada Alliance for Workers Rights pushed Kiss My Foot with imagination. They demonstrated in both Reno and Las Vegas and received coverage in state and national media for over two years.[37] Eventually, they succeeded in forcing several casinos to drop their high heel requirement. Kris felt the publicity helped women who were afraid that protesting would get them fired. "Pretty soon it's like, 'Well, this is public. So if you want to fire me, go ahead. But I'll be in this paper and on this radio and TV station tomorrow morning, letting them know that you fired me because I disagree with you and you're causing damage to your workers. You're having them work in an unsafe, unhealthy environment, and you don't care.' "

In the next chapters women like Alicia, Valerie, and Kris take their experience housekeeping and cocktailing and turn it into something much, much bigger. It is the story of Nevada's Culinary Union, a labor organization that would not have been built save for the contributions of women like them.

Part II
UNION WOMEN

"I'LL ALWAYS LOVE THE UNION"

**Once you become active in something, something happens to you.
You get excited and suddenly you realize you count.**

—Studs Terkel

The first thing Mary Burns did when she graduated from high school in Tallulah, Louisiana, in 1971 was buy a bus ticket to Las Vegas. Her brother, sister, aunts, and uncles all had jobs there, and as far as she was concerned, they'd made the right decision in getting as far away from Louisiana as possible. They were not alone. Black Southerners had been making their way across the desert to Las Vegas since the early 1940s when jobs for African Americans first opened in numbers.[1] By 1970 when Mary Burns arrived, 14,000 African Americans lived in Las Vegas, up from 165 in 1940 and 9,600 in 1960,[2] and they were key to the city's rising economy. "Black people," said one Mississippi migrant, "are really the people that built this town—we all were here working in the hard jobs."[3]

To Mary Burns and other African Americans, the South they left was never-ending work. Mary had first gone to the fields with her mother when she was six or seven, "trying to pick cotton." Winters she was out "picking up stumps, just doing everything we had to to survive. We worked from sunup to sundown. You know what I'm saying? When the sun came up we was in the field. When the sun went down we was in the field. And you still only got paid $3.00 a day.... I'll never forget those days. Practically we were working all our lives."[4]

In the early 1940s, word began passing along the Mississippi of an alternative 1,500 miles west. Las Vegas positively glowed in the stories of early migrants. "People would...come back and forth, every year, bragging about Las Vegas," Essie Jacobs, an early migrant remembered. "They would talk about all the big money downtown, and all you had to do was stick your hand in there and then just get a handful of it. It just made it so exciting."[5] Others agreed: "There were a lot of stories that there was a lot of money [out west]. And people back in the country in Alabama and North Carolina, we wanted some of that money."[6]

A remarkable system of drivers, mostly black Southerners themselves, literally ferried a whole population west, arriving in Mississippi Delta towns like Fordyce, Arkansas, and Tallulah, Louisiana, with news of well-paying jobs and the offer of a ride across the desert. The trip from the South was legendary. Eight, nine, and ten adults and children crowded into cars, loaded up with baskets of food—"big boxes, you know," another migrant remembered, "cakes and chicken and this and that."[7] It wasn't that the travelers appreciated home cooking—there would be no stops except for gas during the two-and-a-half- to three-day journey. African American drivers pushed right on through, declining to risk the segregated South. Texas was an especially dangerous place, Jacobs remembered. "When you got there, you had to be extra careful. You see, they had black dummies hanging in the trees, and you know, saying blacks is not welcome.... We couldn't use the bathrooms.... We never slept in a hotel.... We didn't stop, nothing but gas up."[8]

Arriving in Las Vegas, black Southerners quickly discovered the city's downside. The intense desert heat was relieved neither by the South's familiar humidity nor by spreading trees. "It was so hot!" Burns remembered. "I [took a shower right away]...and I almost drowned. [In Louisiana] all we had was the number 10 tubs and stuff." More important, Las Vegas was a Jim Crow town, and life was divided white and black, rich and poor as completely as it had been in the South. African Americans' "place" was the west side, which in the 1940s was little more than a tent city. Ten-by-twelve tents with outside toilets and cook fires housed the new residents, and the desert dust and soaring heat made life a misery.

But there was work and plenty of it. Men worked principally at Hoover Dam, Basic Magnesium (the enormous federal weapons factory just outside Las Vegas in Henderson, Nevada), and later at the Nevada Test Site, where just sixty-five miles northwest of town the aboveground tests of atom bombs were being conducted. Women found jobs in the hotels, restaurants, casinos, and, as always, private homes.

Mary Burns at eighteen was eager for life and a job. She babysat children for awhile, but it wasn't long before she and her aunt made their way to the one place that provided entry to casino jobs: the Culinary Union hiring hall. "We put our names on the book, and we both were called out to the Frontier," Burns said. At the Frontier she, like nearly every African American woman, was assigned work as a maid. Her first paycheck was for over $100, and it both floored and terrified her. "They paid me too much money!" she remembered thinking. "We were used to making like $13 a week, you know...going into the fields and stuff. Come here and get this big check, I was scared to cash it. Heck, they paid me too much money and didn't catch it."

To Mary Burns, the work was not hard—"compared to what I did in the South, no." Others disagreed—making beds and scrubbing bathrooms left most of the women exhausted. But what they liked was the camaraderie. "Back then there were only two races of people in the casinos," Burns said, "black and white—and everybody stuck together when it came to crunch time…all the maids on our floor. One girl wasn't going to leave without the other girls having, you know, linen and things. We looked out for one another back then, believe me."

Burns wasn't ashamed of being a maid. Later, when the edge of hardship had eased in black Las Vegans' lives, people sometimes would say to her, "You came in and worked as a maid?" and she would reply, "You know, I came from the South…and that was a step up from the cotton field. I was in air-conditioning. I wasn't in the sun all day. So I'm thankful. I really am."

There was a bitter side, of course. Viola Johnson, a woman who had made the trek west in the 1940s, expressed the two-sidedness of working in such a glamorous atmosphere well. "During the time when I was working as a maid, oh, I would just stand and look and just wonder if I would ever, ever get to that point to, you know, relax and do like they did. Women could come out so nice in the evening, going to dinner, this and that, and me working, making these beds and washing toilets."[9]

Mary Burns had her own way to describe it: "I always told them we were like the squirrel. We were just getting the shells; we wasn't getting none of the nuts."

A union was new to Burns and nearly all the African American women. Fighting back and overcoming, however, were not new, and in the 1970s the civil rights movement was never far from the women's minds. That was particularly true for Hattie Canty, another woman who migrated from the South, who in time would become president of the Culinary Union. Hattie had left St. Stephens, Alabama, in 1957 at the age of eighteen, first for San Diego and later for Las Vegas. Hattie had not been active in the civil rights movement. St. Stephens was well removed from most civil rights activity, she explained, and her family "was just farmers, and we didn't do a lot of going places." She said, "But there was a lot of talk. I was there at different times when different things happened. And my mom made sure we respected what was going on. We would listen to the radio. And [my mom] would try to explain different things about what was happening."[10]

Hattie Canty didn't need to be directly involved to know what it was all about. "I never shall forget," she told us, "when I was in high school, we all—black kids and white kids—we caught the school bus at the same place, but we didn't ride the same bus. And we all liked to play. So everybody would put their lunch on a little fence sitting out here. So one morning I runs up and I get my lunch and I'm going to the bus, and I looked down. This wasn't my lunch. I had some white kid's lunch. And I said, 'Oh, my God. They're going to get me this evening.' And all day there were a fear that they were going to get me when I got off that bus." That day and its terror lived on for Hattie. She brought it and a hundred similar experiences west with her, and they became in time the lens through which she would see the struggles of casino workers.

It would be difficult to overemphasize the importance of the civil rights movement in the lives of the African-American women who arrived in Nevada in the 1950s, 1960s, and 1970s. Only a few had had the opportunity to participate directly, but everyone had observed, and in that process developed a growing consciousness of how poor people could talk with one another, organize, rise up. The paternalism, violence, imposed silence, and isolation all had been breached, and no African American coming out of the South could fail to know that intimately. It was both terrifying and exhilarating—a beginning awareness that they as poor women could be subjects, people who together could act upon the world, and in so doing win for themselves a fuller life individually and collectively. The world began to emerge as a "problem to be solved," and Hattie Canty was going to be part of it.[11]

In 1970 Hattie and her family moved to Las Vegas where her husband had found a union job with Silver State Disposal. In Nevada Hattie raised her growing family and worked on and off in private homes and casinos. But in 1975, the family's world collapsed overnight with the unexpected death of Hattie's husband. Hattie was left with ten children to raise on one quarter of the family's previous income. Suddenly, a paycheck and benefits became deadly serious. Hattie remembered times when there was hardly any food in the house. "But we could always put together rice or potatoes, chicken and bread," she said. "I did sewing for all of my daughters. I made everything they wore. And then I went to the thrift shop for my boys. I made their shirts. I did all of that."[12] Hattie reached deep inside for the strength she was determined to show her children. "They saw that when I didn't have but a little money, I could yet put a decent meal on the table. They don't remember the lights being ever out or the water being cut off because I was always the type of person who took care of business."[13]

To pay the bills, Hattie took a full-time position as a casino housekeeper. For the first time she sought out the union. It was an encounter that would shape the rest of her life—and the union's as well.[14]

For most observers, then and now, the Culinary Union at mid-century had just one face, that of Al Bramlet, the poor boy become mob titan who dominated union politics in Las Vegas from 1954 to 1977. With good reason: Bramlet built the union, and according to many workers opened doors in Las Vegas that were closed to union workers elsewhere. For no group was that more true than for African Americans.

Born in 1917 on a farm in Jonesboro, Arkansas, Bramlet grew up intimately familiar with southern rural poverty of the white variety. At fourteen, he escaped Arkansas, finding work eventually as a dishwasher in Illinois. After World War II (he was a Navy man), Bramlet landed a job tending bar in Los Angeles, where he became active in the bartenders' union.

In 1946 Bramlet was sent to Las Vegas to help the Culinary Union get on its feet. "It was a match made in heaven," the late historian Hal Rothman wrote. "Bramlet had the traits the young city prized: toughness, competence, energy, and flamboyance. He walked the walk, talked the talk, even if he willingly bent the rules, and some said, was a little crooked."[15]

Las Vegas, young and on the verge of something big, had everything it needed—except a workforce. Set in the middle of the Mojave Desert with the nearest labor pool hundreds of miles distant, Las Vegas casinos cried out for reliable housekeepers, valets, dealers, cooks, cocktail waitresses, and others. Those workers were Bramlet's avenue to power, and he put his considerable organizing skills to use in delivering a steady supply of them to southern Nevada casinos. He made dozens of recruiting trips east and south. "In small towns in the South," Rothman wrote, "he'd pull up to a gas station or talk to waitresses in a diner, ask if anyone wanted to make real money. He'd collect a carload of excited young workers, ferry them to Las Vegas and put them to work."[16] Bramlet had dreamed of escape himself and knew exactly the words to use.

By 1954 Bramlet had become general secretary of the Culinary Union and had established a smooth relationship with casino owners who, despite Nevada's right-to-work laws, generally felt it was easier and better to go with Bramlet, the union man, who supplied the labor, vetted it, and delivered it through a union hiring hall—the very same union hall that sent Mary Burns and her aunt out to their first casino jobs in 1970. Of course, mutual mob ties made labor-management cooperation attractive, if not mandatory. Bramlet built the union from the ground up, increasing its membership from two thousand in 1954 when he took over to sixteen thousand in 1967. He negotiated contracts himself in the early days on the basis of a handshake. They were "very good contracts," too, D. Taylor, current secretary-treasurer of the Culinary Union, reflected, adding with a smile, "He had employers over a barrel."[17] Bramlet hung with the best of Las Vegas's semilegal scene—he smoked good cigars, courted beautiful women, and arrived at picket lines in a silver Lincoln Continental.[18] The excess would in time divide him from workers, but for many years Bramlet was beloved by the poor and disenfranchised who made up most of his union.

African American women appreciated how Bramlet looked out for workers' interests. He drew them into the union where they found community and a place for their civil rights spirits. "[Al Bramlet] was a really strong man," Mary Burns remembered decades later. "He was always talking about fairness and telling you nobody's going to give you nothing if you don't fight for it.... He talked, and he inspired us to really go talk to the other people in the hotel. Get them involved." African Americans were well aware that Bramlet was mobbed-up, but that did not diminish his stature in their eyes. Essie Jacobs, the early Arkansas migrant, when asked how the black community saw Al Bramlet and the mob, answered, "Good. I don't care what they say, it was good. When the mob was in the hotel, you had no problems. That's right. It didn't bother us. [Al] was a genius. He was one of the most gracious [men] I know. Honey, we had a union, and we had a place to go to. That's the reason I told you, we had a joyful time. We did our work, and we had no problem because if you did, you called Mr. Bramlet."[19]

But Bramlet, for all his mob-greased power and organizing capabilities, does not explain the strength of the union, not then and not later. "African American women built that union," Ruby Duncan told us when we talked with her in 2008. (Duncan, community organizer *extraordinaire,* founded the Clark County Welfare Rights organization on Las Vegas's west side in 1971 and for years has stood for poor black women in Nevada.[20]) Essie Jacobs seconded that analysis, remembering the early days and the African American leaders who took Hattie, Mary, and other newcomers under their wings: "When Amos Knight was there, Sarah Hughes was there, all those peoples was good agents. They was there for you. They was there. Oh, honey, for every one of them, I could call their name. They were there. The union at that time [mid-1960s to mid-1970s] was really run by a lot of blacks, and it was a union. They was there for you."[21]

Chief among the African American leaders was Sarah Hughes, without whom the Culinary Union would not have been built. Hattie Canty remembered early being amazed at the sight of a black woman—Sarah Hughes—walking through a construction site complete with hard hat. Hattie knew immediately she was a woman to reckon with: "Whenever she spoke, people moved. She was a shaker. And I don't care if it was management or the maids."[22]

Sarah Hughes, who began her Las Vegas career as a night maid at the Desert Inn, for twenty years served formally as a Culinary Union business agent and informally as the heartbeat of the union, tied equally to Bramlet and the union's African American base.[23] Hughes was everywhere—meeting nightly with Bramlet and small groups of African American workers on the west side, explaining proposed actions, collecting dues, and always on the lookout for natural leaders like Hattie Canty or Ruby Duncan. Her talks got people, especially maids, going. "Right away," Ruby Duncan remembered, "she just made me feel so comfortable, and she was so strong. 'You don't take anything that you don't have to take,' she told us. 'Stay and do your work right because I can't fight your battles if you haven't done everything the way it ought to be. But don't ever let them walk on you.'"[24] Rachel Coleman, the African American woman who would go on to represent the union in eighteen hotels' housekeeping departments in the 1970s and 1980s, recalled of Hughes: "She always taught us that the members *were* the union, and if we stick together we would have a strong union."[25]

Sarah Hughes thrived under Al Bramlet as did many African American women. And for years it seemed to be a two-way street. Bramlet enjoyed the women's company as much as they enjoyed his. "When [Al would] get tired," Ruby Duncan recalled, "sometimes he'd come right over to Sarah Hughes' house on the west side and sit down and spend the evening."[26]

Hughes went out of her way to organize women, whom she was convinced made better leaders. "We are patient," she said, "while the hard labor-minded business agent may forget to remember that the employee is a person. Women take time to listen."[27] She also encouraged women to take on leadership positions, and as a member of the NAACP, the Democratic Party Central Committee, and the Central Labor Council, set an example still widely followed by women unionists of being active politically and in the community.[28]

Sarah Hughes died early, long before people outside the union became conscious of her work, and she left with scarcely more than a minor newspaper article to mark her contribution to Las Vegas, the Culinary Union, civil rights, and women workers. "God bless her soul," Hattie Canty said, remembering a recent Memorial Day when she passed by Hughes's grave. "I said to my daughter, 'You know what? If I had a bunch of flowers, I'd put them on her grave.' ... So my daughter said, 'Wait just a few minutes,' and she went and got me flowers and we placed flowers on Sarah's grave. And that's just how much that lady mean to me. She was a woman's woman. She was a black woman that represented strength. That's what I saw in her. I saw strength. I saw courage. I saw a woman who were willing to do the job."[29]

But Sarah Hughes and the union's black membership garnered little of the spotlight during the next period when the public's attention was riveted on the enormous changes that were occurring in Las Vegas with the arrival of Howard Hughes and corporate casinos and the precipitous decline of both mob influence and union strength. In 1967 the Corporate Gaming Act removed the requirement that casino stockholders pass a Nevada Gaming Control Board background check, and in so doing opened the Strip to corporations and their vast access to capital. Gaming's mob resources quickly became obsolete. As Hal Rothman wrote, "In a few seconds, Wall Street could muster a great deal more money than organized crime ever could."[30] Corporate moguls, who believed in the "supremacy of capital over labor, of managers over workers," also brought with them a considerably more hostile attitude toward labor.[31] While the mob had seen a place for all, Hughes et al. had nothing but scorn for the union's efforts to include workers and their unions in decisions impacting the city's working families. Bramlet's handshake agreements were out, as were contracts negotiated without work stoppages. For some workers, it made the syndicate's old, sometimes savage paternalism look benevolent. "I think the old Mob always figured that there was plenty to go around, and they didn't want any trouble," said one union leader, "so they kind of took care of people....But this new mob only cared about the bottom line and you were just another number."[32]

The biggest indication of the shift was the strike of 1976, Las Vegas's first major citywide walkout. For sixteen days, thirteen thousand workers struck fifteen properties represented by the Nevada Resort Association, chief among them Hughes's Summa Corporation casinos. Workers were angered by management's threats to reduce the guaranteed workweek from five to four days and to increase the number of reasons for which workers might be discharged. But even more worrisome was management's demand for a no-strike, no lockout clause and a requirement that Culinary Union members in certain situations agree to cross other unions' picket lines (management was especially worried that Bramlet might support dealer unionization).[33] Workers by a three-to-one margin gave Bramlet the go-ahead to call a strike, and on the evening of March 11, 1976, thousands of casino maids, bartenders, cooks, and waitresses turned out to picket the fifteen resorts. The Teamsters, building trades unions, and Yellow Cab Company drivers all refused to cross Culinary picket lines, and by morning guests were cleaning their own bathrooms and making their own beds. The next day most resorts closed their doors, leaving twenty-three thousand employees without work. Outside, strikers battled desert winds to form militant picket lines. A strike kitchen at the union hall served sandwiches and coffee, and member-organized day-care centers watched children whose striking parents moved around the city in flying squadrons lending a hand wherever it was needed. At rallies, Bramlet heaped scorn on Howard Hughes: "This is a trap by one of the richest men in the world who pictures his Las Vegas hotels as pawns and playthings," he told cheering strikers.[34] Over the next two weeks the city lost, by estimate of the Las Vegas Convention and Visitors Authority, thirty conventions, 225,000 tourists, and $20–$26 million.[35]

Seventeen days later, with the considerable assistance of Governor Mike McCallaghan, a settlement was negotiated. The NRA resorts were forced to accept a wage increase, and Bramlet assured workers that it was a union victory.[36] But beyond that increase loomed hard times ahead for the union whose access to power had changed irrevocably.

As for Bramlet himself, seduced by power, greed, and fabulous living, he drifted away from the workers he had helped assemble and empower, and in the mid-1970s entered an increasingly shadowy, violent world. He bought businesses whose contracts were greased by his own casino connections and in time locked horns with Tony Spilotro of the Chicago mob who was intent on establishing his dominance in Las Vegas. In February 1977, following a bizarre episode in which Bramlet refused to pay for botched bombings, he was found, as they say in Nevada, dead in the desert, shot through the head and both ears.

Bramlet's murder sent the union into a tailspin, and during the next several years, under the leadership of the much-compromised Ben Schmoutey, it declined rapidly. Agents kept themselves locked in their offices, removed from the membership, and according to most reports corruption ran rampant.

The growth of corporate power and the union's disorganization set the stage for the union defeats of 1984, when garbage contracts gave away most of the benefits that Bramlet had negotiated. The union beat back owners' plan to knock organized labor out, but lost four casinos in the process. It was a near-death experience.[37]

Except the union didn't die, and in that story Hattie Canty, Mary Burns, and tens of thousands of new workers, many of them immigrants, played a central role.

The year 1984 mobilized Hattie Canty who was by then a uniform room attendant at the Maxim. She had long since learned "how beneficiary it was for me as a poor black female to belong to a union. I needed that union salary. I needed the health and welfare" (the popular name of the union's benefit package).[38] When a cancerous growth in his ear sent one of her sons to the hospital, Hattie used her health insurance plan to get him an operation. Without the union, she said, "I would have been on welfare, totally on welfare."[39] Hattie had no intention of letting the union go.

Canty, a careful observer of her world, understood clearly what was happening. "These corporations are coming here, and they'll blow a worker out of the water," she said, "so the workers got to get involved."[40] In 1984 on her days off, she began joining the picket line at the Marina Casino, and when that battle was lost she picketed more. "I really got involved," Hattie said, "and things began to happen in my mind. I began to see that we had lost all these hotels. And if I got active, if I did what I could, you know maybe this wouldn't happen. I was thinking about what I could do."

The labor movement resonated with the civil rights movement, and that was particularly important to Hattie. "Coming from Alabama," she said, "things had laid dormant in me for a long, long time. I was thinking, 'This seemed like the civil rights struggle.' But I couldn't connect it. And then I got to thinking, it does connect. We was fated for a different thing, but actually for the same thing that we're fighting for here. So the labor movement and the civil rights movement, you cannot separate the two of them."

And so it was that in the mid eighties, when activists countrywide were lamenting the general silence and unions were in full-scale retreat, that Hattie Canty, mother of ten, put her foot on the road of change for herself and the union.

> I don't have a lot of pride [Mrs. Canty said]. That I don't have. But guts, I got guts. And I got what it takes to get certain things did. I think it's the Alabaman that I have in me. Whatever mom gave me from Alabama, it's that. I'm just a Southern country girl, and one who will not take no for an answer. One who if you said, "can't be done"—[I'd say] "why it can't be done? Let me try it." And one who [is] not going to be beat down by the system. I guess that's what makes me a little different. I got what it takes to overcome, what Reverend King was—I got that. Everything that Reverend King was talking about, I got it. And I cherish that. And I don't forget it.[41]

Hattie was not the only person moving. On the ground skilled rank-and-file leaders such as Jim Arnold pressed on, refusing to give in to the conventional wisdom that the union couldn't survive corporatization and its determined anti-unionism. In 1987 Arnold and others asked for help, and in response the international union sent in a crack team of young organizers, D. Taylor and Glen Arnodo among them.[42] A synergy between the sizeable grass-roots base around Arnold and the new team developed quickly, and on that basis the union began slowly and steadily to turn. Hattie captured it well: "It had to take all of us to stop what was going on in this town. We didn't stop it in '84, '85, '86, or '87, but we began to work on it."

The strategy was simple: organize. Like the new union movement elsewhere, Culinary emphasized a rank-and-file intensive strategy that included worker committees, house visits, a focus on issues like justice and dignity, solidarity actions on the job that promoted worker militancy, leadership development, and worker empowerment. It developed campaigns characterized by sophisticated research and financial analysis, circumvented the National Labor Relations Board—widely perceived to be biased against unions—and promoted card check and neutrality agreements.[43] The strategy was to change the workplace by building a popular movement within the industry and creating a new generation of union leaders. Resources shifted dramatically to organizing organizers and the painstaking job of building ten- to fifteen-member "committees," one member at a time. Knocking on doors, talking with workers on breaks and at lunch, and educating, educating, educating would turn the tide, leaders believed, and in that kind of work, Hattie shone.

Hattie's focus shifted in 1988–1989 to winning a contract at her own casino, the Maxim. She was a committee leader, and her job was to "talk to the girls about the union and to get them hopefully feeling like I was feeling." She told her fellow workers, "'Look, we really got to get this thing together, because if we don't we're not going to get no contract.'" They replied, Hattie continued, "'Oh, we'll get a contract because the Maxim has always [done]…the right thing.' And I would tell them, 'This company is like any other company. The right thing for them is the dollar. They are not thinking about the workers. We've got to get ourselves together. If we don't we're going to lose.'"[44]

At a memorable moment, Hattie called Maxim's CEO a "liar" and said his repeated promises to move toward a contract and health benefits were words, nothing more. Everyone gasped; Hattie's job seemed to hang in the balance. Hattie, too, was afraid, but, she said, "I don't show my fear. I keep right on going." The incident brought her to the attention of Roxana Tynan, one of the Union's top organizers. "Hattie was the lady that all the other housekeepers talked about," Roxana said. "It was like, 'Go see Hattie.' As soon as I met her, I knew."[45]

Hattie worked from 4:00 to midnight, and when she got off, Roxana would be there. "She would always make her way to me," Hattie said, "and we would talk about what was going on in the hotel." Roxana taught Hattie everything she knew. "When I didn't know what I was doing, [Roxana] was sitting right at the table to direct me," Hattie said. "She taught me how to move people, how to push people, how to get people to do the things that the union need for them to do. Doing that, she also taught me more about the union because nobody can push you to do something for the union if you don't know what the union is all about, because most of us have a bad taste in our mouths about the union, what we have heard or what we have seen on TV."[46]

Roxana talked later about her own experience organizing. It was the "the scariest job that I could have imagined," she laughed. "You'll knock on the doors of total strangers.…Then at some point, most of the workers hate you, because you're asking them to do something that they really don't want to have to do—that is, risk their jobs." She concluded, "In a way, as an organizer you're sent out to look for Christian saints. And you find them, which is even more impressive—they're always out there."[47]

Winning workers to the union was never automatic. Sometimes when Hattie sat down at lunch, everyone at the table would get up and leave. "They did not want to talk to me because they knew I was talking about the union," she said, adding, "every day you take a beating."[48] It was not surprising. Few workers had experience with trade unions, and even fewer came with an understanding of how collective action—which they correctly perceived as dangerous—might advance workers' rights and, in time, guarantee a measure of safety.

No matter how often fellow workers got up and left, Hattie kept at it, passing along the idea of the union. The hotels are "just prospering," she'd say, "and the workers are not getting anything—we [want] our fair share of that pie, not a sliver." Paying dues would not be sufficient she told everyone, voicing the message of the new union movement. "Just because you're a member, that don't make you be union. [People think] 'when I pay my money, that is all you're going to get from me.' But that's not all I need from you. I need your participation. And whatever we're doing or whatever rally there is, we all need to be together because [we] cannot afford [for] the union to be blown out of here because too many people depend on these salaries."[49]

Hattie and Roxana as organizers tended to gravitate toward women in general and to maids in particular. "Some of the toughest people in this city is housekeepers," Hattie said. "You know, women are over one half the people in this union...and [they] are very aggressive. Women—we know what to do and that's to take care of responsibility. Take care of the membership out there. It's much easier to organize women than it is to organize men. Men are so fearful of the boss, where most women—the first thing they say is, well, I was looking for this job and I came here, and when I leave I'll be looking for a job. And they don't want to be pissed over all the time...and they know the only way to stop it is a group of women get together and they go to the boss."[50]

In Roxana's experience, too, women were always more willing to step forward, "anytime, anywhere." She said, "Women are always braver, without question. I think it's partly because women have less of a problem with the notion of the collective good. They have fewer ego problems."[51]

By the late eighties, as Hattie said, "We was full-blown—full-blown." The union had recovered from the body blows of 1984 and also had succeeded in charting a course through the corporate waters of gaming's emerging global empire. While corporatization had brought casino owners untold wealth, it had also bequeathed two soft spots. The first was cash. Gaming corporations from the mid-1980s on had expanded exponentially, financing their billion dollar construction projects with junk bonds that brought unprecedented capital but at the same time made the corporations dependent on uninterrupted cash flows to service their debt and satisfy investors' constant quarterly report inquiries.[52] Second, gaming's drive to expand its market and to drive up Las Vegas visitor numbers depended on a Disney-esque public image that did not include, as Courtney Alexander, the union's research director, put it, "large-scale labor brawls."[53]

The union expertly exploited both arenas. Its precise analysis of industry economics was greatly enhanced by the work of its never-say-die research department, which dug into every corporate report and expansion plan with zeal, probing the empire's vulnerabilities, advising potential investors of them, and in general "educating stock analysts and bond buyers that the most successful operations in Las Vegas embody the spirit of a labor-management partnership."[54]

"The research department, that is a weapon," Hattie said. "That's a big weapon. In your research department you know everything these people [the corporations] are doing—they can't do nothing without you knowing it. We kind of follow you around because every move you make, we should know something about that. And that sophisticated research department, that's what they're all about—to let us know."[55]

"Partnership" was the message the union pushed with passion to owners. Casino management had only one choice, the union said repeatedly: partner with labor. Dependable, skilled union workers were casinos' best asset, the *sine qua non* to serving the fifty million visitors that annually visited Las Vegas. Ensuring workers' access to a stable, middle-class life style was entirely in the casinos' interest, they argued. Owners, explained D. Taylor, needed "workers who actually knew this industry, who actually knew how to service customers, who knew how to clean beds, who knew how to serve a drink in the kind of volume that's demanded." Taylor continued, "So they were incentivized to have a continuation of health and welfare, our pension plan, and the security of a union contract. It was a combination of the priority the workers put on card check neutrality and also the understanding the companies put on what needed to be delivered in this town, the kind of product that should be delivered."[56]

Victories steadily emerged. In 1989 the Union sat down with Steve Wynn's Golden Nugget, Inc., and negotiated a landmark agreement, one that Courtney Alexander wrote, "took vision on both sides of the table."[57] The union relinquished its right to take economic action against new casinos, and Wynn agreed not to oppose the union's efforts to organize future properties—notably the Mirage, Wynn's megacasino that was already on the drawing board in Las Vegas. The "card check neutrality" agreement that emerged from the 1989 negotiations— that allowed workers at new properties to simply vote yes or no on union representation (workers invariably chose union in Las Vegas's strong prounion environment)—was key to the union's rapidly expanding membership.[58]

Hattie Canty was pleased, too, that the union was "squeaky clean," and that Schmoutey's legacy was well behind them. "Anything about this union," she said, "how much money this union got—all of that is public knowledge. Any member of this town or anybody, just about anything you want to know, you can go down there and get it."[59]

In 1990 Jim Arnold, the union's secretary-treasurer, asked Hattie to run for president of the union on his ticket. "I can't do that," Hattie told her best friend. "That's too much responsibility.... What am I going to do? I got my babies."

"You're going to take that job and you're going to do good," her friend laughed.

Arnold's ticket won, and Hattie moved into her new office in the Culinary Union, suddenly at the center of the battles that kept relentlessly emerging. In 1990 the union successfully took on Benny Binion's Horseshoe Casino, a profitable family-owned operation; later, at the MGM, they stood up against CEO Robert Maxey's determination to remain nonunion; and for nearly seven years at the Frontier Casino, workers manned the picket lines and resolved to stay out "one day longer" than owner Margaret Elardi.

But before that story unfolds, another needs to be told: that of the immigrant women who in the 1980s and 1990s arrived in Nevada by the tens of thousands. They would dramatically change the face of casinos' workforce and test whether women could unite across boundaries of race and immigration status.

"HERE'S MY HEART"

The union is a wonderful place for women to thrive and organize and find their power. Especially immigrant women. They walked here, some came in a trunk. [Now] they're finding this leadership. Here we're always in battle mode. People take care of each other. It's not like some organizations where you go to one meeting a month. No, here it's "here's my heart." When you're in battle mode, people have commitment and they make it work. Within the union and immigrant community, there's this feeling, let's pitch in.

—Pilar Weiss, Culinary Union Political Director

By the mid-1990s, Nevada casinos had changed dramatically and the union with them. The corporatization of gaming begun by Howard Hughes two decades earlier had catapulted Las Vegas into the top ranks of global cities and had created within the gaming industry major global empires. Family- and mob-run casinos were edged out of existence as new megacasinos drew patrons and their cash from around the globe. As for the Culinary Union, it emerged by virtue of members' extraordinary efforts as the "biggest union organizing success story in the United States in the last quarter century" and Las Vegas as the "hottest union city in America."[1] In four years during the mid-1990s, union membership increased by 50 percent; members unionized every new hotel, bringing union density in the industry to 65 percent and on the Strip to an amazing 90 percent.[2]

Mary Burns's "black-and-white" world of the 1970s gave way as thousands of immigrant workers flooded to Nevada's casinos, pushed by economic crises and civil wars in their countries of origin and pulled by global gaming's insatiable hunger for workers. The stories of the immigrant women both mirrored and substantially differed from those of the African American women who preceded them. Of every race and multiple languages, the new workers were (with some exceptions) poor people who shared with their African American coworkers a legacy of endless work and struggle. But unlike native-born workers, immigrants, who had often lost both families and homelands to war, globalization, and U.S. imperial dreams, struggled to survive in a new language and within a culture that did not appreciate and often actively disparaged them.

All too often the appearance of new workers—immigrants, women, and in earlier times, African Americans—splits the labor force, setting collective struggle back considerably. U.S. workers sometimes share the country's xenophobia and worry, too, that immigrants, particularly if they are undocumented, will be easily intimidated and more readily accept inferior wages and working conditions. Immigrant workers, for their part, at times take on the prejudices of the dominant society and hold themselves aloof from earlier workers' struggle. How would women from Mexico, El Salvador, Nicaragua, China, and the Philippines, view Hattie Canty and Mary Burns? How would Hattie and Mary interact with them? Would there emerge among the new workers women who were not just carried along by the tide of globalization, but who would find in themselves the will to be subjects not objects?

In this chapter migrating women describe their lives and the confrontation between themselves and global gaming—not as a series of events that might be reported in the newspaper but rather as a process of transformation in which ordinary women, unwilling to turn away from suffering and in the context of a grassroots union open to their leadership, take on responsibilities that unite them in struggle with others. In time—in Las Vegas—this alliance would result in the construction of an extraordinary base of worker power.

The story begins in Reno with the remarkable journey of Josefina Huerta.

In Reno it was Josefina Huerta who everyone agreed held the heart of the union. Born in Mexico in 1955, the third of nine children, she grew up on her grandparents' ranch knowing neither her father nor her mother. The ranch was "nothing fancy," Josefina said, "no water, no electricity, no nothing," but it had cattle and horses, and Josefina loved it. Mornings, she and her sister, cups in hand, would follow their grandfather to the barn to get warm milk from the cows.[3]

At six, Josefina met her mother for the first time, and it was not a happy occasion. Her mother, who had been away working, came to take Josefina back with her to help care for her younger sister. Josefina's world changed overnight. "I wanted to stay with my grandmother," she said, "but I went to my mom's house.... I must have been like maybe six years old. In Mexico—well, my experience is that we start taking care of our brothers and sisters at a very young age." When her grandmother died the next year and her grandfather a short time later, Josefina was devastated. "Losing my grandmother, it was just terrible. It was like losing a part of me," she said. All the children came to live with their mother, and Josefina at seven was taking care of the family, cleaning, cooking, and doing laundry on a washboard.

Eventually, the family, all ten of them, moved to Mexico City. They had no money and lived in one room, their mother's bed in one corner and the children's cardboard pallets in another. Just when things couldn't get worse, Josefina's mother fell ill and could no longer work. "*Then* we were in trouble," Josefina said. Her older brother, who was fourteen, made a little money shoe shining, but many times they had nothing to eat. Eventually, they were evicted from their one room and had to move into the storage room of a local church, where the only water was a faucet two blocks away.

Josefina's mother's health continued to deteriorate. By the end, Josefina said, "she was so skinny that we used to pick her up from bed to put her in the tub to give her a bath." When their mother died, Josefina, who was ten years old, took all the children to their aunt's house, many hours away by bus. "It was like a never-ending-losing-family all over the place," she said. "Everybody was just dying."

The aunt had eleven children of her own, and thrown together the two families struggled. But at least in the new town there were jobs, and four of Josefina's siblings, all under age sixteen, found work. Josefina and her younger sister worked in her aunt's restaurant, went to school, and took care of all the children. At twelve, Josefina, tired of her aunt's beatings, walked to the home of a woman in town who had five children and asked if she could live with them. "The only thing that I'm asking you for is clothes and food," she told the woman. "I'm not requiring payment, and I'll take care of your kids." Her new "mom" gave Josefina twenty pesos every day for expenses. "I don't care what you do with the money," she'd say, "as long as you feed the kids."

"So I was very good at that," Josefina laughed. "The girls and I got along really good. I used to say, 'If you guys want to do something on the weekend, you have to help me do the laundry, the ironing, the cleaning and everything.' They liked flour tortillas, and I was good at making them. One of the girls was really white complexioned and she used to call me 'Nigger' because my skin was dark. And she goes, 'Nigger, would you make flour tortillas?' And I'd say, 'Yeah, if you do the laundry.' I used to have one doing the laundry, another doing the ironing, and I would do the tortillas."

On Sundays, Josefina would drop the children at the movies and tell the movie operator to watch them while she went across the street to dance. "Everybody knew me in town," she laughed. "I lived in the middle of the town, and that was the center of getting together.... Everything was a celebration. They had a car with speakers and drove around town telling everybody about the movies... and if we had anything going on in my house, we used to tell that, too. That was really good. Dances all the time and good times."

One day Josefina's "mom" met an American man thirty years her senior who wanted to marry her. He agreed to bring all the children, including Josefina, to the United States and get them papers. After several attempts, the family crossed the border in Tijuana on January 9, 1969, a day before Josefina's fourteenth birthday. "It was exciting," she said. "We finally crossed the border. My birthday present—my first birthday present that I remember—was a baby doll. I had never owned a baby doll before."

The family settled in Vinton, California, just north of Lake Tahoe, where the husband bought a house with a grocery store, gas station, and post office attached. English was a problem. "I couldn't talk to anybody," Josefina said, "and that was not like me, you know? Having to sit in there—no dancing, no Mexican music, no friends." But the elderly woman who worked at the post office told Josefina not to worry, that she would teach her English. "So every day I used to sit down with her and read a book," Josefina said. "I didn't know what I was reading, but I had to pronounce the words. Well, six months down the road, I could speak to her and have a good conversation, and the store was doing good."

Three years later, Josefina moved to Yerington, Nevada, where there was a larger Latino population. She met her future husband, an occasional ranch hand, there. He didn't have a house or much of a job, but Josefina had a tiny trailer she'd managed to buy and her husband's car. That car opened up Josefina's life. She knew many people in Yerington and was bilingual, so she became a kind of taxi and interpreting service. "I could do things for other people," she said. "I was taking the whole town—all the girls…and that's how I started helping other people. After I had struggled myself for years and years."

Life was getting better, but the marriage wasn't. Josefina's husband drank, and once when she was pregnant with her second child he went to the grocery store and didn't come back for three months. At that point, Josefina moved to Reno where she got a series of jobs bussing and cleaning motels—she was a hard worker, and it wasn't difficult finding work. Josefina eventually became lead housekeeper at one of the motels. It felt good being in charge, she said, because she could do right by employees. "As long as I didn't overdo the budget I could work people the way that I thought was good for them. I used to train a lot of my own maids. And [when] people [came to me] that didn't have legal papers—back then everybody was working with no legal papers—[I] would say, 'Don't worry about it. Get a piece of paper.' I'd invent a social security. 'Here you are. Don't lose it because this is your social security number.'"

In 1990 Josefina got a job as a cook at Reno's only union house. "The benefits," she said, "were great. They were free. They were free!" This was Josefina's first experience with a union. But she worked an entire year before joining it, because like many workers she thought, "Why join? You get the benefits either way." The union was not too strong at that time; in fact, it was little more than a tape recorder. Employees could call in and leave messages if they had problems. But Josefina began to think more seriously about it when she started seeing the abuse that workers, especially immigrant workers, encountered. "That's one of the things that really bothers me," she said, "when people try to take advantage of people [who] don't speak the language. They think that they can do whatever, and we're going to take it just because they're better than we are." She remembered one early incident with an arrogant assistant executive chef, just twenty-two years old, who "press[ed] on people [and gave] them a hard time." Josefina remembered, "We all got together and complained about this guy. By all of us getting together, he was terminated—even though he had the power and thought that the world was under his feet, especially when it came to minorities—people who didn't speak the language." Josefina started watching out for other people, and her reputation as the workers' "lawyer" grew. "Learning about the union was a good experience for me," she said, "because I knew at that point that there was something else that I could do besides interpreting for people and taking them to the doctor." She became a shop steward, and in 1997 was elected president of Hotel Employees, Restaurant Employees (HERE), Reno Local 86.[4]

Josefina by that time was convinced that "if we wanted to change the future of work in [Reno], it was going to be by union contract," and she wanted to be a part of it. "I struggled a lot to get to this point," she said, "but not as bad as a lot of people.... You have to do what you have to do to survive, but to have dignity ... well, I'm proud to know that there is hope out there, and to be able to work as a human being with dignity, you're going to have to have a union contract." It was not the title of president that made her proud, she said:

> I know that I'm the president because my coworkers believe in me.... When people trust you and believe that you're going to be there for them, well, mostly it's people's respect. If you don't have people's respect, you're nothing.... I care about the workers. I care about all those people that don't have the courage to defend themselves. That's what I mean, the commitment. You do it for other people. You do it for the things you believe. You do it for doing the right thing. If you're not ready to accept that, then it's not going to happen.

There was no doubt about the level of support, indeed love, workers felt for Josefina. Consuela Hernan, a fellow activist and native of El Salvador, put it well: "I think right now [Josefina] is giving a lesson to everybody that she is a woman so strong that no matter what happens, she's always going to stand up for everybody.... Josefina *is* the union ... and they know everybody follow her.... I have seen all her struggles, and I know there is a lot more to come for her, but we will be there for her. She used to go out at 4:00 in the morning to get together, because that's when the people come out of work. Anytime, any day ... she was just there. We couldn't get any better president of the local. She's amazing. And everybody knows."

Josefina reflected on her immigrant background and what brought her to leadership: "I think that I'm really proud of coming from Mexico from an orphan family and stuff like that," she said, "and end up to be the president of the union. All those years I was struggling—I know that a lot of people in this town know me and I help[ed] a lot of families." Josefina also thought that being a woman helped: "I think that women are taking the lead," she said. "I think that us women raise our kids, and we have that organizing with the house. I used to tell my kids, this week you do this, next week you do that. And I think that that's where we start. That's where we learn to care for other people.... We may not be very good with husbands, but—!"

Josefina, like other union activists, developed a strong sense of historical consciousness. "It's going to take a lot of years, but I think that eventually it will change," she said.

> I love doing this work. I know that it is the right thing to do.... This is the time to make the difference in this town. If we go to sleep again, people are going to have to work two jobs the rest of their lives. I have lots of dreams—that [when] Reno becomes unionized, we won't have to work two jobs. Families will be a lot happier. We won't have to be worrying about... gangs and drugs, because I think the parents will have more time to raise a family, a happier family.... So I want to stick around. I don't want to go anywhere.

Josefina Huerta's story and those of Geoconda Kline and Mirna Preciado (in chapter 1) and Alicia Bermudez and Raquel Marquez (in chapter 2) provide access to the world of migrating women who, as Gilberto Arriaza writes, "defied all odds to reinvent themselves and open up new possibilities for their children."[5] While each woman's story was unique, there was a pattern, too, in their experiences. For most, the pain of uprooting was excruciating and the struggle to insert themselves in a culture foreign to them, enormous.[6] Many women reported feeling torn for years between hopes of returning to their homeland and the slowly dawning realization that the move was going to be permanent. Consuela Hernan, a Reno restaurant waitress who came to the United States from El Salvador in 1980, had that experience. She was studying to be an architect at the University of El Salvador when the war and her family's economic need forced their decision to leave. "I didn't want to come," she said. "To me it was like, what happens to me in the United States? I'm here studying, and here are my friends. I didn't see myself in this society." Settling first in Los Angeles, Carmen studied English and worked at Kentucky Fried Chicken. "I didn't like it at all," she said. "I didn't like a thing...I was feeling really lonely and out of place. There were no real friends. [There wasn't] anything for me [to do] besides go to work and do nothing."[7]

Casino work was a shock to many, especially for those like Geoconda, Consuela, and Raquel who had never worked as maids. But it was the reality, and the women took it on, becoming impressive workers, a constant theme in their narratives. In important ways, pride in work well done sustained all the union women with whom we spoke. The women shared whatever they knew with everyone, stood up for shy or fearful coworkers, learned English, and kept working, working, working.

It was the women's sense of justice and their response to suffering that provided for most the path out of the grimness. In this, finding the union—or being found by the union—was key. Estela Contreras, a Reno food server originally from Mexico, told her story. After six years of standing up for herself and others, Estela went looking for the union. Workers in her casino had already experienced one failed union drive, and, as she said, "nobody wanted to say nothing."[8] Eventually, she found the Culinary Union—in the bathroom. "All our meetings was in the bathroom, right?" she said. "A waitress was talking about Culinary this and that, and I said, '[Tell me] who's in charge, because I want some information.' [So I talked with the leader] and said, 'I want to learn. I want to know what my rights are.... If I'm joining the union, I don't want to be a signing-the-card person. I want to be a leader. If you train me, I'll sign the card. If you don't, I don't do [any]thing.' The union person said, 'If you want to be a leader, I will give you the training you need.' She came to my house every day. She talked for hours until I got it."

There was a dramatic difference between union and nonunion immigrant women we interviewed; we could see it, and the women referred to it often. Union activists like Geoconda, Mirna, and Josefina without exception described a kind of coming into their own, an opportunity to develop themselves, to realize their humanity. Consuela Hernan, the women whose dreams of becoming an architect were interrupted by war and migration, described the change in herself: "I have seen myself more outspoken. No matter what, I can always fight for my rights. I have grown mentally. It was a big step in my life. Before I didn't know what was happening around me...go to work, come home, do my shopping—that was my life. Now I see a lot.... [I have had the] opportunity to meet so many different people, many different cultures. In the end we are all together—we're fighting for our life."

It was collective action, however, that provided the real catalyst for change. On-the-job contact between workers of varying ethnicities and nationalities provides important lessons in unity—Valerie Miller's friendship with her Vietnamese "brothers" is an example. Still, workplace interaction, limited to on-the-job experience, is as likely to produce tension as it is friendship. Collective action, particularly under the leadership of activists with expansive world views, like Geoconda Kline and Hattie Canty, brings workers together in an entirely different way and opens the possibility that life can be much more than one ever imagined. This was played out in the most dramatic way possible in Las Vegas from 1991 to 1998 in the longest strike in U.S. history.

Mary Burns, the young African American woman who had come to Las Vegas from Louisiana in 1970, looked out on the Strip on a cold December night in 1992.[9] Below, twelve thousand people sang and chanted in support of the 550 striking Frontier Casino workers. Mary, a maid at the Frontier ever since that day in 1971 when she and her aunt first visited the Culinary Union hiring hall, was one of them. "On the line! Shut it down! Vegas is a Union Town!" Enormous, Teamster-driven garbage trucks rumbled past, blocking access to the Strip. It was Mary's first big rally, and tears rolled down her face: "To me then it was so fulfilling," she said.

> You know who I could see among all those people walking down there was Martin Luther King. 'Cause everybody was together. Every race, color, creed, kids—the whole nine yards was together. And it was just so emotional. It looked like Martin Luther King was saying—to me he was saying, "Now my people coming together."

The strike at the Frontier Casino provided for union women like Mary Burns, Mirna Preciado, Geoconda Kline, and Hattie Canty, all of whom were intimately involved in the strike, over six years of impossibly hard collective struggle. It served to unite not only the 550 Frontier workers but also Las Vegas's entire casino workforce, forging in the process an unshakable Culinary Union identity that announced to the world in general and casino owners in particular that Culinary workers were united and not going away. One Day Longer!—the rallying cry of the strike—captured strikers' resolve to stay out one day longer than the Frontier owners. It was a cry that got into the very soul of the union.

It all began not as one might think in the fabulous megacasinos that made of the 1990s Strip a virtual construction zone of global empire but in an anachronistic little operation, the Frontier Casino. The Strip in the 1990s was postmodern, extravagant, corporate, and scripted to within an inch of its life—but not unidimensional. Scattered among the giants were older, family-owned enterprises that operated close to the bone, *sans* stage shows and choreographed fountains, where tourists with fanny packs fed slot machines hour after hour.

Chief among the small operations was Margaret Elardi's Frontier Casino. In 1989 Elardi and her sons, Tom and John, cash rich from the $112 million sale of a Laughlin, Nevada, casino, had purchased the Frontier from Summa Corporation, Howard Hughes's holding company. Lacking both the vision and the deep pockets of gaming's giants, the hard-operating Elardis' strategy was to cut costs wherever they could, and that was principally on the backs of their workers. In short order they proceeded to dismantle everything the union had fought for, slashing pay and health insurance benefits, discontinuing pension contributions, and breaking the contract in multiple ways.

By 1991 working conditions at the Frontier, where Mirna Preciado waitressed and Mary Burns worked as a maid, had become intolerable. With all options depleted, on September 9, 1991, 550 workers walked out [of the Frontier], Mirna and Mary among them. "Course, I was really scared," Mirna remembered. "But we was so united, all the workers. And we did it." For the Frontier strikers and Las Vegas workers in general, there was but one option: win. "The fact is," said Heidi Hughes, Mirna's fellow picket captain, "if we gave up on this we might as well give up on this town and be a minimum wage town. Once management or corporations or the rich people that run this town know that they can get the workers to give up and walk away, then it becomes open season."[10]

It got very hard quickly. The Elardis were vicious in their efforts to break the strike, violating numerous federal labor laws and announcing in their raw way to the press, "If the union wants to make war in the state of Nevada, the Elardis will make them wish they never started." Blind to the fact that they lacked the political connections and vast resources that undergirded big gaming corporations' power, the Elardis forged on, consistently underestimating the union's strength.

The Frontier strike continued from September 19, 1991 to January 31, 1998, the longest strike in U.S. history, "a showdown," in historian Hal Rothman's words, "of mythic proportions."[11] During that whole time, union members led by Geoconda Kline and Joe Dougherty and a full complement of picket captains such as Mirna Preciado maintained a twenty-four-hour picket line. Not one striker crossed it. "You never know what somebody is made up of until it's put in front of them," D. Taylor, secretary-treasurer and for twenty years Culinary's respected leader, commented later. "Those strikers were made of steel."[12]

Strikers on the picket line, who hailed from nineteen countries and spoke seven or eight languages, found in time that their differences could be a source of strength. Joe Dougherty laughed, "We noticed as we got on into the strike that everybody liked everybody." On cold mornings, he said, strikers who had in the past been prisoners in Siberia would let everyone know that it wasn't as bad as it could be. Everyone had their own experience of hardship to share, their own ways to help.[13]

Support for the Frontier Strike spread throughout the nation, and as it did strikers came to understand their importance to the labor movement as a whole.

It was all part of the transformation of which Mary Burns spoke. "I'll tell you, it changed me," she said a decade later. "It was five hundred of us walked out, and it was like we had a bond that nobody could break no matter what. Nobody walked back across that picket line. I don't know if there was Jesus or what it was, but nobody walked back across there. I say that was to prove to the nation, the country, that people could stick together." It was hard, she said, and sometimes heartbreaking, "because we walked in the cold, in the rain, and we felt like some-time people had let us down when nobody comes, you know.... But we stayed, we stayed out there. Some people got jobs and left and went other places, but 250 of us, I think, still stayed out there in that rain. It was lonesome a lot of times. And it still brings tears to my eyes. Still today."

Mirna Preciado agreed. "I changed totally," she said. "I was happy, because for the first time in many years—you know—I feel strong. I could do something on my own. I'm a woman from Mexico. I don't even speak good English, but I could fight for my rights. That's the beauty of when you learn about what the union is, 'cause the person that I am right now, the woman that I am right now, it's what I learned in the union."

On January 31, 1998, six years, four months, and ten days after the strike began, the Elardis sold the Frontier to industrialist Phil Ruffin, effectively ending the strike in victory for the union. Every worker who wanted returned to his or her job with full seniority; every individual got everything to which he or she was entitled, including pension credits for the time they were on strike. Thousands of strikers, families, and supporters gathered outside the Frontier on the evening of January 31 for Jesse Jackson's ceremonial cutting of the ribbon allowing strikers back to their jobs. Cooks, maids, and waitresses glowed. Mary Burns, tears run-ning down her face, said, "My husband always told me, you can break a rich man, but you can't break a poor man." Lydia Joffrion, a cashier at the Frontier, asked, summing up more than six years of struggle, "What do I want in the future? I want to work in the hotel I fought really hard for. I want to be able to buy myself a home, which I'll be able to do now I've got my job back.... I want my son and my nieces and nephews to be able to come into a workplace and say, 'I'm not going to be paid pennies, I'm not going to be paid minimum wage, because my mom, my aunt, my cousin fought so I didn't have to scrape to get by.' "[14] It was a legacy that would sustain everyone in the difficult years ahead.

After the Frontier strike, union members continued to construct a bulkhead for working people in Las Vegas's booming global economy. Fired by victories like those at the Frontier, the MGM, and the Rio, women unionists began to discover new roles for themselves beyond the casinos' walls. They responded to crises, notably 9/11 and the unprecedented decline in gaming revenues that followed the economic downturn of 2008 (see chapter 12); built an unstoppable grassroots political machine; and extended members' vision of the American dream by developing programs like the Culinary Training Academy (CTA) and the Citizenship Project. In every case, members' activism was central.

In 2008 we picked our way through the construction zones that surrounded the Culinary Training Academy (the Academy is adding a $7 million, 25,000-square-foot space to its already substantial building on Las Vegas's west side). Inside, we were delighted to be greeted by all three of the Culinary Training Academy's executive officers: Sterling Burpee, chef and chief culinary officer; Pam Egan, chief financial officer; and Steven Horsford, CEO (Horsford, just twenty-nine when he took on the leadership of the Culinary Training Academy in 2002, is a Nevada State Senator and the Senate's first African American majority leader).

The Culinary Training Academy, designed to meet the gaming industry's growing demand for skilled workers and at the same time provide advancement opportunities to both union and nonunion workers, was the brainchild of Las Vegas chef George Seess. It was begun in 1993 as a joint labor/management educational program between Local 226, Bartenders Union Local 165, and twenty-four major resort properties on the Strip. Each property contributed a negotiated per-worker sum to cover operating costs, and an executive board composed of representatives from management and labor oversaw the CTA's operations. Widely cited as an example of a successful training partnership between labor and management, the CTA, for a relatively modest input from industry, provides casinos with "work-ready" employees in large numbers, including skilled men and women able to service the chef-designed gourmet and specialty restaurants that increasingly characterize Las Vegas. There is a high demand for graduates of the CTA. Hotels, who frequently send recruiters to CTA graduation ceremonies, report that turnover is 50 percent lower among CTA graduates than employees hired off the street.[15]

"You're worth more than minimum wage!" proclaimed a huge banner in the Academy's foyer, a slogan repeated on all CTA material. Inside students of all colors and nationalities crowded into classrooms, as the Westside Bistro, a restaurant operated by CTA students training for advanced jobs in casino restaurants, geared up for the day's lunch traffic.

The Academy is the largest provider of training for entry-level and incumbent workers in Las Vegas. In 2006 it enrolled 3,000 students, a figure it hoped to double in two years, placing 85 percent of them in good union jobs.[16] Workers who have more than six months' seniority at one of CTA's twenty-four "partner hotels" can enroll for free in CTA courses that provide training for culinary apprentices, fine-dining servers, professional cooks, sommeliers, and wine servers. New workers (60 percent of CTA's students) may enroll (often with the support of federal or state grants) in these and other entry-level courses that prepare them for positions as barbacks, guest room attendants, porters, and food servers.[17] CTA students under the supervision of instructors also cater events and help feed thousands of Las Vegas children and hungry families through the "3 Square" program.[18]

Our young guide for the day enthusiastically toured us through the academy's kitchens, dining halls, and classrooms. Photos of board members, including corporate grandees, hung on the walls, but it was the spirit of the union and its insistence on dignity that walked the halls. In every classroom, the pride and love teachers had for students was apparent. Bernice Thomas, a long-time CTA instructor, currently was mentoring young welfare moms training for jobs in the gaming industry. "A lot of these girls have never worked before," she said, "and they have low self-esteem. After two weeks, they're bubbly, they're smiling. They know they're ready for work."[19]

At noon we waited in the academy's Westside Bistro, a popular lunch spot, for an appointment with Hattie Canty, and watched from across the room as she made her way to us, speaking with dignity and warmth to everyone who called her name—which seemed to be everyone in the restaurant. "Where did the idea for the academy come from," we asked when she made it at last to our table. "You were at the start of the CTA—is that right?" Canty laughed, "Yes, I was on the Board. But it was George Seess that had the idea. I wish it were mine, but it's not." She continued, "It's amazing what this labor movement has done. I've seen people here in the Culinary Training Academy grow like you won't believe." Mrs. Canty admitted it was not always an easy sell—a steady job as a cook's helper is not necessarily the dream twenty-year-olds have in mind. "[I tell them], if you've got to start in the kitchen washing dishes, get it, because once you get into the hotel after you've been there for six months, you can come back here free and take any class you want to, because that's one of the benefits that the hotel will pay for. We have a lot of upgrades coming in from the hotel, and as long as they come here, get that certificate, the hotels give them a shot at that job. What we're doing here at the Culinary Training Academy is good for our city—the whole city."

In addition to job skills, the CTA also provides language classes. One of our favorite stops was the VESOL (Vocational English for Speakers of Other Languages) classroom. Funded initially with a $1.9 million grant from the U.S. Department of Labor, VESOL serves both students eager to learn English and employers who need skilled, English-speaking workers. Over 2,500 immigrant workers have been trained in the English language, 80 percent of whom have gone on to get jobs in southern Nevada's hospitality industry.[20]

Closely associated with the Culinary Training Academy is the Union's Citizenship Project, another area of union activists' involvement. "We were finding that huge numbers of our members wanted to become citizens," Pilar Weiss, the Union's young political director, told us when we sat down with her. "Las Vegas had very few immigrant lawyers—not all of them ethical. [We heard stories of] people spending $8,000 for an immigration lawyer [who then] absconded with their money."[21] Pilar continued, "So in 2001 we decided to be the free way to become a citizen." The nonprofit Citizenship Project was the outgrowth of that decision. In 2005 the project helped 750 people with immigration issues; a year later that number grew to 1,200.[22] "Twenty percent of all naturalizations in Nevada come through the Culinary Union program," Pilar said with pride.

In addition to the Citizenship Project's direct aid to immigrants seeking citizenship (free to members and nonmembers alike), the Culinary Union dedicates considerable resources to educating all its members to the importance of unity and immigrant rights and to fighting the toxic atmosphere that so often surrounds issues of immigration. "Forty percent of Culinary Union members are recent immigrants," a 2006 Culinary Union Newsletter reported. "That means 40 percent of our power with the casino industry comes directly from our immigrant brothers and sisters who are also our coworkers. We need each other to stay strong. We work in an industry that would run right over us if we divided ourselves along immigrant and nonimmigrant lines."[23]

In 2003 Culinary Union members, with citizens and trade unionists from around the country, participated in the Immigrant Workers Freedom Ride. Over one thousand "Freedom Riders," Geoconda Kline and Mirna Preciado among them, boarded busses in Los Angeles, San Francisco, Seattle, Portland, Las Vegas, Reno, Dallas, Minneapolis, Chicago, and Miami for the long journey to Washington, DC and New York City, stopping in cities along the way to educate Americans about the importance of immigration reform.[24] In Reno and Las Vegas the send-offs were gala events—smiles all around, mariachis playing. D. Taylor, the union's secretary-treasurer, spoke to the crowd. "Immigrant workers work hard," he said. "They pay their taxes and they sacrifice a tremendous amount for their families. Here in Las Vegas, they build our houses, they clean our hotels, they take care of us when we're in the hospital. They are us."[25] Union member Asela Martinez added, tears running down her face, "We've had enough with all the injustices done to us. We are hardworking people and are as honest as anyone in the U.S. I immigrated in 1985 with my four children. Never will I forget that day when in my arms I brought my three girls and a boy. When we had to come in a horse trailer as if we were animals. It breaks my heart because I know all the sufferings we are going through. That is the reason I am going…to carry the message to the president and Congress."[26]

Meetings with Congress in Washington, DC, and a rollicking rally of over one hundred thousand in New York's Flushing Meadows, where U.S. Representative

John Lewis, an original Freedom Rider, welcomed the "new" riders, concluded the journey. Those huge events, however, were nearly eclipsed by the emotional stop in Little Rock, Arkansas. Hattie Canty and Mary Burns were not there in person, but their spirits and those of the tens of thousands of African Americans who went before certainly were. At the evening gathering on the steps of Central High School, Minnijean Brown Tricky, one of the Little Rock Nine, welcomed riders to "hallowed ground," and chants of "si se puede!" intermingled with the strains "We Shall Overcome." Across the street a group of counterdemonstrators added their opinion: "What do we want? Mexicans out! When do we want it? Now!"[27]

Finally, from the 1980s forward, the Culinary Union has focused enormous effort on building a grassroots political power base in Nevada. "There's probably not a more highly political industry than ours," the Culinary Union's legendary political director, Glen Arnodo, commented. "By its nature, it's a political industry, so every struggle we have, from contractual to organizing, is going to have a political manifestation in some way, shape, or form."[28] In this effort the union had several advantages, the first being its size. With sixty thousand members and behind them family, friends, and neighbors, the union outranks in sheer numbers any other entity, save the Democratic and Republican parties in the state. Those members, the union was convinced, could become knowledgeable, skilled, and committed political actors. The union also realized that gaming corporations, although often arrayed against union members, also could benefit from the union's support in locales into which it wished to expand and in Washington, DC, where gaming was constantly under legislative scrutiny. "In most states outside Nevada...[the industry] is not held in very high esteem," explained D. Taylor, "and in order to get certain things done legislatively...or establish itself in a new market...sometimes they need our assistance."[29] The union drove a hard bargain, and in exchange for "assistance" demanded recompense, which in the 1990s chiefly meant the industry's agreement to honor card check neutrality.

At the heart of the union's political initiative, as always, stood its members. Pilar Weiss, who in 2005 stepped into Glen Arnodo's shoes, understood that well. Pilar, who is nearly always the youngest person and often the only woman in meetings of Nevada heavy hitters, introduced us to Jeanette Hill, a member of Culinary's political team.

Jeanette Hill, who arrived in Las Vegas in 1974 in the same wave of African American migration that brought Hattie Canty and Mary Burns to Nevada, is the kind of woman who brightens any room. A maid, porter, and runner at the Las Vegas Hilton, Jeanette often worked in the early years "up there where Elvis Presley used to be at all the time," struggling, she laughed, with "all those round beds."[30]

In 2002 after nearly twenty years of employment, Jeanette's life took a new and decidedly more interesting direction when Pilar Weiss asked her to "come out" on a political campaign. Jeanette loved the excitement of the campaign, which was Steven Horsford's first bid for state senate. "The thing about it," she said, "is you're doing it for a cause, and it's a good cause. So even though I might get some doors slammed in my face, that's okay, I keep going.... I always end up with one [vote]. If it's not one, maybe two the next week." Early on Jeanette learned the union's approach to political campaigns: look a long ways out, choose battles carefully, and win every race you enter. "Every campaign that I have worked, we have won it," Jeanette said. "Every one. And it's a great feeling behind it, too." She said, "I don't come out to work a campaign and lose. I don't even use that word."

Jeanette hadn't been interested in politics before she started "coming out." But afterward, she said, "[all of that kind of stuff] started getting my attention." She continued, "[Now] when they get to talking about stocks and different stuff on the news and different campaigns, you know, I find myself just like...glued to the TV." At the time we interviewed her, Jeanette was "out" on political campaigns and union organizing drives as much as she was in the casino working. "Now I tell people," she said, "'you know what? I'm on this path. But I don't know where this path is going to lead me. But I can tell you this, one day I'm going to be a great leader. You just wait'." We all laughed, quite sure Jeanette was not kidding. "But with me," she went on, "it's going to be all different races. You see like Martin Luther King, he had a dream. I had a dream as well. And my dream was I going to be a leader, and I was going to lead all people. All generations and nationalities. That was my dream."

"This union is such a place [for women] to thrive and organize," Pilar Weiss told us when we returned to her office.[31] "The majority of organizers are women. Geo is critical. I have teams of workers on leave of absence for political election cycles—forty to sixty women, women who become these powerhouses." She went on, "There's a woman porter at Harrah's. She has three kids. At first she seemed very shy. But now she's willing to go up to someone she doesn't know, convince them to vote, and tell them who to vote for. You see these women leaders who blow you away. It's so grueling, and for women with family obligations, it's a big sacrifice."

"This is an opportunity for women to find their power," Pilar continued, "especially immigrant women. They walked here, came in a trunk. It's really grueling, but they're finding this leadership."

Here we're always in battle mode. Everyone will find a way. People take care of each other. [So many] kids grew up on the Frontier picket line—and they're wonderful kids. You see this leadership rise up. It's not like other organizations where you go to one meeting a month. No, here it's "here's my heart." When you're in battle mode, people have commitment and they make it work. Within the union and immigrant community, there's this feeling, let's pitch in. We have a lot of Culinary families. It's easier for people to be an activist. It's not a secret culture.

"Here's my heart"—that seemed to sum up the stories of women union activists. Today for working people it is often a legacy of defeat that is passed on to future generations. But among members of the Culinary Union and for women like Hattie Canty, Mary Burns, Geoconda Kline, Josefina Huerta, and Mirna Preciado, it is a legacy of triumph, a stunning one given the propensity of global capital to extract every penny from workers and made even more impressive by the fact that there has not been one month, one week, one day during the last twenty-five years that the union has not been embattled. And while the successes are due to many things—leaders, strategy, research, and the particular history of union concentration on the Las Vegas Strip—we doubt that anyone would dispute the centrality of women in constructing that legacy.

Part III
NONUNION WOMEN STAND UP

DARLENE *JESPERSEN V. HARRAH'S* ENTERTAINMENT, INC.

> When you think about it, women are always put into a category...told how to look and how to dress and sometimes how to act....It's for men's gratification and because casinos made $300 million and it wasn't enough. It made me angry.

—Darlene Jespersen, Bartender

In the spring of 2000, Chuck Whitaker (not his real name), manager of the Food and Beverage Department at Harrah's, Reno, sent a letter to all food and beverage employees detailing Harrah's new appearance and grooming standards and launching the corporation's "Personal Best" initiative. It was a letter that shortly would jettison Darlene Jespersen's twenty-year career as one of Harrah's top bartenders—and land the corporation in the midst of a major legal battle, as a consequence of which "Jespersen" would become a cause célèbre and near-household name to lawyers and law students across the country. At issue was the right of a massively wealthy employer attempting to brand its particular form of entertainment to require a female employee to wear a heavily made-up, stereotypical "Barbie" face to work, even if her job, done successfully for years without makeup, involved lugging cases of beer.

"We have a great opportunity right here in the Beverage Department," Whitaker wrote, "to raise the total service performance of the beverage team from where we are now, which is good—to where we want to be, and that is, truly great."[1] Truly great? Darlene Jespersen felt uneasy. She had no trouble with service, having consistently garnered praise for her work at the Sports Bar. Still, she had grown somewhat suspect of Harrah's efforts at improvement, which seemed always to focus on employees and their alleged inadequacies and rarely on what she and other workers perceived as the corporation's declining standards for customer service.

The Personal Best Initiative was all about "looking your personal best and delivering the best in service to our customers," Whitaker went on, assuring employees—none of whom were represented by a union—that Harrah's would provide them with "the tools and training to ensure [their] success."[2] As part of the Personal Best program, he wrote, employees would be required to attend Image Training where Personal Best Image Facilitators would make them over and instruct them on how to maintain their "personal best image." At the end of the training, Harrah's would photograph everyone looking his or her Personal Best. The photos would be filed in a Rolodex on supervisors' desks and copies given to employees to take home to refer to in dressing for work. Employees would be required to report every day ten minutes before starting time so that supervisors might measure their appearance against the Personal Best photographs.[3] Employees' failure to maintain their Personal Best Image would result in discipline up to and including termination.

Twenty of Harrah's twenty-eight properties nationwide announced the Personal Best Initiative at about the same time. The standards required that beverage service personnel be "well groomed, appealing to the eye, firm and body toned, and comfortable with maintaining this look while wearing the specified uniform," and delineated specific guidelines for men and women in each job category. Standards for men seemed to dwell mostly on what they couldn't do: they couldn't wear colored fingernail polish or eye and facial makeup. They were to keep their hair above the top of their shirt collars and couldn't wear ponytails. Their hands and fingernails were to be clean with nails "neatly trimmed at all times." Strangely, the guidelines did not forbid beards or moustaches.[4]

Female employees' appearance standards, Harrah's claimed later, were no more restrictive or onerous than those for men. Women's hair "must be teased, curled, or styled every day [they] work[ed]" and "must be worn down at all times, no exceptions." Stockings were to be of "nude or natural color consistent with employee's skin tone. No runs." Nail polish could be "clear, white, pink or red color only. No exotic nail art or length." Finally, *a lot* of makeup was required— "lip color... foundation/concealer and/or face powder, as well as blush and mascara applied neatly in complimentary colors."[5]

It was the makeup that worried Darlene Jespersen.

Darlene Jespersen, when we first interviewed her, had been working at Harrah's for nearly twenty-one years, the last nineteen of them as a bartender. From the beginning, we enjoyed being with Darlene. She is delightful—a tall, unassuming woman with a dry and ready wit.

Darlene told us she moved to Reno when she was three and had lived there ever since.[6] Growing up, she never wanted to work in a casino—"it seemed like everybody did"—but one night she compared notes with a bartender friend and discovered that he made a lot of money. "It was like, 'I want that job,'" she laughed.

Bartending, then as now, is a prize casino job. Harrah's didn't hire people off the street as bartenders or barbacks—you had to transfer into the job—so Darlene applied for a job as a dishwasher. "They never called me," she told us, "so I went in there a couple times a week. I just kept coming in bugging them, bugging them. That's how I got a [dishwashing] job at Harrah's. I had to torment them!"

After three months of washing dishes, Darlene put in for a transfer and got a job as a barback. Barbacks, Darlene explained, "do all the dirty work—wash dishes, cut the fruit, get the ice, get the beer, stock the bar...clean the floor and clean the drains." After six months of barbacking, the bartenders nominated Darlene for bar school, a real compliment, especially for a woman (there were hardly any women bartenders in casinos at the time).[7] Commenting on the bartenders' favorable review, Darlene said, "Well, I didn't call in [sick]. I was there on time. Whenever I went into work, I always tried to do the best I could for that day. That's just the type of person I am. I have value in how I do things."

Darlene thought those values came from her mom. Her parents divorced when she was nine, leaving her mom with the bills and nearly all the responsibility for raising Darlene and her sister. Her dad was a compulsive gambler. "He kind of had a sickness," Darlene said, "and even though he was supposed to pay child support—a lot of times mom didn't get it. It was really hard, but she got through it. She's a very strong woman." Even though her dad dropped the ball on child raising, Darlene in her gentle way was philosophical about it. "It was kind of sad because at one point he was working two jobs, yet he was broke. But after my sister and I turned eighteen, he made up for it. He kept paying Mom until it was all paid up. He was good like that. A lot probably wouldn't have done it."

Darlene was surprised how much she liked bartending. She enjoyed the customers, and like most of the women we interviewed built many relationships. "I was at the Sport's Bar for over ten years," she said, "so [customers] knew me.... You know, you see them through all parts of their lives, weddings, divorces, deaths, births. For awhile there at least once a week, I'd have a minimum of one customer call me or send me a card."

Darlene liked her fellow bartenders as well, but thought some of the men went out of their way to harass women. "There were very few women [bartenders] when I started there," she said, "only one or two. I don't know if it's Harrah's bartenders or just men, but they try to give you a hard time....They try to make you cry and stuff. Not all of them, but a good percentage. If you did something wrong, they'd really get on your back." Cocktail servers are supposed to call drinks in a certain order, Darlene explained, which makes it easier for the bartenders to remember. "And maybe she'll put the tonics before the collins," she went on, "and they'll get after her for it. It's no big deal. But they make it like she almost ran over their mother. It's stupid. I think they try to show their authority. It's a lot easier if you talk nicer."

Darlene's description of her work day said a great deal about her character. When she came in, she said,

> I would wipe the whole bar down and clean all the ash trays. [I want to] have them a certain way. Right by the napkins. I mean, I do. I don't like one here and five down there. It's got to have balance to it. And then I would stock everything, and usually I overstock because that way during the day you wear it down, but you don't have to do it at the end of the day because sometimes you get real busy. I kept up on it. You know, kept everything neat and clean. Because when I walk up to a bar, I don't want to see cigarette ashes or whatever.... That's how I liked it—neat and clean looking.

Darlene looked out for the company's interests as well. Bartenders are allowed to give away free drinks while a customer is actively playing, she explained—about one drink every twenty minutes. When people tried to scam her and get a drink every five or ten minutes, "Well," she said, "we have that rule to fall back on—because it is a business also, and I respect that."

Darlene got many compliments for her work, and her file steadily filled with letters from customers and positive reviews from supervisors. One guest wrote that Darlene "always greets us with a smile and a friendly word. We all look forward to seeing her each time we are in Reno, which is four or five times a year. All the people that work at Harrah's are great, but I feel Darlene deserves extra recognition."[8] Another customer reported enthusiastically, "My friends and I always do lotsa video poker at the Sports Bar. We call it 'Darlene's Bar' cause she's just great!"[9] Darlene's supervisors regularly complimented her as well. In 1988 one rated her as "highly effective or exceptional" in all areas, including appearance, commenting that Darlene's "attitude is very positive and *exceptional* & she is an asset to our dept."[10] In 1996 another supervisor nominated Darlene for an outstanding performance award, noting that she "makes a lot of Harrah's guests feel good and this is proven by her guest comments. Darlene has a subtle manner that makes a positive impression on our guests."[11]

During these twenty years of superlative performance, Darlene did not wear makeup. Like many women she simply did not feel comfortable with it on her face. She was always neat and clean, and by and large that seemed enough for Harrah's. Once, in an early and desultory effort at cosmetics management,

the company made appointments for female employees with a makeup consultant. The consultant, Darlene said, plucked her eyebrows and made up half her
face so she could see the difference:

> He told me the colors and stuff to buy, and I went out and bought all
> this stuff. I tried it for a couple of weeks, and I felt really bad about it. I
> did not feel comfortable. I mean, here I am a barback, and I'm picking
> up two, three cases of beer.... I just felt totally degraded. So I went home
> one day, and I threw it all in the garbage. And they never said [anything].
> Sometimes they'd say, "Your face looks really washed out behind the
> bar, and you need to have something on so you don't look as washed
> out." So I just said, "Okay," but I never did it.

Makeup was never mentioned in her annual evaluations, and Darlene continued to be a model bartender.

Shortly after Chuck Whitaker sent out his letter about the Personal Best initiative, Harrah's Brand Operations division began scheduling makeovers for all
Food and Beverage employees at the Reno Convention Center. The makeovers
were to be done by a Las Vegas firm, The Winning Edge, which specialized in
"corporate training, business and personal coaching and image consulting," and
is one of many firms riding the current wave of frenetic self-improvement.[12]
Reimi Marden, its owner and founder, says her company's mission is to "empower people with their own greatness, help them to define what winning in
life means to them and show them how to lead themselves to the next level of
personal and business success."[13] (Marden was named a southern Nevada "Distinguished Woman" for her contributions to Las Vegas industries and to the
Community College of Southern Nevada where she teaches Professional Dress
and Grooming.[14]) More interesting is Marden's former position as sales director
for BeautiControl Cosmetics, an international direct sales company—a reminder
of how Harrah's commitment to making over thousands of female casino workers nicely combines the profit interests of the gaming and cosmetic industries
(the latter enjoyed $25 billion dollars in profits in 1999[15]).

The makeovers were not cheap. In Las Vegas the cost of the makeovers was pro-
jected to be $3,000 per employee.[16] Why would Harrah's pay that much money to
"improve" employees? The answer lies in a decade-old marketing strategy.

In June 2005 Harrah's Entertainment, Inc., acquired Caesars Entertainment
and in so doing became the largest casino company in the world with forty casinos in twelve states and three countries. The acquisition, which united Harrah's forty-six thousand employees and 2004 revenues of $4.55 billion with
Caesars' fifty thousand employees and revenues of $4.21 billion, solidified Har-
rah's Entertainment's position as "the world's largest provider of branded casino

entertainment."[17] *Branded* is the word to note. It is the business strategy that is key to Harrah's success. It also stands at the center of the Personal Best Initiative and Darlene Jespersen's life.

Harrah's first began to consider the issue of branding in the mid-1980s, when former CEO Phil Satre noted that customers who gambled at Harrah's in one city tended to gamble at Harrah's in other cities.[18] That went against the conventional wisdom that gamblers were in general a fickle lot who gravitated not to any particular casino but rather to the biggest show in town. Based on this thinking, megacasinos spent millions on spectacle, constructing volcanoes, fountain shows, and Venetian palaces to lure customers in.

Satre, convinced that the popular wisdom was wrong, at least in regard to Harrah's, which always owned more properties than other corporations, shared his ideas with John Boushy, Harrah's senior vice president of brand operations and information technology.[19] In the 1990s Boushy and Harrah's new COO Gary Loveman took Satre's vision and ran with it.[20] Instead of spectacle, Harrah's under Loveman and Boushy sank money into a winner's information network (WINet), the industry's first national customer database. Previously, each Harrah's property—Atlantic City, Las Vegas, Reno, Tunica, etc.—had maintained its own database and its own customer-reward system. The databases could not "talk" to each other, and consequently Harrah's Atlantic City had no way to know the gambling habits of a Harrah's Las Vegas customer when he or she arrived in Atlantic City. Nor could the Las Vegas customer use his or her "credits" at the Atlantic City property. WINet changed all that. By the millennium all the customer databases were combined in a vast information system that tracked customers' preferences and habits in a single national player card system—Total Rewards—in which members acquired points for gambling and used those points for hotel room discounts, meals, birthday presents, rounds of golf, and other "once-in-a-lifetime experiences" at any of Harrah's forty casinos.[21]

The integrated, coast-to-coast system parted the customer from his money very efficiently. According to Marc Cooper in his provocative reminiscence, *The Last Honest Place in America,* the goal of the new technology was to "not only maximize customer 'seat time,' but also to increase REVPAC—Revenue Per Available Customer."[22] Cooper quotes Randy Fine, Harrah's Vice President of Total Rewards, who talked about deciding which Harrah's gamblers to reward with free lodging and other comps:

> We have a world-class [database of twenty-five million customers] that tells us if we should give a customer a room at what price. This has driven up our gaming revenue fifty to sixty percent. Our problem isn't just filling a hotel, but with whom we fill it. We want the best players, the players

who are going to give us the best revenue while staying in that room.... We have twenty years of data on the same people. We know everything about you; what you play; how much you play; when you play.... In short, if there's anything to know about you, we're gonna know it.[23]

Harrah's also set about building an attractive and powerful image across all its properties so that when customers walked into any Harrah's they would be swept up in a familiar and fabulous ambience, one they had enjoyed before. That included "branding" not only games, but employees' looks as well, and that is where the Personal Best policy came in. As Harrah's spokesperson Gary Thompson said, standardizing employee appearances was "a necessary ingredient in the company's efforts to establish consistency at its properties nationwide."[24] He added, "We see this effort as an important step in branding ourselves as a corporation. We want to make sure our customers can expect a consistent level and quality of service at all of our properties."[25]

It seemed to work spectacularly well, at least on the financial side. In 1999 the company's growth in "cross-market revenue" increased 33 percent, and profits more than doubled since introducing the loyalty card.[26] John Boushy became the first casino marketing executive to be included in the *Advertising Age* list of one hundred top marketing executives, and Gary Loveman was named Best COO in the gaming and lodging industry by *Institutional Investor* magazine.[27]

With the acquisition of Caesars, Harrah's branding strategy seemed positively brilliant. The day after the merger was announced, harrahs.com was bouncing with information about how customers could get the "same great service and all of the excitement at more locations than ever." It announced, "The upcoming year will bring a combined rewards program to offer customers full portability when visiting any of our casinos," encouraging everyone to sign on to "Total Rewards."[28] It all promised to reshape the world of gambling.

Although branding in company parlance connoted something positive—fun, excitement, reaching for the stars—that was not the only message Harrah's was conveying. Behind the rah-rah of the Personal Best policy lay a darker, more aggressive message, occasionally revealed in public statements in which managers worried that employees, unregulated, might slip to their Personal Worst.

Gary Thompson, Harrah's spokesperson, likened the standardized appearance requirements to those found in the fast food industry. "It's not unlike (the consistency) you would expect at McDonald's," he said. "You wouldn't want burgers and fries served to you by somebody who hasn't washed in weeks."[29] Hasn't washed in weeks? Was he talking about casino workers' hygiene practices? Casino workers, Darlene Jespersen would assure him, were proud of their presentation—hygiene included.

Similarly, beverage supervisor Michele Little of St. Louis noted that the ban on upswept hair was aimed at women who "would throw [their hair] up in combs" because they got up late and were in a hurry. "Obviously, they're not at their personal best," she snipped. Little welcomed the initiative because with it she could consult her Rolodex and discipline shaggy employees. "It's a way for me to hold them accountable," she said.[30]

Marilyn Winn, Harrah's senior vice president for human resources, echoed Thompson's and Little's remarks. "Beverage departments were picked because they consistently got the lowest ratings in customer questionnaires," she said, adding that the company had "broad authority to set rules covering everything from the one-inch minimum heel for women servers' shoes to the color of their nail polish.... There are all sorts of rules in any job," Winn lectured on. "In my mind, that's why they call it work."[31]

Workers quickly picked up on the darker tone and, interviewed off the premises, described the Personal Best policy as rigid and intrusive. They asked for anonymity for fear of reprisals. "Harrah's is a good company to work for, but I just find this extremely restrictive," one waitress said. "It's like our own judgment isn't trusted."[32]

Meanwhile, back in Reno, Darlene and the other food and beverage employees were filing into the Convention Center for their makeovers. Tables were set up in a giant horseshoe with Winning Edge consultants on one side and seats for employees on the other. Meeting with the makeover consultants took about an hour, Darlene remembered, and attending the hair consultant class another two hours. Most of it seemed silly to Darlene—"you'd already been doing this stuff for twenty years or more. I mean, shampooing your hair?" Both men and women attended the makeover session, but "it was short and sweet for the men," according to one male employee.[33]

After the consultation, Harrah's scheduled appointments for employees to have their Personal Best pictures taken and sign a "Beverage Department Image Transformation" pledge. Darlene had her pictures taken, but declined to sign the pledge which read in the pseudoenthusiastic language so common to this kind of endeavor:

> Yes, I want to be my personal best! That means I:
>
> - commit to meeting the Personal Appearance standards
> - commit to maintaining my own "Personal Best" standard as my photographs show.[34]

Darlene talked at length about those difficult weeks in mid-2000 after she said "no" to Image Transformation. Her relationship with Department Manager

Chuck Whitaker, who continually pressed her to sign the pledge, was particularly poor. Whitaker had been Darlene's barback at one time and later was promoted to supervisor and eventually manager. In one exchange Darlene remembered telling Whitaker, "I will not wear makeup. It's against my belief. It's degrading. It's humiliating that I would have to do that to do this job that I've been doing for twenty years without it."

"Well, Darlene, it's not my decision," Darlene remembered Whitaker saying. "It's corporate. You know, I think I have good-looking legs, but they don't let me come to work in shorts."

"That was his mentality," Darlene said. "I don't have respect for him. A lot of times his attitude is, 'if you don't like it, go somewhere else.' If I were a manager, I'd want good harmony with my people, and I'd stick up for them. But he isn't like that."

Chuck Whitaker's good-looking legs provided one of the few light moments Darlene experienced during the spring and summer of 2000. In an effort to get some clarity on Harrah's position, Darlene finally requested a meeting with Employee Relations. At that meeting, she remembered, a female manager said, "Let me call Corporate in Las Vegas and see what they say about a twenty-one-year employee not doing this, and we'll get back to you." Darlene jumped every time the phone rang. After two months of stress and worry, she told the general manager, "I deserve an answer. I don't feel that Harrah's should disrupt my whole life.... You guys owe me an answer." She surmised, "They were checking all the legal stuff."

Six weeks later when she went to the office for her inspection, Chuck told Darlene that if she had time—"if I had time!" she laughed—there'd be a meeting that morning in Human Relations. At the meeting, Darlene remembered that Whitaker and managers above him told her, "You have to do it."

"I won't," Darlene replied.

"Well, then," she remembered them saying, "you can resign."

"I'm not resigning over this," Darlene replied, adding, "you know, in our society women are always being pushed around. For twenty years I haven't gotten caught in this bullshit, and I'm not starting now."

"Their eyes bugged out of their head," Darlene laughed later. "It's like, 'I'm not starting. You don't pay me enough to degrade myself. And I will not do it for you." She went on, "When you think about it, women are always put into a category...told how to look and how to dress and sometimes how to act....It's for men's gratification and because casinos made $300 million and it wasn't enough. It made me angry. And [one of the upper managers] goes, 'I sense a form of hostility here.' We all laughed at that."

We asked Darlene what gave her the courage to fight back. "I don't know," she replied, "but I remember those times that I did that makeup when I was younger and how bad I felt about it. And the fact that I was a woman and I was being told that. I mean, Gary [a fellow bartender] isn't told that, and he's older than me—and I've got more hair than he does. I had to do it because I was a woman, and I thought, 'I will never let that happen to me again.'"

Harrah's reassigned Darlene back to personnel, meaning she had thirty days to find a different job within Harrah's with no guarantee of the same hourly rate. She called it the "thirty-day-we're-going-to-fire-you mode." Darlene went in at least once a week to look at the job list, and there was nothing there.

At the end of thirty days—on August 10, 2000—Darlene Jespersen was terminated.

"I saw it coming," Darlene told us, "so I tried to prepare for it as best as I could." Her first efforts led nowhere. She called the Nevada Equal Employment Opportunity Commission and talked to its director. "He basically said that the employer has the right to ask women to wear makeup as long as it's a reasonable request," Darlene remembered. "'Yes, it's been proven,' [he said.] 'It's been tried in court, and it is okay that women can wear makeup and men aren't supposed to.'"

Next she talked to someone at the State Labor Board who said that in Nevada, a right to work state, "Your employer can fire you for any reason." That message was confirmed by two lawyers she consulted. It was a predictable dilemma—few lawyers in Reno, a virtual company town, would risk going up against a giant in the gaming world, one with endlessly deep legal pockets. Darlene by that point was "real depressed."

During those awful months, Darlene dragged herself to a party given annually by a cocktail server. "There was a lady there," Darlene remembered, "who said 'you need to call this lady named Kricket.'" Kricket, she said, was affiliated with the union. "And I'm like, okay… that's not going to do me any good. I'm already going to be drop-kicked out the door. They're just deciding which shoe is going to do it. So I didn't call her. Then I got terminated, and another cocktail server called me up and said, 'You've got to call this lady named Kricket.' God, Kricket again. So I called up Kricket, and she's affiliated with the Alliance for Workers Rights. It was about 10:00 or 10:30 at night… and I said this is Darlene Jespersen and I'm—"

"She goes, 'I know who you are.'

"And I go, 'You do?'

"And she goes, 'Yes, I've been waiting for you to call me.'"

A few days later, Darlene, Kricket Martinez, and Tom Stoneburner, the director of the Alliance for Workers' Rights, met. In short order they consulted with the American Civil Liberties Union, found a lawyer who was enthusiastic about taking the case, and went with Darlene to talk with him.

"[The lawyer] says, 'Give me a week and let me do some research, and I'll get back to you.'" Darlene remembered. A week later, he was smiling when Darlene walked into his office. She asked him: "Did they violate my civil rights?"

"And he goes, 'You bet they did.'"

On July 6, 2001, Darlene Jespersen filed suit against Harrah's Operating Company, Inc., in the District Court for Nevada. Word of Darlene's case spread quickly helped by people at the Alliance for Workers' Rights. "After that my phone was ringing off the hook," Darlene said. "A lot of it was support, too.... I've had a lot of women call me. A lot of men, too." Darlene all of a sudden was at the center of media attention. Articles about her appeared in Nevada papers, *People Magazine*, and *Mother Jones*.[35]

Especially exciting was Darlene's appearance on *Good Morning America*. We, like most of progressive Reno, were up to watch her. In a split screen "dialogue," Darlene was paired with Jan Jones, the mayor of Las Vegas from 1991 to 1999, an unsuccessful candidate for governor in 2000, and at the time vice president of Harrah's. It was not much of a dialogue since the two women were in separate Las Vegas studios and could neither hear nor see each other. Jones, who clearly enjoys makeup herself, succeeded in alienating herself from many female supporters with her public opposition to Darlene. Jones talked with Paula Zahn, host of *Good Morning America*, about how she was sure Paula could understand getting up in the morning and preparing for an audience. Well, Jones assured Zahn, that was all that Harrah's was asking their employees to do. Darlene was angry about it months later: "It made me feel like I didn't get up and prepare even though I took my shower and I brushed my hair and I brushed my teeth and did all that, and I was neat, clean, and well-groomed but it wasn't enough according to Jan Jones.... The message that I got was that if you don't wear makeup, you're not professional."

Popular support did not guarantee legal victory, and on October 22, 2002, the District Court for Nevada rejected Darlene's claim, holding that the Personal Best policy "did not run afoul of Title VII because (1) it did not discriminate against Jespersen on the basis of 'immutable characteristics' associated with her sex, and (2) it imposed equal burdens on both sexes."[36] The court went on to note that "some men may feel the same way with regard to the male makeup policy.... [P]rohibiting men from wearing makeup may be just as objectionable to some men as forcing women to wear makeup is to Plaintiff."[37]

The District Court ruling was a blow, but it served in some ways to usher in a higher level of legal activity. In late 2002, Lambda Legal Defense and Education Fund, a national organization "committed to achieving full recognition of the civil rights of lesbians, gay men, bisexuals, transgender people and those with HIV through impact litigation, education and public policy work," took on Darlene's case.[38] Jennifer Pizer, senior counsel at Lambda Legal, said in the press release announcing the organization's involvement: "This is a classic sex discrimination case. Harrah's fired Darlene because she wouldn't adhere to the most extreme stereotypes of women, even though her supervisors praised her and her customers loved her."[39] Pizer immediately requested that the Ninth Circuit of the United States Court of Appeals hear Darlene's case. Based in San Francisco, the Ninth Circuit is the largest of the U.S. Appeals Courts and is generally considered the most liberal.

Cases like Darlene's are brought to the court under the provisions of Title VII of the Civil Rights Act of 1964, which makes it an "unlawful employment practice for an employer to fail or refuse to hire or to discharge any individual or otherwise to discriminate against any individual with respect to his compensation, terms, conditions, or privileges of employment, because of such individual's race, color, religion, sex, or national origin."[40] Very occasional exceptions to the antidiscrimination rules are allowed "in those certain instances where religion, sex, or national origin is a bona fide occupational qualification [BFOQ] reasonably necessary to the normal operation of that particular business or enterprise." (For example, an advocacy organization like the National Association for the Advancement of Colored People might claim that race was a BFOQ in hiring an executive director.)

Since the passage of the Civil Rights Act, "appearance cases," that is, cases in which employees are protesting employer discrimination in hiring, promotion, and firing based on appearance, have regularly appeared before the courts. Case law in this area is substantial and complex, but in general, the courts in their rulings have shown a clear desire to prohibit sexual discrimination and have steadily broadened their thinking about what constitutes discrimination.

In way of history, the first appearance issues to appear before the court were seven "haircut cases" brought by men challenging workplace regulations banning long hair. The courts in all seven cases ruled in favor of the employers. Long hair, the courts reasoned, was a "mutable" characteristic, and employers' aversion to it did not constitute sex discrimination. Title VII, the courts said, prohibited discrimination on the basis of immutable characteristics like gender or race, but mutable characteristics were not the court's concern.[41] H.L.A. Hart summed up this line of reasoning in *The Concept of Law*: "In contrast with morals, the rules of … dress … occupy a relatively low place in the scale of serious importance. They may be tiresome to follow, but they do not demand great sacrifice: no great pressure is exerted to obtain conformity and no great alterations in other areas of social life would follow if they were not observed or [were] changed."[42]

This was a discouraging beginning. It was not long, however, before the courts began to broaden their interpretation of Title VII, and in 1979—in *Carroll v. Talman Federal Savings and Loan Association*—the court took a decidedly more open stance in regard to grooming codes.[43] Mary Carroll, the plaintiff, was a model employee at Talman Federal Savings and Loan where female employees were required to wear color-coordinated "career ensembles"—skirts or slacks with a jacket, tunic, or vest. Men, on the other hand, were allowed to come to work in "appropriate business attire" of their own choosing. On certain "glamour days," women could dress as they pleased. Mary Carroll announced after one such glamour day that she would no longer be wearing her career ensemble. She was terminated without pay.

In this case the court elected to pass over the "mutable characteristics" argument and ruled that Talman Savings and Loan had discriminated against women by "subject[ing] on the basis of sex … two sets of employees performing the same functions … to two entirely separate dress codes."[44] It went on to link grooming codes to power relationships in society, a critical legal advance. "The disparate treatment is demeaning to women," the court wrote. "While there is nothing offensive about uniforms *per se*, when some employees are uniformed and others are not there is a natural tendency to assume that the uniformed women have a lesser professional status than their male colleagues attired in normal business clothes."[45]

The court's reasoning reflected growing scholarly and legal awareness of gender differentiation—"the enforcement of a set of distinguishing characteristics in order to set the sexes apart."[46] Feminist legal scholar, Mary Whisner, writing in 1979, linked gender differentiation with the maintenance of patriarchy and argued that *in an unequal society,* "preserving distinct categories of how men should look and how women should look, invariably carries with it the potential for subordinate status for women."[47]

The court in *Talman* also found offensive the employer's reasoning that the career ensemble requirement was necessary because women tended to exercise very poor judgment in their choice of business attire. A company representative told the court, "[Women have worn] the slit skirt and … the mini which often barely qualified as a skirt. High boots have alternated with spike heels and sandals. … Women frequently now wear slacks, an accoutrement in previous years regarded as being the exclusive province of the male."[48] In the court's opinion, Talman Savings and Loan sexually objectified women by concluding that they were inclined to wear sexually provocative clothing and lacked judgment about appropriate business attire.

Sexual objectification was again ruled discriminatory under Title VII in *EEOC v. Sage Realty Company,* a case that was brought by Margaret Hasselman, a lobby attendant for Sage Realty in Manhattan.[49] Sage Realty stimulated potential customers' interest in their business by having lobby attendants greet them wearing interesting uniforms. In 1976 Sage brought out the "Bicentennial"—a uniform consisting of a red, white, and blue poncho which attendants were to wear with blue dancer pants, nylons, white shoes, and nothing else. The poncho, according to observers, was particularly provocative as it moved and shifted as the attendants walked, and "you never knew what you were going to see next."[50] Hasselman tried wearing the uniform for a couple of days during which lobby customers made lewd comments, vied to take pictures, and propositioned her. After that Hasselman refused to wear the "Bicentennial" and was laid off for being out of uniform. Again, the court ruled against the employer and for Hasselman, noting that the employer's "requirement that Hasselman wear the Bicentennial uniform, when they knew that the wearing of this uniform on the job subjected her to sexual harassment, constituted sex discrimination."[51] (The courts have generally ruled that sexually objectifying women, that is, regarding them "primarily in terms of whether or how they arouse men sexually," is discriminatory.[52])

Courts under Title VII also have been concerned that policies not impose unequal burdens on women and men. In *Frank v. United Airlines, Inc.*, for example, female flight attendants argued that United Airlines' weight restrictions violated Title VII because women were required to maintain the weight of women of "medium" build, while men were held only to the standards of men of "large" build. The court ruled in the stewardesses' favor, concluding, "although employers are free to adopt *different* appearance standards for each sex, they may not adopt standards that impose a greater burden on one sex than the other."[53]

A significant advance in the court's thinking came in the case of *Price Waterhouse v. Hopkins*. Ann Hopkins, a Price Waterhouse employee, was repeatedly passed over for partner in the firm. She was too "macho," the company told her in a series of amazingly indiscreet statements—she behaved aggressively at work, perhaps, they surmised, because she was "overcompensat[ing] for being a woman." If Hopkins would wear makeup, dress in muted colors, and have her hair styled, "she might have more success," they thought.[54]

The court ruled that the actions of Price Waterhouse constituted sex discrimination in violation of Title VII and in language that positively rang with disapproval, noted: "we are beyond the day when an employer could evaluate employees by assuming or insisting that they matched the stereotype associated with their group."[55] Employers, it held, could not under Title VII fire or sexually harass employees on the basis of their "failure to conform to commonly accepted gender stereotypes."[56] The courts have applied the Price Waterhouse ruling in several subsequent cases such as *Nichols v. Azteca Restaurant*, a case in which

Nichols, a waiter at a pizza parlor, was harassed because he carried his tray "like a woman" and didn't act "as a man should act."[57]

Overall, as the American Civil Liberties Union would later argue in support of Jespersen's case, the court "has held that Title VII prohibits a wide range of sex-based employment practices that impede women's ability to participate and succeed in the workforce."[58] It seemed an excellent foundation on which Darlene could build her case.

Jennifer Pizer and the Lambda Legal lawyers' appeal to the Ninth Circuit claimed that Harrah's "demand that female bartenders and cocktail servers wear facial makeup including foundation, blush, mascara and lip color, while male employees are told simply to keep their faces clean, imposed a greater burden on female than male employees that discriminates "because of sex" in violation of Title VII, and that the requirement forces women to "conform to restrictive gender stereotypes as a condition of employment" in a way that also discriminates "because of sex" in violation of Title VII.[59] In the appeal Lambda Legal was joined by the National Employment Lawyers Association, the Alliance for Workers' Rights, The Legal Aid Society—Employment Law Center, the American Civil Liberties Union of Nevada, the Northwest Women's Law Center, the California Women's Law Center, and the Gender Public Advocacy Coalition, all of which contributed to *amici curiae* briefs.[60]

The case was solid and the support impressive. Because of this, the blow when it came in late December 2004 was all the more devastating. The three-judge panel in a 2–1 decision ruled against Darlene. Ignoring several decades of case law, the court returned to the haircut cases, saying that makeup was a "mutable" characteristic, and further, that Darlene had provided no evidence that there was an unequal burden—if applying makeup cost women more in money and time than washing their faces cost men, that evidence had not appeared in the record. Finally, the court declined to apply the *Price Waterhouse* ruling to Darlene's case.[61]

Judge Sidney Thomas in a ringing dissent argued that "Jespersen easily satisfied her burden." Any reasonable fact finder, he wrote, could determine that "the policy impose[d] a requirement on women that is not only time-consuming and expensive, but burdensome for its requirement that women conform to outdated and impermissible sex stereotypes."[62] He further noted that Harrah's "stringent" policy in effect required "a uniform of makeup," adding that it was a "classic case" of *Price Waterhouse* discrimination. Like Ann Hopkins, the Price Waterhouse accountant denied a partnership because she didn't wear makeup and act sufficiently feminine, "Jespersen was fired," Judge Thomas concluded, "from a job she also excelled at, for exactly the same reason," adding in an important note on social class, "the court cannot protect professionals and fail to protect service employees."[63]

Public response to the decision of the three-judge panel quickly spilled over into newspapers and onto the Internet. Traffic on the website of Nevada labor activist Andrew Barbano—a major source of information about the case—soared. Tom Stoneburner of the Nevada Alliance for Workers Rights wrote:

> This is not a story about one employee and not just about a very courageous Darlene. It's one that impacts all women in America who are treated differently in the workplace due to their gender. It's a case of a powerful industry crushing a small sign of rebellion in the servants' quarters.... We at the Alliance for Workers Rights... are disappointed at the decision but the fight is not over. I guess the court's decision and the "pleasure" expressed by Harrah's management at the plantation workers once again being put in their place tell us how far we have to go in achieving equality.... Darlene will always be a heroine to us at the Alliance for Workers' Rights.[64]

Young women in particular reacted strongly to the ruling. Blogs and websites bristled with indignation. Annalee Newtiz of Alternet.org wrote, "This is your government, helping cosmetics executives to get rich on state-enforced gender norms."[65] Another young woman asked in reference to the Court of Appeals' ruling that Harrah's makeup policy did not impose an unequal burden, "If being robbed of one's feeling of self-worth on a day-to-day basis is not an 'unequal burden,' what is? How could any court possibly rule in favor of Harrah's?... It is not fair. It is not acceptable. And it is certainly not equal."[66]

Darlene's lawyers responded to the ruling with a small legal roar, immediately requesting an *en banc* hearing—one before a full eleven-judge panel. In the first positive court response, the request was honored in May 2005 and fast-tracked for a June hearing in San Francisco. On June 22 we crowded into an imposing marble and polished-wood Ninth Circuit courtroom along with dozens of young lawyers and law school students—the case's "buzz" was by now increasing exponentially. Everyone's neck craned to get a glimpse of Darlene, who entered the courtroom with Jennifer Pizer and Lambda's legal team, warmly greeting the people she recognized. We sat with a young lawyer friend, who interpreted the legalese and bristled every time anyone referred to Darlene as someone who did not meet stereotypical female standards of beauty: "She's beautiful!" the young lawyer whispered. "They shouldn't say she isn't!"[67]

En banc hearings are nothing if not exciting, and the audience leaned in to follow the judges' rapid-fire questions, trying to gauge each judge's opinion, noting shamelessly which of the women judges wore makeup and which didn't. Patrick Hicks, Harrah's clean-cut, expensively suited lawyer, calmly laid out Harrah's case. The atmosphere overall felt hostile, even disrespectful at least to lay observers.

Ten long months later the decision came down: 7–4 against Darlene. It was a heartbreaker. Chief Judge Mary Schroeder in her twenty-seven page decision reaffirmed, "Jespersen did not submit any documentation or any evidence of the relative cost and time required to comply with the grooming requirements by men and women," and as a result "we would have to speculate about those issues in order to then guess whether the policy creates unequal burdens for women."[68] Judge Alex Kozinski, funny at the *en banc* hearing and funny in dissent, wrote: "You don't need an expert witness to figure out that such items don't grow on trees," adding that reasonable jurors "easily could agree with Darlene that those not accustomed to makeup could feel demeaned to an extent that it would impair their ability to work," and offering that *he* probably would feel that way if required to wear makeup when taking the bench.[69]

In the years following, Darlene's case spawned multiple law review articles and a major conference at Duke University Law School, "Making Makeup Matter," where Jennifer Pizer was the featured speaker.[70] Legal scholars set about deconstructing the "trivial" issue of makeup.[71] At issue for many were global corporations' new and enormously intrusive efforts to "brand" employees' look, and they called upon the law to expand its conception of appearance and its relationship to power and rights in a new economic age. Of particular interest was Diane Avery and Marion Crain's journal article, "Branded: Corporate Image, Sexual Stereotyping, and the New Face of Capitalism."[72] In it the authors argued that "sophisticated forms of marketing and branding," processes that when successfully done yield high profit margins, create "a property-like interest that is engrafted onto the faces, bodies, and psyches of service sector workers through appearance codes." Workers thus become "uniformed, painted, smiling, talking billboards mirroring the cultural stereotypes of the employers' target market," providing extra service and extra value for which they are unacknowledged and uncompensated. While legal challenges will be important in defending workers' rights, Avery and Crain wrote, so too will be union building: "Only by standing together might workers have the strength to demand appropriate compensation or to resist branding," they concluded.[73]

Jennifer Pizer returned to the human dimension. "Periodically," she wrote in her article summing up the Jespersen case, "American women have been blessed with determined visionaries who have put their bodies, jobs, and lives where many just put rhetoric." Darlene Jespersen, she said, was "one of those rare and inspiring souls." Pizer continued:

> Darlene is a hero without pretense. She resisted one of the wealthiest companies in America because she believes the law's promise of equal treatment for working women should mean something, and that her twenty years of exemplary service to Harrah's Casino likewise should have earned her a measure of loyalty in return. Darlene is not naïve. But she does care about fairness and being treated in a respectful manner. She also believes individuals can make a difference. To this author, Darlene embodies integrity and a centered sense of self like few others. It has been a privilege and pleasure to represent her, and even more so to call her friend.[74]

Today, a decade after it all began, Darlene works as a greeter at Sam's Club. She continues to live in the small manufactured home where she cares for her mother who is fighting cancer. We asked her how the case had changed her. "Well," she said, "I tend to rebel against authority a little more, because, for me, for a long time I've done a lot of things to please other people, but I haven't really looked out for me. And sometimes—we can all relate to this—you make yourself feel where other things are more important than what you really want. But it got to where, 'unh unh, not that one. I'm not going to do that....I wouldn't feel comfortable covering up my face. I'm comfortable with myself.' I just said, 'I'm not doing it.'"

As for her reduced financial situation, Darlene was philosophical: "I appreciate things a lot more. Like every year I had money. I could go out, because I had my tips. Now I've got to really watch how I spend money, and that's okay. Because I think that's a good lesson for me."

"Maybe we should have the Million Woman March, just women," Darlene mused. "A million of them would come forward and say, you're not pushing us around. So hopefully, we'll do it. That'd be exciting. You two would be there, huh?"

LIBERATION THEOLOGY, PIT BOSS STYLE

I am a shepherd who, with his people, has begun to learn a beautiful and difficult truth: our Christian faith requires that we submerge ourselves in this world.... It is the poor who force us to understand what is really taking place.... The poor are the Body of Christ today.

—Archbishop Oscar Romero, 1980

Edna Harman, white-haired and in manner somewhere between a nun and a truck driver, dealt cards and pit bossed at a top Reno casino for twenty-six years. Less than an hour into our conversation, she reached into her bag and pulled out a copy of Jack Nelson-Pallmeyer's *School of Assassins,* an exposé of the School of the Americas, the infamous U.S. government-funded military training center for Latin American soldiers at Fort Benning, Georgia.[1] What was seventy-year-old Edna Harman, pit boss, doing with that book in her bag? "Oh," she said, "[The School of the America's] is the place where I've been protesting for the last three years. I got arrested this year with 1,700 others."[2] Sorting through her bag again, Edna picked out a laminated card (she had dozens). "Here's one," she said. "'I was hungry and you formed a humanities society and discussed my hunger. Thank you.'" She grinned, "I thought you'd like that."

The lessons of Edna Harman's life lie at the heart of this book. Born into the poverty and bigotry of a rural Nevada town, Edna spent her early adult years following a well-trod path to casino work and addiction. She hated her work as a dealer and numbed her alienation and despair with ample quantities of alcohol and tranquilizers. But in the 1980s in a small miracle she found the Maryknoll sisters and a whole world opened up to her: one of commitment to justice in Central America and service to the poor. Suddenly, she found herself in the company of missioners, activists, and the poor themselves.

Edna Harman grew up "really poor," she said, in a small and generally narrow-minded Nevada town. Her dad, who had only made it through eighth grade, farmed, and when farming failed, made a business for himself hauling scrap.

"But he was smart," Edna said. "He read *Newsweek* and *Time* and the paper. He educated himself." Growing up, Edna hated injustice, including her own father's racial prejudice. "There used to be signs," she said. "'Nigger, don't be in town after sundown.'" She guessed her father's mentality came from "back in those days when they used that word...and we did, too, as kids," she remembered. "It was supposed to be funny."

Edna joined the Navy after she graduated high school and when her tour of duty ended returned to Reno where she landed a job dealing at the Nevada Club. It was 1957, and she was twenty-one. In short order she married, got pregnant, and had a son. But after just a year, she realized she had to find "a real job—something that would make me feel good about myself." So she picked up her baby (it was a short marriage) and set off for California. There she found work in the electronics industry, but starvation wages eventually forced her to return to Reno and another job dealing. She took classes at the university, too, where she struggled to get Bs. One day her advisor, whom she worshiped, told her, "You can do it, but only when you want to...and one of the reasons that you haven't done it is because your mother doesn't think you can."

Edna half-laughed: "It was true. My mom always said, 'What do you want to go back to school for? You're not going to make it.'" Her mother, a teacher, had different plans for her. "She came home one time," Edna remembered, "and said, 'You know what I'd love to see you do?' And I said, 'What's that?' My mom replied, 'I'd like to see you be a pit boss.' I just said, 'Oh, Mother.'"

Edna made pretty good money dealing, but there was no challenge in the work. She grew so bored that she would make up elaborate story problems—"if a car leaves San Francisco, traveling at so many miles per hour and so on and so forth"—to occupy her mind. So when she was offered a job pit bossing, she jumped at the chance. As a pit boss, Edna supervised the table games—craps, roulette, and 21—and oversaw a team of dealers and the processes and policies they had to follow. She checked decks for flaws, changed them regularly, and handled thousands of dollars every hour. "If I screwed up," she said, "I could lose my job."

Edna had mixed relations with management. Over the years she thought they had been "really, really good" to her. But she was never averse to giving them an earful when they needed it—which was frequently. Edna loved to tell stories about being on the casino's Board of Review, especially ones that involved women employees standing up to managers. The Board of Review heard employees' appeals and grievances. Some of the women discounted the Board of Review as a management tool, but Edna served on it for nine years just to make sure workers had a voice. Early on, a dealer named Norma asked Edna to go with her to the Board of Review because she was getting so many late shifts. "Oh, man,"

Edna worried, "they'll dump on me." But she thought about it for a while and asked herself, "Well, are you who you say you are, or are you chicken?" At the meeting Norma asked, "How come I'm getting all these late shifts?"

The managers replied, "Well, you see, Norma, we have to utilize people."

"Utilize. Utilize," Norma replied. "Is that the same as screw?"

Edna beamed remembering it. Later, Edna went on, management told Norma that she couldn't go on vacation. "There were three guys in there [who] were steadily crawling up the ladder," Edna smiled. "And one of them said, 'Fire the broad. That'll put her on vacation.'" Edna said, "Well, an executive walked by one day, and I said, 'Can I see you for a second?' And he said, 'Sure.'" Edna continued, "I unloaded everything that was going on and how people were being treated, and boy, I'll tell you, shit hit the fan. Those people that were crawling up the ladder, they got bumped back down, and they never did go anywhere, except supervisor."

Edna's experience mirrored that of many long-term dealers who appreciated and drew upon their contacts with management and even executives in the old, precorporate days. Edna considered the casino's owner "brilliant, a perfectionist. He could walk in and spot a light out across the club."[3] But like others, Edna was not impressed with the changes that corporatization had brought, like speed-up. The "game pace" at her club stood at 450 hands an hour, up from 270. "You know," she said, "it's gotten so people who run the club—the people in the highest places—don't really know a lot about gambling. It's turned into just a plain old business."

Inevitably, the negative energy got to Edna. The atmosphere was so toxic, she said, that she used to cry before it was time to go to work. Finally, she talked to her doctor who prescribed tranquillizers. "I'd come to work," Edna remembered, "and pop a tranq as I walked in the door. And if they said to go over to the craps pit, on my way I'd touch my shoulder. For me it was, you know, 'Spirit, please. Please help me. Help me deal with these thugs. Help me not to make a mistake....' So I literally lived on spirit and tranqs to just help me get through it."

Alcohol helped, too. It got bad enough that her friends began to notice. Eventually one began needling her, "You're not alcoholic. You don't go to the meetings," or "You're not alcoholic. You're never sober." They laughed together awkwardly, but when her university advisor asked, "Have you ever thought you could be an alcoholic?," Edna began to look at her world. "Alcoholics Anonymous is a wonderful organization," her advisor told her. "Should you find the need, they are in the phone book." About six months later Edna picked up the phone.

As the cloud of alcohol cleared, Edna began to change; her relationships at work grew better. One day she was called upstairs, and her boss, Bob (not his real name), was sitting there. "[My boss] was a guy who—oh, he was just a pig," Edna said. "He really liked to dump on women. Really liked to belittle them." Bob turned to

Edna and said, "You know, nobody upstairs respects you." Edna laughed, "Well, when he said that I took this key to my brain, and I just went click."

And I said, "You're right, Bob."

And he said, "None of your peers respect you."

And I said, "You're right."

"And everything he said," Edna grinned, "I just agreed with him."

"Are you listening to what I'm saying?" Bob yelled.

Finally, Bob got so mad, Edna said, that he just sat there and stared at her. "Are we done?" she smiled—and got up and walked out.

On a later occasion, Edna noticed that Bob was coughing uncontrollably. "Bob," she said, "you sound terrible. Is something wrong?"

"I got the flu," Bob replied. "I am so sick I don't know what to do."

"You know, Bob," Edna said, "my hairdresser gave me some Chinese stuff that dumped my flu fast. If I make up some packets for you, would you take them?" Bob didn't say no, so Edna made up four packets and drove down to the casino and gave them to him.

"When I walked in," Edna said, "Bob asked, 'Did you come down here just to give me those?'

"Yes, I did," Edna replied.

"Well, God bless you."

After that, Edna said, "well, I started praying for him. I mean I was so angry that I thought—I'm going to kill myself with anger. I've got to get this off of me. I'm letting them hurt me. So I went for a walk one day, and I'm just down-to-earth, call-it-like-I-see-it, even when I'm talking to the Lord. I figure that the Lord is right here by my side, my best buddy, and we went for a walk. And I said, 'Lord, how do you pray for some son-of-a-bitch you'd like to kick down the escalator and then pick up and slap the shit out of?' And I walked and I walked. And I did that every day until I found myself saying, 'Lord, bless them. If they knew better, they'd do better.' And you know, down the road I went to work one day and I had a new jacket on, and one of the higher-uppers said, 'Wow, what a beautiful jacket. You look really nice.' And I said, 'Well, thank you.' And just down the road things got better. My appraisals got better, and everything smoothed over."

Years later Bob was himself the object of a giant corporate screw. By that time, Edna said, she was beginning to respect Bob. "Well, actually, I don't respect him in that he doesn't respect women," she corrected herself, "but I have no animosity toward him." Bob, along with eight other pit administrators, was let go in a familiar corporate restructure:

> They announced that [they were reducing those eight jobs to five]. They could all put in for it, and whoever got it would get it, and the other ones just wouldn't have a job. All they did was change the name [and]

add the responsibility, so they divided everything the nine did by five. They did that over and over at [the casino]. They eliminated this, eliminated that. They cut down their workforce. They shoved more work at everybody.

In the end, Edna felt sorry for Bob, who didn't make the cut: "He just thought he was a shoo-in forever because, you know, he was a shift manager. I don't think he's ever gone back to work."

For Edna, however, there were much bigger changes in motion than the ones at work. In 1986, when she was thirty-three and had just quit drinking, she met three Maryknoll sisters. Edna had grown up Protestant, but from the first time she had seen sisters in her hometown, she liked them. "I used to follow them down the street," she remembered, smiling. In 1986 the Maryknolls talked to Edna about peace and justice, and she just couldn't get enough. "We started a friendship," she said, "that turned my life upside down."

The Maryknoll sisters in the 1980s were brave beyond brave and at the heart of the liberation theology movement in the United States and Central America. Arising out of Vatican II, liberation theologians, particularly in Central America where the chasm between the poor and the wealthy yawned obscenely wide, believed that that the church is "of and for this world as well as for the next" and that "here and now are the place and time for the beginning of the kingdom of God."[4] Leaders like Archbishop Oscar Romero in El Salvador, expressing a "preferential option for the poor," called on believers to be advocates for the voiceless and the powerless. It was dangerous ground—assassinations of religious and lay leaders dominated the headlines. Two Maryknoll sisters, Ita Ford and Maura Clark, were brutally murdered on December 2, 1980, in El Salvador alongside two other religious women, Dorothy Kazel and Jean Donovan, just months after Archbishop Romero himself was gunned down while saying mass.[5]

While this was going on, Edna was meeting Maryknoll sisters from Africa, Hong Kong, Chile, Bolivia—all over the world. One day she phoned a sister and said, "I'm embarrassed to ask you this, but what is 'Third World'?" She laughed, "And boy did I get an education." Another time she asked a sister what she was reading.

"It's on the Sandinistas. It's on Nicaragua," the sister replied.

"What is it about?" Edna asked.

"Well, we're having a meeting, Citizens Concerned about Central America," the nun said. "Would you like to come?"

Not long after Edna began attending meetings, one of the Maryknoll sisters told her she was leaving for Bolivia. "You have to come and visit me," she said. "Gee," Edna thought. "This is really nice. But Bolivia? That's halfway around the world." Still, she couldn't get it out of her mind. She had gotten involved in

Citizens Concerned about Central America and felt energized learning about what was happening there and the response of Nevadans like Maya Miller to the war.[6] "So I decided I was going to go to Bolivia," Edna laughed.

But how to get off work? "Those [casino management] people can't make a decision for tomorrow," Edna thought. "How are they going to make a decision in August for me to go to Bolivia in January?" The next day, Edna walked into the personnel office and said, "I'm going to Bolivia in January. I will need my three weeks off and two weeks extra, and I need your answer in two weeks so I can pick up my ticket. Okay?" To her surprise and delight, two weeks later they agreed.

"So I went," Edna said. "And I just fell in love with the people. It [was] still the Sandinista thing going on then…and the sisters were all talking about the United States funding the Contras, and I was hearing it first time, firsthand, from these missionaries—the things they witnessed. And so I knew these things were true." She went on, "I cried and cried. And I thought, 'I've got to be a part of this. I have to be part of it.' I felt so called…and I thought, 'Me? Give up everything?' But when I was in Bolivia, I was sitting in the house one day, a mud house with cement floors…and I thought, 'God, I am so happy. There's nothing I need. I don't want anything.'"

All of a sudden Edna's world opened up, and her spirits began to soar. "My heart and soul is in mission," Edna explained. "We visit people, orphanages, the blind. We walk with the poor. We try to be a voice for the voiceless."[7] Everywhere she went she asked, "What do you need?" In response, the next time she came to Bolivia she filled her suitcases with coats, eyeglasses, and other useful things. "I'd get on the scale with my suitcase," she laughed. "You could have seventy pounds. My suitcase would weigh sixty-nine." Edna sold her house and bought a mobile home so she wouldn't "have a house to hold me back," and with that money, a small inheritance from her parents, and her casino earnings, she was able to afford the airfare. Eventually, she went on eight Maryknoll missions to Mexico, Bolivia, and Nicaragua.

Edna even thought about giving up her job and her life in Reno, but the nuns encouraged her to be thoughtful about how she would support herself. In Bolivia they told Edna, "You know, we need people like you to be a voice for us. We need people from North America who will speak out." That was when Edna began writing Congress and making trips to the School of the Americas. She also made sure that everyone in the casino knew about her commitment, and from the big bosses on down, casino people contributed to her cause.

The missions also changed Edna's relationships with fellow employees, including the many Central Americans who in the 1980s were flooding north for sanctuary and jobs. Edna didn't know Spanish, but she would pick up a phrase or two and talk to people in the back of the house. "I could say, 'Hi. How are you?'" she said. "You know, 'Mucho trabajo, poco dinero, huh?' "[8] If her Spanish was off, the employees would correct her—and Edna liked that.

Edna also began to bring liberation theology right into the pit. One time, she said, a dealer named Ximena was trying to bring her children to the United States from El Salvador. She had been to the Immigration and Naturalization Services office where she'd stood in line and gotten very poorly treated. "She wanted [her kids] so badly," Edna said. "So I said, 'Okay, Thursday I'll go to Immigration with you. I'll stand right there beside you.' " On Thursday, Edna, wearing her cross, stood next to Ximena and just smiled at the INS worker. "The lady was so nice," Edna laughed. "It was unbelievable. My feeling was, 'you say one rude word to her, I'm going to raise a ruckus.' And so anyway, she did get her kids over here."

Edna spent all her free time working and organizing. She would arrange community lunches at the casino on her days off and invite all the nuns in town along with anybody else who wanted to come. One day, after Ximena's daughters arrived from El Salvador, she had the girls, who were now her goddaughters, come and meet the sisters. Another time a Guatemalan refugee woman came to the university to speak. "Can you get some people to translate?" the frazzled organizer asked Edna. So Edna brought a couple of dealers from El Salvador and Mexico up to the university. One Salvadoran dealer told the audience after the presentation, "You know, this lady is telling the truth. I'm from El Salvador. Most people won't speak out. They're afraid to lose their green card." He added, "There's no such thing as neutral in El Salvador. You're either in the military or you're a rebel. And if you're in the military you have to torture and kill your people. I was a rebel. That's why I'm here."

Edna began to read fellow employees' name tags to find out where they were from. When the Gulf War broke out, she said, "I went home and pulled out my encyclopedia. I don't know that much about the Middle East...and I'd pull the book open and say, 'Oh my God. Ahmed lives there. He's from there.' Then I'd go to work and say, 'Is anybody in your family hurt?' "

Edna loved immigrants—her view in general was "bring them on," but that sat poorly with some of the coworkers. When one waitress commented, "Look at them [the employees]! Chinese! I thought we were in America!" Edna replied, "You know, when you die, you might find out that God's Chinese." Later someone asked Edna, "Why don't these people speak English?" and she said, "It's because they're probably working two or three jobs and have to go home and cook a meal; they don't have time to go to class because they get paid so little!"

Other issues engaged Edna as well, particularly domestic violence and low wages. The biggest problem in her opinion was "that people are having to work a lot of jobs, and they're not home with their kids. So they don't have the family unit, and I think that this leads to family violence and drinking." She befriended a dealer who was living with a man from Kenya, who, according to Edna, "was from money…and beat [his wife] up regularly." Edna said, "I always tell them if you need me, I'm in the phone book." One night the woman called Edna, sobbing.

"Where are you?" Edna asked.

"I'm outside in the phone booth."

"I'll be there in twelve minutes max," Edna replied. "Wait somewhere where you can see me. I'll flick the lights as I drive up. Run out and get in the car."

Edna took the woman to the hospital. "Eventually she left him," she remembered. "But you know, she'd come to work and her makeup—I knew he'd beat her up again. Sometimes I'd be right in the pit with her, and I'd say, 'That son of a bitch hit you again.'"

Edna was unique among pit bosses who, according to many dealers, have a reputation for rude and abusive treatment of dealers. She had seven dealers assigned to her and was always looking after them. "You treat my dealer mean in my area, and you're out of here," was her attitude. "We don't allow our dealers to be abused," Edna said. "I've thrown people out. Lot of money…but you're out of here." Edna suspected her treatment of dealers negatively impacted her tenure at Harrah's. "One of the things they used to tell me in my appraisal was I was too dealer-oriented," she remembered, "but I couldn't let go of the fact that I was once a dealer. For me, I guess the biggest thing is that we don't have enough people that really care for the employees."

Edna worked continually at creating a culture of caring in the pit. She sat with dealers whose family members had died and with alcoholics, including customers, on the edge. "I'm not trained to counsel someone," Edna said, "but by God I can throw my arms around them and cry with them. And they need that sometimes more than they need anything else." Sometimes whole families came to Nevada with nothing but the clothes on their backs and money for an apartment. Edna discovered a casino laundry worker in that situation. "I was telling one of the dealers, and someone said, 'Miss Edna, I've got two chairs that you can have,' and someone else said, 'I have a bed,' and someone else, 'I've got a couch.' And, you know the next day we got a U-Haul and started picking stuff up. A guy from slots came and said, 'Can I help? I could get a dolly from the slots department…and Clyde says he'll come, too. We each got a truck.' And so in like less than a week we had them completely furnished. I think that's really good."

It was one of many occasions when dealers reached out to help each other. "I think it's typical that you have good people in all the clubs," Edna said. "Among the workers, you have people that can fly in together fast when something happens to somebody. We had Black and White picnics every year—black and white because that's what dealers wore." One year graveyard threw a party and auction for a coworker who had stomach cancer. "We raised $5,000 in one day," Edna said. "I mean, people brought things. I brought a brand new hedge trimmer. Hadn't used it yet. And people brought like homemade pickles. One of our guys, he loves to sew and he loves to cook, and he makes an almond toffee tart. Every time we had a party, I would bring at least fifty bucks. I was going to outbid anybody for that toffee tart!"

"I'm a practicing Catholic," Edna explained. "And I feel no contradiction whatsoever between my religious beliefs and the gaming industry. I feel that God meets people everywhere, and I see a lot of Christianity here, both in our customers and in our people."[9] Still, she hated what corporate politics was doing to the gaming industry: "I mean, there's no feeling. There's no thought, no caring for the employees. They're just a commodity. They're something that you just throw away when you're through with them." But Edna always held out hope. "We need to be more kind as a people," she said. "And it's got to start somewhere. It's got to be somewhere in these corporate giants. Someone's got to get a heart and realize that you can make so much more money when you're kind to people."

In 1998 Edna retired from the casino. She found that she could pull $1,000 a month from her 401K, and that along with Social Security paid the bills. Retirement meant she could go to all the meetings and retreats she'd missed while she was working. She went to Maryknoll gatherings, peace and justice conferences, and Central America meetings all over the United States. "I just boarded a plane and took off," she said. She especially looked forward to participating in yearly watches at the School of the Americas, where she was proud to be arrested with others. And every year on December 2, the anniversary of the murder of the four religious women in El Salvador, she renewed her vows of peace at the beautiful Carmelite monastery overlooking the lights of Reno.

Today, health and the economy have slowed her down a little, but Edna still gives away books and laminated cards. In her gentle way, she reminds us that commitment to the poor and suffering is a daily affair that requires not the formation of a "humanities committee to discuss hunger," but action. In the spring of 2006, more than five thousand Reno immigrants and their supporters joined protesters across the nation raising their voices against the criminalization of undocumented workers and for the rationalization of U.S. immigration policies. It was the largest demonstration in recent Reno history. On a cold and rainy day, workers and students poured out of casinos, schools, and homes; flags of the United States, Mexico, Nicaragua, El Salvador, and other countries waved briskly. Edna had been asked to speak. Helped by organizers onto the enormous boulder that served as the dais, she spoke loudly into the bullhorn: "Usted estan mi familia! You are my family!" The crowd, many of whom were casino workers who knew Edna, roared back its approval. For Edna Harman, the poor really are family. It is liberation theology at its best. We do not need to be theologians or even religious to appreciate the witness of this working-class woman who changed her life so that she might serve God and the poor, even in the pit of a casino.

Part IV
DEALERS
The Illusion of Power

DEALING
The View from Dead Center

I am reading an article in *Psychology Today* comparing schools to prisons. It says, what other place do you have metal detectors and are under constant surveillance? I think: my casino!

—Cynthia Bowen, Reno dealer

Jeanine Carter had dealt roulette at a high-end Reno casino for twenty-two years, and from her position near the center of the gaming floor she closely observed both players and the house. The view, exciting at first, in time became deeply disturbing. "On Friday, Saturday, and Sunday on a busy weekend," she said, "you can see the people come in. They're frantic. They're all pumped up, and they're pushing and they're trying to get their arms in [to play].... It's a momentum—they're pushing their will on us and they're trying to break us down. I mean, that's how I envision it, because you can see their franticness, their excitement. I deal roulette so it's like this—people just trying to gamble frantically. And the noise!"

"By Sunday," Jeanine continued, "people have lost their money. They're beaten down, depressed. The whole thing changes. People comment on it. Dealers comment on it. And we all know it. In the end, they're desperate because they have lost. A lot of these people have lost a lot of money, have gone way overboard.... You see the same ones. For me it's sad. I would want to help these people if I could."[1]

Jeanine Carter's view is from dead center of the casino enterprise, the place where money is transferred from players' hands to the coffers of the gaming corporations. The noise, the smoke, the drinks, the frenzy, the action—all are sidebars to the fundamental exchange that is taking place. It is the crux of the gaming industry and the source in Nevada in 2008 of $11.6 billion in gross gaming revenues[2]—and dealers' hands are on most of those dollars.

"Lefty" Rosenthal, an early casino executive, described just how relentless that movement of cash is:

> The name of the game is win. From my experience, as far as being able to win,…99.9% of the public, including myself, have two chances: one is slim, the other is none and Slim's out of town.… Winning is virtually impossible. Anybody can get lucky, but if you're attempting to sustain yourself over a period of time and take money out of a casino…, you're better off climbing Mt. Everest by yourself. [The reality is] you're going to give it back; there is no two ways about it. There is no way, legally, to beat any form of gaming that I'm aware of.[3]

Because dealers handle the money, casino owners from the beginning have left nothing to chance in their relationship with these employees who ostensibly sit at the top of the non-managerial pyramid. At the heart of their strategy is absolute control. Dealers in nearly everyone's assessment are the most highly controlled employees in the casino.

A key aspect of dealer control is the creation of a privileged strata of employees with strict standards for admission and certain limited but not insubstantial benefits, including a place at the center of the action, perceived access to management, tip income, and in earlier times, special parking lots and dining rooms. This was all part of convincing dealers, in MGM Grand President Bill Hornbuckle's words, that "dealers and [the] management team work on the same side of the table."[4] For dealers who missed the point, elaborate and frequently changing policies for dealer behavior—including protocols for handling chips, cards, and dice; interaction with customers; and "game pace"—provide the house with inexhaustible reasons to discipline or terminate them. Also in play is casino management's positively ferocious opposition to union organizing. A Las Vegas executive, at the conclusion of yet another failed attempt to organize Las Vegas dealers, commented, "There is no way there is going to be a dealers' union. I will replace every one of the dealers if I have to, and you know how long it would take me? Half a day."[5]

Control of dealers' bodies is key. Dealers, particularly at blackjack tables, operate in a very narrow space, deal a prescribed number of hands per shift, handle chips and cards in prescribed form, breathe prescribed air, and smile a prescribed number of times per hour. All this is enforced by a multimillion dollar system of dealer surveillance, including pit bosses, "mystery shoppers" who visit gaming tables, and the famous eye-in-the-sky cameras, good for catching gambling cheats and even better for monitoring dealers' every action. These mechanisms of control—all legal and all "normalized," that is, accepted as part of the job—combine for one purpose, to ensure the house's take.

In this chapter women dealers' stories provide a window onto life on the gaming floor and onto the changes that have accompanied corporatization, including the commodification of smiles and other human interactions. They provide as well clues to a critical question: why is it that Hattie Canty, Mary Burns, Geoconda Kline, and Josefina Huerta, all objectively in much riskier positions and with far fewer financial reserves, were able to stand up to corporate gaming, but dealers submitted to stricter and more abusive control?

Our story begins with Alejandra Lomeli.

Alejandra Lomeli, short and feisty, was a veteran dealer. At the time we interviewed her she was leading a popular lesbian discussion group in Reno—something that might have come as a surprise to her bosses and most casino guests. Born in Cuba in the late 1950s, Alejandra and her family came to the United States when she was eleven and settled in New Jersey. After high school, she was accepted at a college, "but," she said drily, making us laugh, "I didn't show up. I got married instead."[6] In 1978 Alejandra and her husband decided to try their fortunes in the West and ended up in Reno where her husband landed a casino job and Alejandra began working at a bank. Two years later, her father, who had been a political prisoner in Cuba for seventeen years, arrived in New Jersey, and to earn money for the trip east to see him, Alejandra took an additional part-time job in a casino as a change person. She had intended it to be short-term, but at the time we interviewed her she had been there twenty years.

Casinos initially confounded her. "It was the strangest thing," Alejandra said. "I couldn't believe people would put money into machines and pull handles.... It was incredible for me to think that people did such things, but I made money there, so it was okay. Let them all come in."

After a year, Alejandra applied for dealing school. She was turned down "many times," she said, "because of height, because of weight, because of looks—"

"Looks?" we asked. "Would they tell you that straight out?"

"Straight out," she replied. "I went in and applied and they take your picture. And I guess my picture was not a 10. My hair was messy, and...they wanted beautiful people." But Alejandra persisted through comments that she was too short or too shy or too plain and eventually got an interview. "I think when I got [hired]," she said, "it was because I had bought myself a blue silk dress on sale....Everybody loved that dress. And not having a silk dress before, I washed it, and that was the end of [it]...but it served its purpose."

Being a dealer was "the thing to be," Alejandra continued. "I mean, if you worked in the casino, everybody wanted to be a dealer. Dealers make more money...and you were looked up to for being a dealer and being chosen to be one, because you have to go through all that." Alejandra attended an after-hours, in-house dealers' school for six weeks, for which she wasn't paid. Prospective dealers were taught how to count and deliver the cards and were expected to practice at home. She didn't like it especially, because she didn't like the whole idea of gambling. "But," she said, "I needed the money since I was supporting my family.... My husband never really worked very hard [and] we lived in a motel. I couldn't stand it."

The money was good, but the work never lived up to Alejandra's expectations. "At that time," she said, "the tables weren't as big as they are now so it was really close contact between the players and the dealers. I mean, they sneezed and *psffft*—it was all over you. It was bad with the smoke, too."

The atmosphere in the pit also wore on Alejandra, especially the pit bosses' often brutal handling of dealers. "I cried a lot when I first started," she said. "I can tell you that. They would call you aside and pick on you. They would even yell at you right at the table in front of everybody for making a mistake or for not doing something that they wanted you to do."

"Also, years ago," Alejandra said, "they would—it's called 'sweat the money' where if you were losing, they would be upset because, you know, the money's not staying at the casino, so they would come by and want you to change. There were... trade secrets, but—well, there are things you can do to change how things are going, but now it's illegal. It wasn't then. Or at least, it was done." Declining to be more specific, Alejandra shrugged, "I guess I really just did my job and went home. I wasn't really interested in anything in there. I didn't like the gaming."

Worst of all for Alejandra was the assumption that she belonged to the casino. She remembered asking her supervisor for a Sunday off for her daughter's first communion. "This is your livelihood. What comes first?" the supervisor asked back. "She expects me to say, my job comes first, but how could I?" Alejandra said. "So I remember being in tears because of that. That has always been the case. If for some reason, they can't do without you on a certain day, tough luck." In the end, Alejandra took the day off and got written up. "Well, what else was I going to do?" she said. Alejandra thought the casino's attitude that they owned their employees was "really bad" on families and couples because "the couples don't see each other as much. My marriage was ruined from the beginning," Alejandra said, "but [I'm] speaking of many others."

Alejandra worked swing shift for thirteen or fourteen exhausting years, juggling work life and her children's schedules. "I came home at four in the morning, went to sleep—then get up, send them to school. Then I could sleep a little possibly. And then they come home, and it's almost time for me to go to work again." Fortunately, Alejandra could drop off to sleep quickly when she got home from her shift. "But that's because I would deal with my eyes closed half the time," she laughed. "And it's true. At times I would be like, oh, my gosh. What did I do? I hope I paid them right, or whatever. It was like you're on autopilot, and that happened a lot."

Close regulation of dealers' work lives heightened substantially in the 1980s with the growth of corporatization and the coming of rational business management. Sweating the money was largely out, and "interaction" with customers was in. In the early days, talking with gamblers was not particularly encouraged, and in some casinos actively discouraged. "You were just your normal self," Alejandra said. "If you were pleasant then you were pleasant, if not you were not." Today, the casino requires more interaction, Alejandra said, "a lot more." She continued, "We are videotaped and watched, and if you don't interact enough, you're out the door.... We have to find out [customers'] names, and use them. Ask how their stay has been, and if there's any problem. Find out things about them so you can remember them when they come back. Make sure they come back. Invite them back. Anything—but just keep talking constantly, as well as deal and keep the numbers in your head. It's kind of hard."

Alejandra herself had nearly lost her job during a period when she was depressed, partly due to a failed love affair. Her supervisor began harassing her, and this went on for months. "I couldn't do anything right," she said. "He said he had my videotapes and that I was just sleepwalking, and that I wasn't even there. It could have been part right... but still the way they went about it was wrong, because they just had no... friendly skills at all or no sympathy with you." That was management's strategy in general—"see the negative"—and Alejandra hated it. "But that's how it is," she said. "I hate it when I talk about it, because I feel like, gosh, how could I put up with that? How come I did? Why am I doing it?"

Corporatization also meant, in Alejandra's opinion, that the quality of customer experience at her casino had fallen off. "It's about service," she said. "The [players] think they're not getting as many free comps as they used to. And all the improvements have not improved the service or quality. Like the dealers are better. I mean, we're all smiling and chatting with the players, but the complaints that I hear from the player is that they don't get as many free dinners or free anything. I think it's because the company's getting selective, and they are only giving to higher-limit players." Management's response, in Alejandra's view, was to blame the dealers. "They'll say, 'You're not smiling enough and you're not talking enough to bring them back.'" She concluded, "But what isn't bringing them back is the fact that if you've driven four hours to get here and you have reserved a room and you go in thinking that you're going to go up to your room and rest after the long drive, they tell you the room isn't ready. Sorry, but I wouldn't even wait. I'd go somewhere else."

Alejandra Lomeli, like all Nevada dealers at the time, was not part of a union. She and her fellow Reno dealers thought about organizing, but they had done nothing to contact a union. "A lot of us," she said, "are thinking that we could use a union... with the way things are right now, but I don't think it will happen. For one thing, most of the people are scared of losing their jobs. I don't know how much the union can do for us. But [the casino] will not allow it. They never have." Her relative lack of will, in this regard, contrasted sharply with the union women's.

Like most dealers, Alejandra expressed surprise and regret that she had stayed in the casino so long. "I didn't think I would be there forever, you know," she said. "I would say every five years, this is it, this is it. And it's been twenty...and now I'm giving myself another five years. I hope this is it though. 'Course, I don't know what else I'm going to do. That's the other thing. You get so involved in it—then most people have nothing else they can do afterwards."

Corporatization swept the gaming industry in the eighties and nineties, bringing significant changes to the casino floor. Long-term dealers like Alejandra were in a particularly strong position to see and evaluate the changes and often spoke passionately about their impact. While assessment of the old varied, no one felt that modern corporations' "rational" approach to extracting every possible coin from players while at the same time reducing dealers to minutely managed automatons had merit. Dealers witnessed the erosion of their meager measure of privilege and repeatedly spoke of a kind of emptiness that left them feeling demeaned, their talents' unacknowledged, their connection with customers reduced to a commodity. As their access, real or imagined, to power diminished, dealers struggled to find ways to assert their humanity against the demands of the casinos—but unlike union women who moved collectively to protect themselves, dealers were often left isolated and dispirited.

The changes that accompanied corporatization were noted by all. Some mourned the passing of a style, a kind of class that might have been illusory, they admitted, but at least spoke to something more than raw financial accumulation. Remedios Cortez, a forty-three-year-old blackjack dealer, said: "Everything has changed now since it became a corporation. When the owner died, everything went downhill from there. Even though, like I said, he [didn't promote] equal opportunity and things like that, he treated people nicely. I remember that we were happy and the place looked very, very nice. Everything was elegant. We were not supposed to talk on the games. We were supposed to be quiet and deal. They played soft music. But then when he died and his widow...sold to this corporation, it all went downhill. The conditions of the building, the treatment of employees, everything changed completely."[7]

Other dealers were not as captured by memories of past elegance. Cynthia Bowen, for example, spoke of trade-offs. "I think if you talk to someone that's been there for thirty-five years," she said, "they'd say, 'oh, it was so much better in the old days.' But I just see trade-offs." She went on, "In a way it was more of a family-type atmosphere back then. Maybe that's what the old-timers felt...that they were a part [of a family]." She continued, waving her hand dismissively, "I never felt that way. But they felt, you know, that they were winning this money for this patriarch or something. So they felt really a part, and they did take it personally if they lost. And I think nobody really cares anymore if we win or lose, because it's like this big corporation who really doesn't care about us anyway."[8]

The institution of the policies mandating "interaction" particularly maddened the dealers. Programs designed, as one woman said, "by a business major somewhere in the upper echelons who has never done this in his life," required dealers to smile, learn players' names, and ask how "things are going"—all in a rationalized effort to secure return customers. In the women dealers' estimation, the programs—labeled with catchy (or appalling, depending on one's perspective) acronyms like PPE (People Pledged to Excellence) and FOCUS (Fast and Fearless Service, Offers and Rewards, Chance of Winning, U Know Me, and Spotless Environment) were "friendly" neither in spirit nor implementation. Dealers were required to attend training sessions and assiduously watched by the eye-in-the-sky cameras that counted interactions and prepared reports for supervisors on employee inadequacies. Connie Hogan, a blackjack dealer, felt they meant "kiss the customer's ass no matter what." Like many dealers, she resented corporate-mandated policies that failed to appreciate the subtleties of dealer-player interaction and personality differences among dealers themselves. "We're supposed to like talk all the time, constantly," she said. "You know, some people are extroverts and some people…I tend to be one who talks all the time pretty much. I'm very good at knowing when people want to talk and when they don't want to talk. If they don't want to talk, I don't talk to them. Also it annoys some of our guests if you're talking to one person and they're really serious about gambling. So I try to balance it. But some people…they are really nice dealers, but they're just not real talkative. And I don't think that really should be a part of our job. It's like if you greet people and treat them with respect and say thank you and good luck and good-bye, I think that should be enough."

Programs such as People Pledged to Excellence also offended women who felt they had always been polite. Not only was friendly interaction a part of who they were, but as tip earners they had become masters at ensuring customers had a good experience. The relentless demand for pleasantry in an emotionally negative environment left many drained. "I didn't want to smile once I got home," Cynthia Bowen said, "and I was in a bad mood most of the time, because I'd had to stuff my feelings all day, and maybe I had seventeen different people tell me what a rotten person I was because I took their money. I was good at what I did, but there was a price tag, and the price tag kept getting bigger the longer I was there." Elaine Enarson, in a study of women dealers, focused on this "emotional work" so critical to corporate casinos' bottom lines. "Dealers pay a high price in inauthenticity," she wrote. "Like other tip-workers…dealers cultivate a façade of sincerity to increase their income. They learn to commodify friendliness."[9]

Dealers also complained that the programs gave too much power to the customer. "You feel like if somebody wants to complain about you," Connie Hogan said, "you have no defense, even though a lot of them—they're drunk and they're just mad…because [they've] lost their money and gone over their budget." Women in particular were afraid that being extra-friendly to players could be interpreted as a come-on.

Management implemented the programs with deadly zeal. The women shared many tales of fellow dealers being called in, disciplined, or terminated for failing to interact sufficiently. "This girlfriend of mine," Cynthia Bowen said, "she's been there for thirty-five years, but they took her downstairs and showed her her video—that she wasn't being interactive enough—and she said she was having a bad day. And they said, 'Well, that's no excuse. David got fired today for the same thing.' So to me, that's just threatening her with her job. She's scared. She's really scared."

With no union and in a fire-at-will state, there was little the dealers could do to protect themselves from arbitrary discipline. Mostly they kept their heads down, but occasionally the cases were so egregious, that they felt they had to act. In the case of one firing, forty-eight dealers signed a petition to have a terminated dealer reinstated. Cynthia had even written a letter:

> Those forty-eight signatures were not just about Bob.…If this could happen to Bob, [dealers were saying] it could happen to me.…I understand the aim of FOCUS and I think it is an honorable one. We need to treat our guests with courtesy and make them feel special. But the problem with FOCUS is that the company forgot to put the fun in it. The F is for fear. If people are fearful of losing their jobs, how can they have fun and make the customers feel comfortable? There is definitely a pervasive feeling of fear and paranoia in the games department. I think we need to build a corporate culture where our differences are recognized and we are rewarded for our individual performance and then we can be stronger as a team.

Corporatization brought other issues as well—like speed-up. Casinos regularly increased the "game pace," or the number of hands dealers were required to deal an hour. Edna Harman, the oldest and most experienced dealer we interviewed, described it as oppressive. "It's like the hand pace, the game pace," she said, "how fast you deal your hands in an hour. They started out at 350 an hour. Then the next year they said, you know, we want everybody at 370 an hour. And pretty soon it was 390 an hour, and then it was 400. And one guy said, '[T]hese people aren't machines, you know, you can't just keep grinding them up. They get older and they work eight hours and how can you expect…? What are you going to do? I mean, do you want any relationship at all with these people?' "

The use of part-time employees increased as well. Full-timers became the minority, and benefits were increasingly hard to secure. "It used to be that most people were full time and just a few part-timers for weekends or holidays," Edna Harman said. "Now, it's the other way [around]. Now the day is going to come when everybody's going to be part-time and on call because it's so convenient for the corporation." Connie Hogan said it had become a struggle to secure benefits (employees who work less than thirty hours a week are not eligible for health insurance or retirement). "They got real stingy about it," she said. "The new ones, what they do is keep them on call.... They haven't had any new benefited dealers for about four years."

In sum, programs such as People Pledged to Excellence and FOCUS, designed ostensibly to create a friendly, customer-oriented atmosphere, have a darker side, the creation of a mindless and often not-very-smart conformity among employees who, if they deviated from the established norm or protested, would be disciplined or terminated. The surveillance and penalties all did their job in the molding of a workplace dominated by fear. Employees kept their heads down and kept to themselves, the desired end product if one's goal was absolute control.

Every woman dealer we interviewed discussed, often with considerable passion, her worries about health. Dealers stood for hour after hour tied to the gaming tables, subject to high levels of smoke and noise, doing the same repetitive motions. The result was a host of physical ailments, not much to worry about initially, but more and more frightening as the years wore on. Women were vividly aware of the toll their bodies were expected to pay and the futility of protesting the abuse. Dealers' stories, more than those of any other employees in the casino, attest to the total control of bodies that corporatization brought about.

Connie Hogan, forty-six, had dealt cards for twenty years at a prominent, nonunion casino in Reno. A single woman with no children, she and five formerly homeless cats welcomed us to her condominium on the Truckee River. "One of my big causes is animal rights," she laughed. "That and women's rights, of course. I belong to People for the Ethical Treatment of Animals, the Nature Conservancy, the Humane Society, and a few other things. Well, you can see 'sucker' on my face, and [the cats] all move in!"[10]

Connie paid a lot of attention to issues of health. As far as she was concerned, it was the primary issue she faced as a dealer, and she was making plans to leave casino work because of it. She was just that worried. "I don't want to be one of those people," she said. "They retire and less than a year later they die."

Connie's principal concern was smoke. (See chapter 10, "Big Tobacco Rides the Strip" for more about the effects of smoke on casino workers.) But noise, an issue we did not automatically associate with health, also worried her. Noise on the casino floor is deafening and constant. "You've got utter chaos," Connie explained. "You've got Wheel of Fortune. You've got ding, ding, ding, ding over here. The announcements on the PA have gotten more obnoxious...loud and fast and real hyper. Anything to get your blood pressure up." A twenty-six-year dealer reinforced Connie's concern: "Both [my husband] and I have trouble hearing," she said. "It's affected our hearing to the point where [both of us] really do have hearing loss."[11]

Connie felt strongly that noise and smoke together had a profound effect on dealers' emotions and interpersonal relationships. "The energy in that place is unhealthy," she said. "It makes you very testy." A male friend had told her that every night when he got home from work he started arguing with his wife. Finally, he realized it had nothing to do with her—it was all about being wound up from work. Other relationships suffered as well, Connie said: "You don't want any noise. You don't really want to talk to anybody. Yeah, it definitely affects your personal interaction with other people and your energy level. Even the part-time people that only work like two days a week, they say there's a whole world of difference between how they feel when they get up after having worked the night before or not having worked. That has a lot to do with the lack of oxygen. Well, the carbon monoxide, you know, from the cigarette smoke...the four thousand chemicals. It's such a physical thing."

Dealers also reported a great deal of body pain. Dealing "throws your body off," the women said, and many went to massage therapists, chiropractors, and foot doctors, whose businesses, they laughed, thrived in casino towns. Feet, knees, backs, wrists all ached. "My feet always hurt," said Grace Ling, a Reno dealer. "Sometimes between my shoulder blades, my lower back. [I have] bunions and lots of bone spurs. It's just from standing. Women my age, a lot of them are ending up having knee surgery."[12] Edna Harman had had her feet operated on three times for neuromas. "Oh, it was really painful," Edna said. "[I went in and said,] 'Doctor, I hurt so bad when I get off work I could crawl out the door. You've got to do something.' I was out four months." Repetitive stress injuries, like carpal tunnel syndrome, were common among blackjack dealers. "A lot of the women," Jeanine Carter said, "have carpal tunnel problems. Some people wear braces....People have gone as far as to have surgery, but I don't know any that have been successful." Jeanine herself had one area on the bottom of her foot that was "pretty much numb." She said, "I'm sure it's from standing for so many years. Shifting around, putting your foot up...helps, but sometimes you can't put your leg up. You have to just stand there. And I don't think they care. They really don't care." In most dealers' opinion, management routinely ignored the complaints or denied they were work related. Alan Feldman, spokesman for Mirage Resorts, Inc., assured the public, "Wrist and arm injuries are simply not a common complaint among dealers."[13]

Women tried to protect their health by taking vitamins and sharing health information with coworkers, but most were afraid to confront management or felt protests would be useless if not dangerous. "There's a lot of us that are really into nutritional things," Connie Hogan said, "and we take our vitamins, take our herbs. There's a whole bunch of us that are trying to take care of our allergies and our sinus problems." But as far as the casinos themselves making changes, she said, "You can make suggestions, but I think they would be on deaf ears. In my perception, dealers—we're bodies in a lot of ways. They don't say this anymore, but they used to say, 'We need a body in Pit 3.' I mean, that was the term! That's what we are! We're not trained monkeys, but a lot of time we feel that way."

In contrast to the union women and their experience of collective power, Alejandra Lomeli had given up on the idea of a union. "We could use a union," she said. "But I don't think it will happen.... The casinos will not allow it. They never have." All the Reno dealers we talked with shared this bleak outlook. Privately and to each other they complained, but for the most part they did not fight back and had built no traditions of militancy. As one dealer said, "You don't even think about talking union, even to your best friend in a casino. You just don't do it."[14]

It wasn't that the women hadn't heard about unions or rejected them on face value. Nearly every woman dealer we interviewed said she would welcome a dealer union. Reno dealer Remedios Cortez was certain that "a lot of people...want the unions to come in." She said, "I think it would be good." But echoing Alejandra, she shrugged, "I believe if you mentioned something like that, they probably would fire you. Not openly...but using any excuse. Any excuse...whatever. Out the door." Furthermore, none of the women mentioned anything she or others had done to initiate an organizing process—no phone calls, no bathroom meetings, no after-hours knocking on doors. Fear, most said, trumped their interest. Maxine Everett, a veteran South Lake Tahoe dealer, recalled an early push to unionize dealers and the terror associated with it. "There was fear in the dealers' hearts," she said, "because there was a rumor—no, it wasn't a rumor. People had come up from the AFL-CIO to unionize a few years previous to that. I heard that they were found floating face down in the Truckee River with their throats cut. And so that sort of squashed the idea."[15] She and the other dealers also remembered their friend, Charlie Perkins, whom Maxine described as "an extremely intelligent black man," chef, and union organizer. "When he started organizing for the unions," she said, "he was literally booted out of the state. Couldn't get a job anywhere. So when that kind of stuff happened, especially if you're supporting a family...most people were real fearful."

The story goes that early on when the mob ruled gambling, a deal was struck between owners and the unions—unions would be allowed, but dealers would not be part of them. "It was a compromise," commented Lefty Rosenthal drily.[16] Gregory Butler, a labor journalist, offered his account of the "compromise":

> Table game dealers and the bookkeepers are all non-union—thanks to a deal that the then-mobbed up HERE made with gangster Ben Siegel out in Las Vegas back in 1947.... They agreed that the union would not represent anybody who handled money in a casino, so Siegel and his "associates" could "discipline" them as they saw fit.... In those days, "labor discipline" in Las Vegas often involved a .45 caliber slug to the head.... These days it's not quite so brutal... bookkeepers get fired instead of murdered, table game dealers get docked rather than having their hands broken... but these workers are still subject to the whims of management, with no union protection.[17]

Ironically, corporate casinos' move to intensify their control of dealers and to replace the "family" atmosphere with rational business practices has been the single most important influence that moved dealers toward union. That had not yet impacted Reno dealers, but in Las Vegas dealers were on the move.

We talked with Tony Badillo, President of the International Union of Gaming Employees (IUGE), who more than anyone else has stood for dealer organizing in Nevada and does not shy away from the impossible. We met Tony at White Cross Drugs, a shabby Las Vegas institution with an old-fashioned Woolworth's-type counter, a short distance from the offices of the Culinary Union and the IUGE. We settled into a worn booth, and Tony, in his seventies and looking fine in a soft flannel shirt, asked "How can I help you girls?"[18]

Badillo's story itself is fascinating. Back from the Korean War, he was walking the streets of Las Vegas looking for a dealing job without success. There wasn't much call for young, Mexican-American dealers (or for that matter, women—dealing was entirely a male domain in the early days). Leaving the Las Vegas Club where he had been turned down again, he mentioned Korea, and the owner said, "You're a veteran? Well, you got yourself a job." Tony laughed at the memory: "I started right at the bottom. Las Vegas Club to the Sands. I know every step."

Tony had a good career dealing 21 and roulette. He knew the Rat Pack—they'd come by his table—and he knew his job (he later published *Craps*, a guide for gamblers). But when Howard Hughes started buying properties and the corporations started moving in, there were "cuts here, cuts there, sick pay cut, floating holidays reduced, more pressure on the dealers," and Tony began worrying. When in the mid-1980s casinos began terminating dealers forty years and older, Tony and other veteran dealers began to move, and in 1989 they organized the Nevada Casino Dealers Association to "level the playing field" in Las Vegas and Carson City.[19] The organization as they conceived it would fight for better wages and benefits, to improve working conditions and job security, and to negotiate improved retirement and health plans, "all through collective bargaining and guaranteed by contract."[20]

The spread of gaming outside of Nevada and its right-to-work laws also resulted in some dealer organizing successes. In Detroit, a breakthrough came when the United Auto Workers formed a dealers union, and Detroit casinos agreed to allow a coalition of UNITE-HERE, the Teamsters, and the United Auto Workers (UAW) to solicit members. Buoyed by its successes in Detroit, the UAW took on six Atlantic City casinos; it won votes (and 3,500 new members) in four of them.[21]

In Las Vegas, the seemingly impossible happened when in 2007 dealers at Wynn Las Vegas voted 444–149 to be represented by the Transport Workers Union of America (TWU).[22] The move was fiercely contested by management, and Steve Wynn himself met with dealers, who had been angered by Wynn's earlier efforts to require dealers to share their tips with pit bosses, a move that some dealers said cost them $20,000 a year in tip income. "That was my mistake and I only have myself to blame," Wynn told dealers. "What [it] caused was the loss of the…family warmth and happiness that we had here. I got it wrong." Wynn continued, "A union comes between the employer, me, and you," echoing the historic management anti-union rationale. "It complicates our relationship. Our future as a family is based on us being together."[23]

Winning dealers' votes was one thing; securing a contract was another, and in both Atlantic City and Las Vegas, dealers in 2009 were still awaiting a contract as company officials dragged out the negotiating process on issue after issue.[24] In response, four national labor unions representing 15 million union members—the Transport Workers Union, SEIU, UAW, and AFL-CIO—put together the Gaming Workers Council to "stand together on behalf of workers in the casino industry" and "jump-start stalled contract talks."[25]

We conclude with two stories—the first, "Menopause Gulch," details veteran Reno dealer Maxine Everett's path from favor to despair; the second, "A Day in the Life," was written by dealer Cynthia Bowen, who shyly handed it to us at the end of our interview with her.

In 1973 Maxine Everett graduated from the University of California, Santa Barbara, and after a fun summer in Europe, headed to South Lake Tahoe where she easily secured a job as a hostess. Casinos were just right for her; blonde, vivacious, and game for anything, Maxine loved the fast pace, glittering lights, and especially the free-flowing alcohol. "It was fantastic," she laughed twenty-five years later. "You could drink twenty-four hours a day."[26] Maxine hiked, skied, and "fed [her] addictions." She said, "I couldn't pack enough booze. I [used it] to come down from the cocaine." She worked swing shift, escorting high rollers into the showrooms and to the head of the line at buffets. At the end of the night, she would retire to a back room with the managers where she watched them tally up the 24-hour take, evaluate the performance of pit bosses and dealers, and identify which "whales" to court. "I was privy to a lot of stuff," she said.

When after six months her position was eliminated, management came to Maxine and said, "You name your job. Whatever you want to do, you've got it." So Maxine chose dealing and was trained on the tables. Dealing was "fun, scary, fast-paced, and...grueling," she said. "You stood for many, many hours." She experienced all the ailments—back, feet, and, what Maxine called "organ problems" ("because the tables would hit us right here and there was a lot of pelvic inflammatory disease, lots of problems with ovaries and endometriosis"). Sexual harassment on the casino floor was rampant. Maxine remembered one pit boss who would run his craps stick "up your legs if you were wearing a skirt." There was a good deal of sexual innuendo, as well. "If you dropped a card," she said, "the pit boss would kneel down to get it and say, 'Is there anything else you want me to do while I'm down here?'"

Young, beautiful, and drug assisted, Maxine rose rapidly in the dealer ranks and was assigned all the best tables and high-limit games. "With or without cocaine," she said, "I was a good dealer, but I dealt a much faster game with the cocaine." Dealing fast meant more money, and the benefits weren't bad either: "You'd get lots of free cocktails," she said, "and there were always plenty of cocaine dealers."

But in time the party faded, and Maxine's highs began to crumble. "I had really, really low self-esteem," she said, "and I think that went hand in hand with staying in the casinos for so long. 'Oh, this is all I know, and I'm good at it.'" Addictions, an occupational hazard on the casino floor, nearly did Maxine in. "You'd have to lean out over the layout," she said, "and sweep the losers, and if you're feeling like you're going to throw up, it was a hard move to make." Hangovers kept her in bed more often than not, and when she did make a shift, people would say, "Oh, Maxine is making a guest appearance in our casino today." The bosses could ignore Maxine's shaking hands and frequent absences only so long before they began exacting penalties. "They would switch my shift," she said. "It was a message that you need to straighten up or we're going to give you these horrible shifts for the rest of your life. I knew they were either going to ease me out or they were going to fire me. So when that started happening I would quit and go to another casino....I'd pull a geographic."

Maxine worked all the casinos on Lake Tahoe's south shore before landing at a "little club...we called Menopause Gulch because that's where the old, washed-up dealers wound up. I wound up there [and] I wasn't even menopausal.

That was the bottom. This is the end of the line, sister. There is nothing after Menopause Gulch."

In fact, Maxine's story did not end at Menopause Gulch. By the time we met her ten years later, she had gotten sober, pulled herself together, and was completing a graduate program at the university. Not every dealer's path ended as positively, though. In the next two chapters we examine, first, the dramatic loss of self-esteem that developed in nearly every woman dealer we interviewed and, second, the efforts of two mega-industries, Big Tobacco and Big Gaming, to maintain lethal levels of smoke on the casino floor.

A DAY IN THE LIFE

BY CYNTHIA BOWEN

It is Sunday. I drive down Wedekind Road to work at ___ Casino where I am a blackjack dealer.... On Sundays I get to park on the street because there are no meter maids issuing tickets, which saves me a few minutes. It is always dark in [the casino]. Usually, I deal Baccarat but today I am dealing 21. I prefer dealing Baccarat because 90 percent of our clientele are Chinese. I have learned a lot about their culture and can even speak a little Cantonese. They are humble people, even the ones that have a lot of money, and contrary to the stereotype of the serious Asian, they have a good sense of humor.

Today...everyone is crazy. There is an old woman on my table who is 79 and looks 102. She asks everyone how old they think she is and they say, oh, about 65, to placate her. She is instructing everyone on how to play their cards and at one point almost inspires a fistfight. I have to referee this table and negotiate a peaceful settlement while enhancing everyone's self-esteem. We have something at [the casino] called PPE skills that we go through extensive training for. We are required to greet everyone at our table, say thank you and you're welcome and engage them in casual conversation. I'm certain [the casino] has spent millions of dollars on the training program, which is contained in that book, *All I Really Need to Know I Learned in Kindergarten.* We also attend classes called Valuing Difference, which is about accommodating different culture and personality. But [the casino] demands that we all be alike. And they have spies to inform on us if we are not. They have people disguised as guests sitting on our games rating our performance, sort of Gestapo techniques. We are under constant surveillance, so if we are not talking or smiling enough we are taken into the office and reprimanded.

...I return to my blackjack game where five women are slamming down straight tequilas. These women are no amateur drinkers. They are coaches' wives. Their husbands are participating in a softball tournament at UNR. They are in their forties and not well-preserved. Too many late nights and cigarettes. One is blonde—you can tell she was beautiful and she still thinks she is. There is a gruffly old Swede from Minnesota, and he starts to tell blonde jokes. I feel the tension. The blonde is simmering. She counters by telling him male-bashing jokes. This is scary for me—just where I want to be—trapped with a bunch of hostile alcoholics. I would prefer to be somewhere where people discuss Proust and Melville and Tolstoy or at least know who they are. I want to live in a world where people listen to public radio and know who Garrison Keillor and Terry Gross are. Naw, I probably wouldn't like those people anyway—too pretentious. But anything has to be better than this. My friend, when she is having a bad day dealing 21, says to herself, would Anne Frank like this? Would Anne Frank think this is better than being locked in a crowded attic fearing that any moment a Nazi could snatch her from her hiding place and send her off to work camp where she could be exterminated along with millions of other people?

I get another break. There is a little coffee cart in the middle of the casino. I like to get a coffee mocha and read there. It makes me feel like I am not really at work. I am reading an article in *Psychology Today* comparing schools to prisons. It says, what other place do you have metal detectors and are under constant surveillance? I think: my casino! The day is filling with more crazy people that I greet and engage in casual conversation. My last hour is a brief respite from an otherwise unredeemable day. I have the sweetest man on my table. He is about sixty and severely handicapped. He can hardly pick up his cards because his hands are so crooked. His name is Lowell. I ask him where he lives. He says in the Bay area. I tell him my daughter lives in Santa Cruz. Lowell asks me what my daughter does. I tell him she is a baker. Lowell scoots five dollars across the table to me when he leaves.

It is 5 o'clock and I swipe my time card through [the casino's] pathetic little time machine. It talks to me and I answer yes. Hooray! I am free. When I leave work, I always feel like schoolkids busting out of their classrooms at 3 p.m. on Fridays. Not a bad day, I think. Anne Frank would have preferred a day at my casino.[27]

STUCK

When we speak we are afraid our words will not be heard or welcomed. But when we are silent, we are still afraid. So it is better to speak.

—Audre Lorde, "A Litany for Survival"

Bettina Aptheker in her memoir, *Intimate Politics*, writes that bearing witness "is a political and spiritual practice in which the participants go to a place of great suffering and publicly acknowledge its existence. They shine a light all over it so that those who have suffered are no longer alone, or forgotten, or ashamed, and so that no one can claim that they didn't know what was happening."[1] In our interviews with casino women, we did not ask that they go to places of great suffering, but in acts of extraordinary generosity, they often did. Nowhere was this more apparent than in our conversations with long-term dealers.

Dealing has an allure unmatched in popular culture. Working at the center of the action, dealers appear to enjoy exciting, lucrative work lives. Ziggy, a male Las Vegas dealer whom Marc Cooper introduces in *The Last Honest Place in America*, wonderfully captures this image:

> After twenty-seven years, every night when I walk up to the table I'm happy. When I have to leave, it's like, ugh. There's nothing else I'd rather be doing. I have fun with the game and I have fun with the people. I talk a lot and the bosses let me get away with it. I enjoy teaching the game; I want to help people play right. The more they win, the more they tip. I just love the people who come to my table.... What can I tell you? I just love my job. Haven't even taken a vacation in four years. I'd like to do this job forever.[2]

Most women dealers we interviewed had equally long tenures in the casinos but a dramatically different story. With rare exception, they ached to escape the casino and had come to detest their jobs. They hated the noise, smoke, and having to work holidays, and even more they hated how the casinos profited from greed and broken lives. But they felt stuck. Dealing cards, the women said, was hardly a transferable skill, and even if they went back to school, the jobs they might get would pay considerably less than they made dealing. Worst of all, they hated themselves for having stayed so long, as if in their staying they had come to be all that they despised.

Being stuck is devastating. Most women have been there, in a place distant not only from our dreams but also from our knowledge of who we are and what we could contribute. Aptheker toward the end of her memoir writes, "Many women and men have a feeling of some deeper sense of purpose. However, fear of change, of rejection, of loss, of the unknown holds most of us in check for a lifetime, or for a very long time."[3] Among the long-term dealers, we discovered many women who felt that deeper sense of purpose and who knew, as one woman put it, that "I had a lot to offer... but didn't."[4] Their pain was boundless.

In the interviews, many of the dealers took the opportunity to "shine a light all over... places of great suffering," and in so doing opened a space where they and others could acknowledge their humanity, explore the structures of power that denied it, and create the possibility of community with others hoping like them to change the world. For other dealers, no light came. These were stories we did not anticipate hearing—we present three here.

Jeanine Carter

When we met her, Jeanine Carter, an attractive, reserved, and articulate fifty-one-year-old, had dealt roulette for twenty-six years, eleven of them in South Lake Tahoe and fifteen in Reno. She was married and had a daughter whom she adored: "I've brought a person out into the world that you guys would love," she beamed. Still, Jeanine was deeply ambivalent about the path her life had taken.

Jeanine grew up in Washington and attended Washington State. "I was thinking excitement a lot as a young person," she told us.

> You know, get away from [Washington]... So I took a map of the United States and thought, where would it be exciting to live? And I thought of Lake Tahoe. I had never been to Lake Tahoe, but I had heard people talking. It sounded exciting. I could make what I thought was good money and live kind of an exciting life.

It *was* an exciting life. For six years Jeanine and her husband, who had a degree in history and dealt craps, divided their time between working in the casino and leading a wonderfully nomadic life. "We would work for seven months," Jeanine said, "save our money and then travel. We went up the coast and camped and got a little cabin in Oregon. I didn't have my daughter 'til I was thirty-one, so we had ten years almost of just that kind of—a little bit of a never-never land."

The money was good in never-never land. "I had bags of money," Jeanine, who once bought a Datsun for cash, remembered. "It was just like, 'Here's $3,000.'" Still, even in those first years, some doubt crept in. Carter remembered telling her husband, "Well, you know, we don't want to be in our fifties or forties and doing this." By the end of her twenties, the doubts had become more insistent. "I can't do this anymore," she thought. "What am I going to do? I've got to do something with my life." Then—in a pattern many women will recognize—Carter became pregnant at thirty-one, and as she put it, "Well, okay, I've got a goal now. I can kind of push those demons down about what are you going to do with your life."

With the new baby, life at Tahoe took on a nicer, more meaningful glow for Jeanine and her husband. Their friends also were having children, and they would hike on weekends, fish, ski, and have a wonderful time. Everyone would gather on Thanksgiving before work, and as Jeanine put it, "I felt connected."

The doubt returned in force when their daughter reached school age, and Jeanine and her husband decided to move to Reno. Both transferred to Reno casinos and continued to deal, but that wonderful community feeling was gone, at least for Jeanine. "I don't think I felt as connected with the people I work with here," she said. "I mean, I had friends at work, but not a real connection with 'Let's do something after work' or anything."

Worse, Jeanine ran right up against the considerable stigma attached to women casino workers. Suddenly, doubts about her career decisions, and more important, her core being, began to seep into her consciousness. It started during school activities—Jeanine's daughter had gotten involved in softball and basketball—where she "would have to go and be involved with these other families." Jeanine said, "And I think that that's what's hard."

> You know, I never felt like I could just say, "Well, I work at [a casino]." I did, of course, because that always comes up. "What do you do?" "Oh, I'm a nurse. What do you do?" "Oh, I'm a roulette dealer." And I don't know if it's my perception—I don't think it is—but there's a wall that comes between.... People size you up. "Oh." Or a lot of times, "Oh, you don't look like you would work at the casino."

Jeanine was puzzled why her husband didn't feel the same way, because he was associating with the other parents, too. "He felt accepted by them," she said, "whereas I always felt like people don't like me as well."

The stigma never abated, but rather worked its way deeper and deeper into Jeanine Carter's life, eventually altering her own behavior. "I didn't allow people to get to know me, because I would rush in and rush out and wouldn't stay," she said. "I didn't feel accepted." Differences between her life and that of non-casino workers began to haunt her, and increasingly she felt outside the community. "And I might not even want to be part of the community," she conceded. "But I can't help feel like when you don't have Christmas off…and other people do."

Jeanine continued working, but for the first time began to experience dealing as "a horrible punishment…like I'd been whipped or something." Working a holiday or busy weekend, she said, "I would get really depressed…it would just be so noisy that you would just feel like—I can't stand it. It's the noise and…when you get a lot of people in a casino, and they're gambling and it's noisy and people are frantic…it's like, 'I can't stand this. What am I going to do? What am I going to do?'" She fought herself all the time to stay there: "You have this family built on this. You have the house payment—there's no way you can leave."

The waste also began to weigh on Jeanine's mind. "Now it's just the same people," she said. "People I've seen over the years.…Same people that come from the Bay Area. And a lot of them are very nice. But the cost depresses me. It's a sad side of life. I look in there, and I'm the type that…sees humanity and what this means. Why are so many people…? Just the waste. I find it so sad because it doesn't make them happy."

After twenty-six years, Jeanine Carter's estimation of herself had plummeted. She began to add up the total of her experience. "I'm fifty-one," she said. "I have no skills. You know, I have no confidence really.…I don't think I had a lot of confidence to start with. And I think that's why I went into this business."

The depression and self-loathing never completely dominated her consciousness, however. In the midst of the bleakness, Jeanine found ways to keep her own and others' humanity alive. She realized she had learned a few good things in the casino, like the ability to talk with people. Brightening, she told us, "The casinos have changed me in a very positive way because they have forced me to be a lot more outgoing. I see a big difference in my personality.…I'm just much more open to people, even in what I see as a hellish environment for me."

> I meet people's eyes. I try to make a connection, and sometimes on the escalator I'll get a wonderful smile, and that will just hold me for awhile. And it's like something has met between us. I have tried to hold on longer by connecting with people—that sort of sense of warmth, humanity, closeness.

Jeanine had tried other means of boosting her self-confidence, too. She was taking a keyboarding class and was playing with the idea of opening "a little vegetarian restaurant." The thought of applying for another job still terrified her though: "You know, it's much safer not to."

Thinking that she would like to be part of a group, Jeanine sought out the Unitarian Universalist Church in town, drawn to them because of their openness to many different people. Standing around after the service, she ended up talking with a woman, and...

> Same thing happened. We were talking and she was telling me a little bit about her life, and then she said, "What do you do?" And I said, "I work at [a casino]." And she said, "Oh, really. What do you do there?" And I said, "I'm a roulette dealer." And I perceived it as being, "Oh." Then a wall. It's hard. You kind of keep with your own....I remember thinking, "Well, when I get another job, and I'm doing other work, I can go back to the Unitarian Church, and I will be accepted." They asked me several times to come to some little dinners and I thought, I'm going to have to sit there and I'm going to have to say, "I'm a dealer," and there's going to be eight people there and there's just going to be silence.

Jeanine ended the interview with the same exhausting mix of despair, hope, shame, and pride. She wondered why she had never left the casino and dealing, because, as she said, "change is good, I mean, you grow." She continued, "And yet, now I'm paying a price for not changing....Monetarily I've provided well for my family, and if I die tomorrow, I can say I've had a great life because of my family. But I come away dissatisfied with a section of my life because I feel like I had a lot to offer, but I didn't. And it's my own fault. I could have done it. But I still can."

Audre Lorde in her extraordinary essay "The Uses of the Erotic," writes of women's deepest passions and how, failing to honor or even see them, we stumble forward, locked often in self-hatred and despair and subject to the powers that control our lives.[5] Jeanine Carter's story rings with the qualities Lorde describes—self-blame, loneliness, isolation. Her life, she felt, had steadily sunk into mire from which she was unable to extract herself.

Clearly, however, Jeanine was not entirely defeated (reminding us that no hegemony is ever complete) for she was still able, as Aptheker writes, to "go to a place of great suffering and publicly acknowledge its existence...to shine light all over it." That light enables us to see several things clearly.

First, and most important, we see that Jeanine works hard, loves her daughter, reaches out to others with compassion, and thinks critically about her life—surely the roots of her self-loathing do not lie in her basic being or some deep-seated inadequacies.

Next, she bears witness to employees'—or at least some employees'—enormous pain. The casino, in contrast to the images of glamour and fun promoted by the industry, makes her ache. "I can't stand this," she says, "What am I going to do?…The waste…I find it so sad." Furthermore, it is a pain that grows over the course of a work life; the emptiness not seen in the early years in never-never land has grown to consume her.

Finally, Jeanine provides evidence that despite the gaming industry's claims that dealers stand on the side of management, they are in fact far from owners' elevated positions on economic and social pyramids—so much so that Jeanine declines to identify herself as a dealer and avoids other parents and even the open-minded Unitarians. Of course, not everyone is tainted by their association with gaming—casino owners such as Steve Wynn do not hide or feel ashamed. Legislators, university presidents, society editors, even U.S. presidents, seek them out, eager for their company, wisdom, and campaign contributions. It is evidence, should any more be needed, of the vast divide between the owning and working classes, with dealers solidly in the latter.

Jeanine Carter's witness allows us to see a great deal. But it is only a beginning, just a crack in wall. What is missing is a consciousness of power, and that is what allows the self-loathing to rush in. Paulo Freire, the Brazilian educator, writes of a culture of silence in which the dispossessed internalize the oppressor's negative images of themselves—a kind of mimicry of the powerful, as he describes it.[6] Dealers were particularly susceptible to this, possibly because they bought into much of management's construction of dealing as a privileged job category. Wanting to preserve their privilege and, not incidentally, their income, dealers failed to unite with others in any meaningful resistance. They complained, yes, and suffered as well, but they did not risk much.

Next we meet Remedios Cortez who, like Jeanine Carter, failed to unite with fellow dealers in resistance but who did find a way to express her desire for a better world and in so doing was able to conceptualize power in a fuller sense.

Remedios Cortez

Divorced and the mother of a grown son, Remedios Cortez had dealt 21 at a high-end Reno casino for twenty-five years. Cortez was a poetry enthusiast, immigrant rights advocate, and political activist who threw herself with passion into the 2004 and 2008 elections, campaigning first for Howard Dean and then for Barack Obama. That she was also a dealer—a twenty-five-year dealer, no less—confounded and embarrassed her. "I never planned on staying twenty-five years," she said. "I wanted to get out, you know, since the first year. I kept telling myself, 'this is temporary,' and that I wasn't going to stay. Year after year I said, 'I'm getting out soon. I'm getting out soon.'"[7] Recently, Mrs. Cortez switched to dealing part-time, because she had taken a job outside the casino as a court translator. She loved translating: "Doing the court job," she said, "I'm providing a service to people, and that's important."

Remedios had followed her husband, who was making good money as a dealer, into casino work. He encouraged her to apply for the job but not without reservation. "I remember when he used to go to work," she laughed. "He would cross himself and say, 'When you go to that place, you need to do this.'" Remedios got a job as a cashier, and as soon as the opportunity to apply for the in-house 21 school presented itself, she grabbed it. She was surprised, actually, to be accepted because she had heard that the casino would not train anyone with an accent (she had recently come to the United States from Mexico) and in addition didn't think she was attractive enough to meet the casino's standards for dealer beauty. Despite her worries, Remedios was admitted to the dealers' school, and as soon as her training was completed, she was broken in at a blackjack table.

From the beginning, Remedios Cortez, who was never attracted to the never-never land that Jeanine Carter so enjoyed, disliked work on the casino floor. "I wanted to get out since the first year," she said. She stayed for the money.

> In one night [she said] we can make $400 in tokes—and that's plus our wages. Normally, it's around $150 a night for tokes. But we have nights when we have somebody [winning] a lot of money. We had a guy recently—he gave the dealers over $20,000 in tokes and tips, so that night, because we share, we made $500 and something—each one of us. That's for eight hours. So that's why [I didn't leave sooner].

The money was important, especially after Cortez divorced her husband and was left with the responsibility of supporting her son, but it never compensated for the distress she felt as a dealer. She never wanted to have other people know that she worked in a casino, and as much as possible kept it a secret. "I try not to tell anybody," she said. "If I can avoid it, I do. For me, it's embarrassing to work in that place. It's very embarrassing. It's just embarrassing. Embarrassing. I don't know...but just to tell anybody that I'm a dealer, that's embarrassing."

For a long time, Mrs. Cortez thought she was the only one who felt the stigma. Then she discovered that her coworkers suffered too. "It's like working in a bar or something," she said. "Everybody there is drinking. Everybody's smoking. Throwing away their money. It's just, you know, totally ridiculous, the whole business. So yes, there are people that feel the same way that I do. We were talking one time about this, and one of the girls said, 'Are you kidding? My neighbors are a minister and his wife. I don't want them to see my uniform.'"

It wasn't only the uniform that embarrassed Remedios Cortez. Her own complicity in casino values deeply troubled her. "I realize now," she said, "that I'm very judgmental about people who are only interested in money. Well, I'm looking at myself—that's why I'm so judgmental. I'm looking at myself....I wouldn't be there if I wasn't so interested in money. I would have left a long time ago."

> If you think about it, I could live more modestly. Once you're there, money is no object. I e-mailed a dealer friend and said, "Well, now that I'm part-time, I'm going to put myself on a budget." And she answered me, "What is a budget?" That's it! Because [when] you want something, you go buy it. There's no problem. When I went to work at the [court job], I was really amazed how the girls [in the office] took care of their money. You know, you get your paycheck every two weeks and you have your budget, and you're very careful about going to lunch....And I was like, "Wow!" Because for us, it's if I want this, I want that, I go get it. Things that I don't need, I go get. So in a way I'm very critical about values, but look at me. I'm doing the same thing. I got caught in this mentality of money, [of wanting] everything.

Remedios thought carefully about power relations within the casino, something that distinguished her from many dealers. It was clear to her that fear of management and its enormous power kept dealers—privileged in some ways but essentially powerless—from speaking up. Management's abuse of workers weighed heavily on Mrs. Cortez, but she kept silent and this troubled her, as if not acting, not protesting in the face of abuse made one, in a terrible turn, complicit. "Nobody dares to say a thing," she said. "If you start making waves, out you go. They don't fire you—they don't do it in an obvious way—but they start picking on you....And that's another scary thing for me that I don't want to get to that point one of these days. So far, they've been good to me, but it scares me when I see people that, if you start complaining, they start picking on you."

The dialogue deepened as did Mrs. Cortez's despair. "It's getting worse," she said. "It's getting worse. The last couple of years I'm just to the point that I want to cry when I have to go to work. That place—the energy in that place is just—it's unhealthy, and in a way I do everything against my values. What is the point of taking everybody's money and hearing these people complain? It's meaningless. It's a meaningless job. It's empty."

Remedios Cortez says with clarity unusual among dealers, "Nobody dares to say a thing—if you start making waves, out you go." Like Jeanine Carter, Cortez bears witness. She is ashamed for doing "everything against my values" and horrified that she stayed so long. But, aided perhaps by her experience as an immigrant rights and political activist, she goes further to talk of power and in so doing enables us to move beyond the feelings of despair and self-blame to begin to analyze the structures that trap dealers.

What can we learn from Remedios? From the start, she is clear about the ability of money to trap dealers in decisions they later regret—for example, staying year after year in jobs they hate or failing to protest when others are abused. She echoes Carter's disgust ("it's just totally ridiculous, the whole business"); speaks openly of the enormous toll dealing had taken on her personally; and is aware that in some measure she has bought into the "mentality of money, [of wanting] everything."

Like Jeanine, Remedios blames herself, but stops short of the all-consuming self-loathing that Jeanine experienced. She tends to talk much more of the owners' power and their positively lethal record in response to union organizing, and she seems in her activism to be more in touch with her commitment to justice and other human beings. Audre Lorde writes, again in "Uses of the Erotic": "For as we begin to recognize our deepest feelings, we begin to give up, of necessity, being satisfied with suffering and self-negation and the numbness that so often seems like their only alternative in our society. Our acts against oppression become integral with self, motivated and empowered from within."[8] No longer satisfied with "self-negation and the numbness," Remedios Cortez opens more and more to herself and to others. It is humanity rising, or in another way of putting it, love.

The issue of connection, of love, brings us to the idea of taking action against injustice in concert with others. Critically, the women dealers, with rare exception, did not describe much in the way of their own activism. Although they certainly complained about work conditions and management, no woman was inclined to organize a dealers' union or even expressed much interest in it. Jeanine Carter had signed a petition urging the casino to rehire a male dealer who was fired for being too slow, but while the abuse hurt her heart, it did not elicit a broader response. For the most part, the women focused on their own lives and the lives of their families. They kept their souls intact by connecting with people on the escalator or by finding more meaningful part-time work, but they did not attempt to organize—at least not in Reno.

In contrast to the union activists whom we discussed in chapters 4 and 5, the women dealers did not benefit from taking action against workplace injustice in the company of fellow workers. Nor did they experience the growth in understanding that comes from actually confronting injustice (a much different process from complaining about it).

The two dealers who took action—in both cases outside the casino—benefited greatly from it. Edna Harman, a dealer and pit boss whom we met in chapter 7, dedicated herself to the poor and traveled to Central America to work with liberation theologians. Remedios Cortez dedicated hours and hours of her time to political campaigns. The efforts of both women brought them into soul-enriching contact with others who shared their passions. In talking about their activism, both women not only brightened markedly but also demonstrated their keen and growing understanding of national and world politics and other structures of power.

How much would be possible should Jeanine Carter and other women dealers discard the self-blame and unite in a purposeful way to share the deep stories of their work lives—joys, despair, hopelessness, strategies for resistance—with the intent of transformative change?[9]

What becomes clear in the light that Jeanine and Remedios so generously shed is that individual solutions, like those that focus on one's own family's well-being, are not solutions for very long. To make a deal with the devil and acquiesce to injustice in exchange for a few privileges—whether the deal is made at a university or a casino—is much more costly than we ever imagine it will be.

We end with Linda Elder, whose story is a sobering one.

Linda Elder

Linda Elder was just a year away from an undergraduate degree in journalism when she saw an ad in the newspaper for work at Lake Tahoe. "Lake Tahoe, wow!" she thought. "Sounds like a fun place to spend the summer."[10] Ms. Elder was confident of her ability to get a job, so she drove to South Lake Tahoe, walked into the largest casino she could find, and was hired immediately. She started out as a change person, "one of the worst jobs in the casino," she laughed. "You just load up [with change] until you can barely walk." It was "miserable"—but perfect for her:

> It was probably one of the most fun summers I ever had because I was with students from all over the country who had come to work there for the summer.... Most of the kids wanted to work [swing shift] because you get off at say two in the morning and then you'd stay and party with all your friends and get home and get a couple of hours sleep and then you'd have the day to go to the beach and the lake and go out boating and stuff like that. So it was actually the ultimate shift for young people in that lifestyle. I loved it. I absolutely loved it.

Linda Elder liked it so much that she returned to Lake Tahoe after she graduated and was hired as a full-time pit clerk. Before long she had worked her way up to the coveted job of dealer. Dealing became the center of her life for the next twenty years, and though she worked at other jobs, including journalism, the casino always pulled her back. "I'd come and work weekends," she said. "I couldn't bear to break that tie."

Part of the draw of casino work for Linda was that it provided her with family. "The people that you work with," she said, "most of them are fantastic. And most of us have been working together now for so many years that it's like family because you spend your holidays there. Well, you have to. Some have been there for thirty years, and they've never had Christmas off." She met her husband, a pit boss, in the casino, and with him and other dealers spent all her free time enjoying Lake Tahoe and its environs. "It's a paradise," Linda said, echoing Jeanine Carter. "We used to call it never-never land because people don't ever grow up there."

Linda also appreciated the casino's flexibility. She loved to travel and had lived out of the country on several occasions. Amazingly, she could always return to her job in the casino without a loss of status and with the same salary, benefits, and seniority. Even when she left for two years to attend graduate school, the casino continued to pay her insurance. "I don't know why," she said. "I just kind of slipped through."

Linda also found pleasure in her relationship with long-term customers, people she'd known for ten or fifteen years: "You know, people that you taught to deal baccarat ten years ago. They're still coming in, and they still look for you—one of your little followings. Even if they don't play your game, they'll come by and talk to you, and you can have fun interactions."

And of course the money was good. Swing-shift dealers at South Lake Tahoe were clearing $55,000, Linda said, adding appreciatively, "They do take care of you. They do care. They'd rather keep you than lose you."

Linda Elder wasn't entirely happy, however. She didn't like having to deal with "bus people," the mainly Asian gamblers who bussed in from the Bay Area. Also, she didn't like that when players harassed a dealer, management seemed reluctant to provide much protection, especially if they were high rollers. Furthermore, corporate ownership had ruined many things for dealers in her opinion. "They keep taking things away," she said, "taking, taking, and taking." They took drink tokes away (the free drink coupons companies attached to paychecks) and Wild Bucks, too (the $1 and $2 coupons the company gave employees for doing a good job). Linda also didn't like the increased scrutiny, especially the mystery shoppers who would "sit down and play in your game and then write up a report on you." She concluded, "Management just keeps taking and never giving back. And all the while they're taking, they're asking more from you."

Linda Elder's complaints, however, never rose to the level of insight or personal self-examination, and in this she differed substantially from Jeanine Carter and Remedios Cortez. While Jeanine agonized ("I can't stand this. I can't stand this. What am I going to do?") and Cortez had her critique ("What's the point of taking everybody's money. It's a meaningless job"), Elder reasoned, "I can make it fun...or I can make myself miserable." She saw no special issues for casino workers relative to family and marital relationships, and saw no sexual or racial discrimination: "I don't think there would be any," she said. Nor did unions interest her: "I don't know very much about [them]. In fact, I don't know anything about them." She talked about alcohol and drugs with the same never-never land sensibility. When we asked if they posed a problem for workers, she replied, "Oh, jeez. Let's see. That's tough, because I'm not sure that I see it." That particularly stunned us, for no other worker failed to comment on casinos' drug and alcohol culture.

Clearly, Linda Elder had hopes and dreams that went beyond the casino. She had continued her education and finished graduate school, worked in other jobs, and traveled widely. But she never stayed away from the casino for long. When asked, "Would you recommend casino work to others?" she thought for awhile and then responded, "No. If you're seasonal [or] a student, it's great...and I would recommend it in terms of working with the public. But it's scary because it's a job you get stuck in. It's easy money, which accounts (for) why a lot of people are not going to college or continuing their careers....You have no incentive to pursue anything outside because you know you could go to work and make $200. Why would you? There's no need."

Recently, Linda and her husband, along with many other South Lake Tahoe casino workers, had moved to Carson City, Nevada's state capital just a half-hour drive from "the Lake" and its casinos. Carson City provided them respite from years of shoveling snow and a "normal community...where people actually go to church." The move evidently did not fill the gaping holes that Linda tried so hard to fill with easy money and her hear-no-evil, speak-no-evil spirit. Three years after our interview, Linda Elder's husband committed suicide, and two years after that, Linda herself died of alcohol-related complications.

BIG TOBACCO RIDES THE STRIP

I had a friend who went in for a physical and his chest x-ray showed that his lungs were absolutely black....The doctor said, "How long have you been smoking? You need to quit now. And [my friend] said, "I've never smoked a day in my life." And the doctor said, "Well, you must have worked in the casinos."

—Maxine Everett, Reno Dealer

Individuals who choose to work in the gaming industry know the circumstances under which they choose to work. They're working in an environment where we try to satisfy patrons' desires and that includes the ability to smoke when those patrons choose to do so.

—Harvey Whittemore, lobbyist for the Nevada Resort Association
and R. J. Reynolds (Whaley 2001)

Teresa Price, daughter of popular state senator Bob Price, had dealt cards at Caesars Palace in Las Vegas for twenty five years. Once an Employee of the Month, she was fun and outgoing, and her personnel file was swollen with customer letters praising her service. Then abruptly in September of 2005 it was over. In the middle of a blackjack game, a player puffed smoke in Teresa's face, an all-too-common experience for dealers. When Teresa blew it back, the customer "started screaming, 'You blew my smoke back on me!'"[1] The casino, which had been waiting for this moment, moved with lightning speed. There were no plaques for twenty-five years of service, no farewell parties. "It was awful," Teresa said, her eyes filling with tears a year later. "People were afraid to talk to me....I put a lot of years into the company. I grew up there, over half my life. Twenty-five years and nothing."

Teresa's problem was that she cared about secondhand smoke and had been pushing Caesars Palace to do something about it for years. Once she had even purchased little fans and taken them into Human Resources with a plea to let dealers use them on the gaming tables. The company denied every one of her requests and in time began the pattern of harassment with which so many of the casino women were familiar—suspensions, bad schedules, anything to make work life miserable. But Teresa kept at it. Eventually, she filed a complaint with the National Institute of Occupational Safety and Health (NIOSH) office in Las Vegas and requested they conduct a study of smoke levels at the casino.

By the time we met her a year after the firing, Teresa had become an activist in the struggle to bring meaningful controls on secondhand smoke to Nevada, which by many experts' estimates has the worst smoking laws in the nation. She had traveled the 450 miles north to Carson City several times to lobby the legislature on smoke—efforts that always failed—and had stood outside stores with petitions to get measures limiting tobacco use in public places on the ballot. A bright woman, Teresa had made a comeback from the humiliation of being fired and when we met her was working as a guide, taking tourists out to the Grand Canyon. "Twice the hours and half the pay," she laughed with some bitterness.

Talking over coffee in Las Vegas we asked Teresa what motivated her. "I had cancer as a young adult," she replied, "and spent time in the UCLA Medical Center Intensive Care Unit. I saw what cancer did to people. It was a huge thing." And after Caesars began harassing me, I asked myself, 'Why am I here? I didn't get married. I didn't have children. Why am I here?' I decided I am here to make a difference."

Smoke scared all the dealers with whom we spoke. Tied to the gaming tables, they literally ate smoke, hour after hour, year after year. They could ask customers not to smoke or to hold their cigarettes away from the table, but most were reluctant to do that as it might impact their tips or, as Teresa found out, cost them their jobs. Remedios Cortez, a dealer at a Reno casino, said, "A lot of people, I don't think they even realize that they hold their cigarette like this in your face. Some people are polite and they say, 'Do you mind if I smoke?' But what are you going to say, 'Yes, I mind'?"[2]

Casinos actively encouraged smoking. When Teresa first began dealing, casinos put cigarette boxes on the gaming tables, and later cigarette girls walked around giving them away for free. "Everybody smoked everywhere," Teresa remembered. "Pit bosses smoked. Players smoked. If you were working for a pit boss who was a chain smoker, he could put his ashtray on your table and leave his burning cigarettes in it all shift."

For dealers the smoke was—and is—terrible. Customers smoke both cigars and cigarettes, freely polluting the entire casino floor. Casinos occasionally provide nonsmoking tables, but they are mixed in with the smoking ones and do nothing to protect either players or dealers. The impact on dealers is massive. As Teresa described it: "Headaches. You blow your nose, and it's all black. Dealers go in the back with their inhalers all the time. They have breathing attacks. They carry inhalers in their pockets. Your lunch bag and your house smell." Maxine Everett, a veteran Lake Tahoe dealer, added, "The places just stink."[3]

Dealers described going home after work reeking of smoke and "zinging from the nicotine."[4] Grace Ling, a Reno dealer, said, "You get home and everything smells, your hair, your clothes. You're in the shower at three o'clock in the morning scrubbing away the film."[5]

Remedios Cortez had a not-so-funny story: "The kids at work laugh," she said, "because I told them one time, 'I even wear special underwear [at work].'"

"Oh, lacy, sexy things?" the guys asked.

"No!" she told them, "I buy the ugliest, cheapest things. My purse, my shoes, everything that I wear in that place, [I buy at] the $1.00 store...because to go to that place, who wants nice things? The smoke is just awful. Awful. That is why I was telling you, I think those are inhumane conditions. I really do."

Many women mentioned asthma and smoke-induced allergies. "The smoke's just oversensitized my body," Connie Hogan, the Reno dealer who rescued cats, said, "and I can think of a lot of other people who have the same complaint."

> Even if you don't have full-out allergies, a lot of people have sinus problems....My friend's husband was so bad—he's a supervisor—he had surgery on his sinuses and antibiotics so many times that it's to the point where it's not even good for him....There's a few that I know have asthma. In fact, there's one younger lady, she's had it. I don't know why she's there, but I guess—well, she's married and has a child, so [she] needs to make money.[6]

Dealers as they aged became nearly desperate with worry about smoke and its long-term effect on their health. Cynthia Bowen, a Reno dealer said, "I'm really concerned about the smoke. Like my girlfriend last night was talking about this woman that had cancer. And I said, 'Do you think that there's a higher rate of cancer here than other places?'"[7] Every year there seemed to be more casualties. Connie read widely in the area of health and talked with authority about the "four thousand chemicals" released in secondhand smoke. "We have lost some fairly young people to cancer," she said, "[including] one lady who left quietly, which I wish she hadn't. She never smoked a day in her life, and she developed a heart and a lung condition in a very short period."[8]

Maxine Everett had a friend who went in for a physical "and his chest x-ray showed that his lungs were absolutely black....The doctor said, 'How long have you been smoking? You need to quit now.' And her friend said, 'I've never smoked a day in my life.' And the doctor said, 'Well, you must have worked in the casinos.'"[9]

In the end the attitude was, the women said, you chose this job. So you have to suffer. "But someone has to do this," Teresa thought, "and it's not right that they have to die. Other people like airline stewardesses didn't have to leave their jobs.... Who made the rule that gambling and smoking go together?"

"But," she sighed, "there's no option. You have a house, kids, bills. People are afraid to stick up for themselves. Look at what happened to me. The casinos have a lot of power and a lot more money."

We did not immediately grasp the health consequences to dealers of second-hand smoke. To be sure, we were sympathetic to the women's complaints but in a removed way—and actually wondered in our first interviews if women like Connie who carried on about "four thousand chemicals" weren't a little over the top. We didn't like smoke ourselves, and often avoided casinos because of it, but in some way probably felt that dealers *should* get other jobs.

In time we became convinced of the extreme danger that secondhand smoke posed to the women's health, a danger that today has no way abated. Critically, we also began to uncover another story—one peopled by extraordinarily powerful economic actors assembled to thwart Teresa and the other dealers' chance at clean air. Curiosities began to emerge—like a study out of the University of Nevada, Reno (our own university) purporting to prove that Nevada's economy would collapse were smoking regulations introduced into casinos. An "independent" university study with findings entirely in the service of the gaming and tobacco industries?: that seemed strange to us as academics and worthy of investigation. Eventually, we made our way to the hundreds of thousands of internal documents from the tobacco industry housed at the University of California, San Francisco Medical School. What emerged was an entire world, well-funded and religiously kept secret, of legal, research, and public relations strategies carefully designed by the tobacco and gaming industries to keep Nevadans smoking and state regulations at bay. In time, Connie's concerns about four thousand chemicals seemed, if anything, understated. Secondhand smoke was, we discovered, a larger and much more deadly story.

Scientists in the last twenty-five years have traveled a significant distance in assessing dangers associated with secondhand smoke (SHS), or as it is also known, environmental tobacco smoke (ETS). Beginning in the early eighties, researchers began to explore its dangers, and in consequence of their work, fully 80 percent of U.S. citizens by the end of that decade believed that secondhand smoke was not just annoying, it killed. It was also during this period that legal and regulatory bodies as well as some businesses began making a series of decisions to protect Americans, including workers, from exposure to secondhand smoke. In 1987 smoking was banned on all domestic flights under two hours, and three years later the ban was extended to flights of any length. State and local governments began to impose antismoking ordinances in public spaces as well.

In 1993 the Environmental Protection Agency (EPA) released a bombshell—a study that classified secondhand smoke as a "known human carcinogen."[10] "The dangers of exposure to environmental tobacco smoke are now well established," the study reported, citing evidence that exposure caused annually 3,000 deaths due to lung cancer, 35,000–62,000 deaths due to ischemic heart disease, 1,900–2,700 deaths due to sudden infant death syndrome, 9,700–18,600 cases of low-birth-weight infants, and 8,000–26,000 new cases of asthma in children.[11] The tobacco industry unsuccessfully sued the EPA, and the report stood, changing the smoking world forever.

By the late nineties, researchers began to focus on two "microenvironments"—home and work—where, they argued, people spent 90 percent of their time. "Populations at greater risk of harm from ETS," they concluded, "are those who live with smokers and those who work where smoking is allowed."[12] In the latter arena, casino floor workers, along with bartenders and restaurant workers shortly became the focus of a number of studies, all with sobering results. For example:

- A 1993 Centers for Disease Control study found food service workers had a 50 percent greater risk of dying from lung cancer as compared to the general population—this increase was attributed to workplace exposure to ETS.[13]
- A 1996 National Institute for Occupational Safety and Health (NIOSH) study concluded that "employees working in the gaming areas of a large casino are exposed to ETS at levels greater than those observed in a representative sample of the U.S. population, and that the serum and urine cotinine of these employees increases during the workshift."[14]
- A special 1998 issue of the *Journal of the American Medical Association* (*JAMA*) identified casino workers as an "occupational group at high risk of disease from ETS," speculating that "the risk-taking ambience and the free flow of alcohol at casinos probably encourage a high level of smoking among gamblers."[15]
- Another study concluded that at bars and restaurants where cigarette smoke is in the air, "women in the study exposed to as little as two hours a week for over six months had a 50 percent greater risk of developing lung cancer than nonexposed women."[16]
- A study of the respiratory health of fifty-three California bartenders before and after that state passed legislation prohibiting smoking in bars, taverns, and workplaces noted a marked decline in the prevalence of respiratory

symptoms and improvement in pulmonary function. It concluded that "in addition to potentially reducing the long-term risk of lung cancer and cardiovascular disease, workplace smoking prohibition appears to have immediate beneficial effects on adult respiratory health."[17]

In short, by the end of the millennium there was plenty of evidence that secondhand smoke killed and that employees such as casino floor workers were among its principal victims. Given that, how did two industries, one determined to sell tobacco and the other eager to maintain casinos as full-smoke environments, convince the public, legislatures, and other regulatory bodies to ignore the scientific findings? Nevada was about to become the test ground for exactly that question.

The story begins in 1996 in Washington, DC, where tobacco industry executives, organized into a high-level "Communications Group," were working overtime to counter a ban on smoking in workplaces that the Occupational Safety and Health Administration (OSHA), pursuing its statutory responsibility to ensure that America's workers have safe and healthy workplaces, had proposed. For the first time, Big Tobacco, accustomed to muscling its way through regulatory threats, felt constrained. On every hand there was trouble. Scientists had been largely successful in their efforts to link smoking with lung and heart disease and now were moving to establish the dangers of secondhand smoke. In Congress the seven tobacco industry CEOs had stood in front of Henry Waxman's committee and declared that nicotine was not addictive.[18] Eight months later, largely because of whistleblower Jeff Wiegand—who despite vicious efforts to discredit him had persisted—the country learned that the executives not only had known of nicotine's addictive qualities but also had manipulated the evidence. It was high comedy to some—the seven executives were everywhere labeled the seven dwarfs—but for Rob Meyne, senior director of public affairs for R. J. Reynolds Tobacco Company and chair of the Communications Group, it was disaster. Furthermore, internal documents were not staying internal. An insider had left a million documents, many revealing an embarrassing trail of tobacco industry machinations, on Stanton Glantz's doorstep. (Glantz was a top University of California, San Francisco Medical School researcher with a history of investigating the tobacco industry.) Lawsuits were proliferating, and billions of dollars had already been extracted from Big Tobacco's pockets by the Master Settlement Agreement.[19] Smoke regulations unthinkable earlier were being approved. Worse, all this had hit popular culture in a way that made Big Tobacco look positively evil. Of course, there had been books such as Kluger's *Ashes to Ashes,* but relatively few Americans read them.[20] Now Russell Crowe was receiving an Academy Award for playing Jeff Wiegand and John Grisham was writing bestsellers about heartless tobacco industry executives![21] The little people were becoming restless.

Less and less able to speak on its own behalf, the discredited tobacco industry rolled out its long-standing strategy of mobilizing third parties who could act as its public voice.[22] Enter Nevada's gaming industry, Big Tobacco's principal candidate for front-person-in-chief.

From the beginning, the gaming industry had promoted smoking, as Teresa Price noted, handing out free cigarettes alongside free drinks. Desires such as smoking, alcohol, and sex just seemed to go with gambling; they were all part of the action. "[The slot machines] sit there like courtesans," Frank Scoblete, gambling's best-selling author and advice giver, laughed, "promising pleasures undreamed of, your deepest desires filled, all lusts satisfied."[23] Andrew Barbano, Reno satirist and labor journalist, concurred: "Casino marketers push for the compulsives. The pros know that their highest effectiveness lies in catering to all seven deadly sins, including gluttony and lust. Nonsmoking casinos have failed because addictives prefer patronizing full-service providers."[24]

Gaming executives, who made a science of keeping gamblers gambling, were apoplectic at the thought of smoke regulations. The entire casino floor—its mazelike layout, the absence of windows and clocks—was designed to promote no-interruptions play, and executives certainly did not want laws that required smokers to leave the casino in order to light up. Furthermore, they were convinced that upward of 70 percent of gamblers smoked. Their perception wasn't supported by research, but nevertheless it made executives extraordinarily fearful of OSHA's proposed ban on workplace smoking and eager to jump on Big Tobacco's bandwagon.

The tobacco industry was delighted at the prospect of a liaison with Nevada gaming. The state's preemptive tobacco laws, gaming's already-established control of the legislature, and the population's sky-high smoking rates together constituted a tobacco paradise. Nevada was one of six states in the country that had enacted preemptive tobacco laws, forbidding cities and counties from imposing smoking regulations more stringent than the state's.[25] Since nationwide most smoking regulations had originated in cities and counties, that severely limited smoke regulation advocates' options. Furthermore, the few regulations that existed were shot through with exemptions, especially when it came to casinos.

The gaming industry also had the Nevada legislature lined up, another plus in Big Tobacco's calculations. Gaming regularly infused campaigns of candidates on both sides of the aisle with cash.[26] In consequence, hardly any politician in either party was willing to go up against the gaming industry. It was political suicide.

Best of all, Nevadans were heavy smokers. Thirty-two percent of adult Nevadans smoked, at the time the highest rate in the nation,[27] and even more young people (39.9 percent) ages sixteen to nineteen lit up (the nation's mean was 34.5 percent).[28] Even better, the state had the country's fewest smoke-free work environments.[29] "We jokingly say Nevada's the smoking section for California," Daniele Dreitzer of the Nevada chapter of the American Cancer Society told newspapers.[30]

That Nevadans' smoking habits were a health disaster did not seem to enter corporate calculations. Because of their smoking and the lack of meaningful smoking regulation, Nevadans suffered the nation's highest death rate from smoking-related diseases as well as the highest incidence of asthma.[31] The Centers for Disease Control and Prevention estimated that 2,600 Nevadans died each year from smoking-related illnesses.[32]

All this provided, in tobacco industry executives' eyes, superior ground on which to play out their strategy to beat back the threat of workplace regulation of smoking. Big Tobacco began to move quietly and aggressively to implement their plans.

In December 1996, six months after the Philip Morris OSHA Communications Group began to meet, the results of a "major university study" predicting dire consequences if a workplace smoking ban were imposed on Nevada were released at press conferences in Las Vegas and Reno. The timing was impeccable. Every paper carried news of the study under banner headlines such as "Survey Predicts Nevada Would Lose Big If Casino Smoking Were Prohibited."[33] The study, which assumed that the proposed regulations would completely ban smoking in casinos, restaurants, bars, and hotel rooms, predicted the following:

- After five years, [the casino sector's] growth could be as little as 38 percent of what it would have been without the OSHA regulations. As many as 7,900 jobs would be lost in the first year.
- Nevadans could lose as many as 50,000 jobs over five years.
- After five years, the total state economy would suffer by as much as $3.5 billion.
- Combined with lost gaming taxes, total revenues lost to state and local government could amount to as much as $94.9 million in year one and to as much as $150.6 million in year five.[34]

Fifty thousand jobs lost in five years! Ninety-four million dollars lost in taxes in the first year alone! Those were sobering figures—even the staunchest smoke regulation advocate could not ignore the economic and human impact that the study foretold.

We were impressed with the figures as well. But we had some niggling doubts. Who was this University of Nevada, Reno professor? Did we know him? And how was it that a UNR faculty member came to conduct a study so clearly in the service of the gaming and tobacco industries? Was this an example of the selling of university research expertise to deep-pocketed corporate bidders? And to be frank, our suspicions were gendered: it was all men, all the time—in the university, big gaming, and the legislature, most very well-heeled in comparison to the women in our study.

But even at our most suspicious, we did not imagine what we would find when we began to tease out the threads. Multiple inquiries later, we arrived at the Philip Morris papers at the University of California, San Francisco Medical School and the work of Dr. Stanton Glantz. The "independent study" predicting big losses was, we discovered, a key component of a nationwide Philip Morris initiative in the mid-nineties funded by Big Tobacco itself.

The Philip Morris OSHA Communications Group, according to Glantz, searched throughout the early months of 1996 for third parties to sponsor scientific studies in key states throughout the nation. These studies would be vehicles by which data critical of workplace smoking bans might be carried to the media. It didn't take long to find the actors in Nevada. By July 1996 the chair of the Communications Group reported: "We have reached an agreement in principle with Dr. John Dobra of the University of Nevada to conduct a separate survey of the gaming industry. Efforts are underway to identify an appropriate sponsor for this survey."[35] Two weeks later, the Communications Group wrote that all was arranged: "The Reno Sparks County Chamber of Commerce has agreed to sponsor the economic study of the gaming industry by Dr. John Dobra. The preliminary work for that study is underway."[36]

The Dobra report was submitted to the Greater Reno-Sparks Chamber of Commerce and the Las Vegas Chamber of Commerce, and on December 4, 1996, was released under their auspices.[37] There was no mention of any Philip Morris or gaming industry involvement, despite the fact that the Philip Morris marketing firm had carefully orchestrated the press conferences. The decision to hide Tobacco's involvement was a conscious one, of course, for headlines announcing, "Tobacco-Industry-Sponsored Study Predicts Nevada Would Lose Big if Casino Smoking were Prohibited" would scarcely carry the same weight.

In December, with the study successfully launched, the Philip Morris Group's chairman in a Christmas memo thanked members profusely, singling out "John Dunham [who] spent many hours with Dr. John Dobra in Nevada to make sure that the economic study showing the economic impact of smoking bans on the state's gaming interests would be beyond reproach."[38]

The opening salvo had been successful.

Ten years later, nearly to the day, we met with John Dobra, an associate professor in the Economics Department, in his office on the University of Nevada, Reno campus. The office was dark, and so was Dobra's mood. We asked Dobra when he had first become aware of Philip Morris's involvement. "A week ago," he replied, "when a reporter called me from a Las Vegas paper."[39] Dobra said he had been approached by the McMullen Strategic Group and the Chambers of Commerce. "I assumed," he said, "that [the study] was financed by the casinos. It was never represented as any more to me. If I had known, I wouldn't have done it."

Dobra hadn't revisited the study in the ten years since it was released. It was not that the study was flawed, Dobra explained—he had used a standard method to assess economic impact. Nor did he have a particular gripe against the casinos. He saw them as having a legitimate interest in the effect of a smoking ban. That a smoking ban would have an economic impact was a "no-brainer," he argued. "Who paid for it is irrelevant to the facts."

Still, there was something sleazy about it, and Dobra knew it. "I wanted to get as far away from it as possible after it was done," he told us.

Did he feel used?, we asked.

"Yes," he replied. "Used. Duped. Pissed off. Yes. I was used."

With Dobra's "independent university study" launched, Big Tobacco focused on the second leg of its strategy—ventilation. Tobacco strategists were convinced that installation of state-of-the-art ventilating systems in combination with an active media campaign to convince the public and regulatory bodies such as OSHA of their effectiveness would be a surefire solution to the secondhand smoke issue, one that would allow gamblers to smoke and at the same time assure nonsmokers' and even workers' comfort (not to mention the two industries' profits). It was a sophisticated, well-coordinated plan—one that would prove highly successful in the years to come.

There are generally two approaches to ventilation, one focused on "source control" and the other on "comfort" levels. Source control involves a limitation or ban on smoking and grows from the idea that "no economically feasible level of ventilation can control the health dangers associated with secondhand smoke."[40] Focus on comfort levels assumes that smokers will continue to smoke and that companies can ventilate the air to a comfortable level. In the latter, language is of particular interest. The terms "comfort" and "state-of-the-art ventilating systems" connote laudable, even scientific business practices. But, as the American public has steadily learned, words in the hands of the powerful often conceal vastly different intentions than their face value suggests. In this case, "comfort" was carefully chosen to shift the focus from "health," something smoke opponents would repeatedly point out.

Communication between the tobacco industry and gaming was generally cloaked in secrecy, but internal memos document their steady meeting of minds in relation to the ventilation "solution." Robert Meyne, head of the OSHA Communications Group, met in early 1996 with Frank Fahrenkopf Jr., president and CEO of the American Gaming Association, gaming's lobbying arm.[41]

> Dear Frank [Meyne wrote following the meeting],
>
> It was a pleasure meeting with you to discuss proposed smoking bans and the impact they would have on the gaming industry.... R.J. Reynolds and the American Gaming Association have a common interest in this issue. Our position is that smoking policies in a casino... should be developed by its owners and managers... and not be imposed on them by government.... I look forward to learning what your board has to say on this issue. R.J. Reynolds is prepared to offer any assistance we can to you, your board, and members. It was good seeing you again. Please let us know how we can help.
>
> Best wishes, Rob Meyne

Meyne enclosed a report prepared especially for the gaming industry by Consolidated Safety Services, Inc., that he "hope[d would] be useful."[42]

Consolidated Safety Services began their report to gaming by arguing that there "are a number of things that can be done to accommodate smokers and nonsmokers before the passage of laws and regulations that will hurt businesses," and recommended "good ventilation" as a means to "reduce the level [of smoke]... that might be annoying to customers and employees."[43] In language clearly not designed to see the light of day, the report described three groups: "smokers, nonsmokers, and anti-smokers." Anti-smokers, in Consolidated Safety's opinion, were a small, "outspoken" minority, "not held to any standard of legitimacy," who increasingly "bombarded" legislatures with demands for regulation, using "free reign to misrepresent, misquote, and manipulate data to better support their opinions." To protect itself from them, the beleaguered gaming industry, in Consolidated Safety Services' opinion, would "sooner rather than later" need to "take a leading role in opposing th[is] school of thought."[44]

"Inventory[ing its] relationships with the Gaming bigwigs" so as to "gain support from as many in this industry sector as [they could],"[45] Philip Morris in a draft budget increased its "special projects" funds from $5.1 million to $8.9 million in order to finance its anti-smoke regulation campaign in Nevada and elsewhere.[46] In this, as in the Dobra report, the tobacco industry kept their involvement under wraps. As one Philip Morris operative wrote, "While Philip Morris is a significant funder of the HCIAQ, sometimes I think 'less is more' when it comes to 'out front' PM involvement."[47] (The Hospitality Coalition for Indoor Air Quality was a group made up of representatives from the tobacco, hospitality, gaming, and ventilation industries.)

The gaming industry was a ready learner, and taking advantage of the rocketing expansion the Strip was experiencing in the 1990s, moved to include and publicize "state of the art ventilating systems" in all its new casinos. Casino executives proclaimed that they were deeply interested in the health and welfare of visitors and employees and extolled the effectiveness of their ventilating systems. Frank Fahrenkopf assured the public that "[newer hotels] are on the cutting edge when it comes to air conditioning systems and ventilation:

> We take the issue of indoor air quality very seriously to ensure both populations [smokers and nonsmokers] are treated well....Any new major hotel-casino in Nevada is going to have the utmost cutting-edge technology designed to drag that smoke out of there so our employees and nonsmoking customers are not affected."[48]

By the new century, it appeared that the gaming and tobacco industries had all but guaranteed that Nevada casinos would remain full-smoke environments. The Dobra study, media manipulation, the discreet but carefully orchestrated contact between the two industries, and the ventilation "solution" all pointed to a big, well-financed win. But in David and Goliath fashion, the little people—Teresa Price and her allies—didn't hear the news that they were outnumbered and outgunned. In the legislature, the courts, the ballot box, and research laboratories, a persistent effort mounted to deny tobacco and gaming their ability to keep casino employees working in smoke-filled rooms. The efforts failed as often as they succeeded, but each failure brought new knowledge of how to find the cracks in the industries' control.

Here our inquiry shifts to 2001 and Carson City, Nevada's historic state capital, where every two years the legislature meets for four months in a modest effort to govern the state. In the spring of that year, anti-smoking groups introduced yet another bill—Assembly Bill 159—this time to ban smoking in public buildings, buses, lobbies, doctors' offices, grocery stores, and day-care centers, and requiring restaurants with more than fifty seats to offer nonsmoking sections. Critically, businesses deriving more than 50 percent of gross receipts from the sale of alcoholic beverages or from gaming operations could be designated as smoking areas in their entirety by the operator of the business, effectively exempting all casinos and bars from the regulation. It was not a very strong bill, especially compared with smoking control ordinances next door in California, but at least there would be no smoking in day-care centers.

The legislature, though hardly a promising venue (smoke regulation legislation was soundly defeated in 1997 and 1999), was the only available arena in which anti-smoking advocates could fight. Preemptive tobacco laws, the artifact of tobacco industry efforts to limit smoking regulations, prohibit communities from enacting laws more stringent than the state's, and in Nevada are strongly supported by the gaming industry.[49]

It was not only the preemptive laws that made legislative action so daunting for smoke regulation advocates. The gaming industry's control over the legislature was nearly hegemonic, and there were few legislators who would risk going up against it.[50] The tobacco industry, although by this point drawing back from direct contributions to legislative campaigns and relying chiefly on its relationship with Big Gaming, had itself contributed to legislative campaigns over the years, although in lesser amounts. From 1990 to 2006, tobacco contributed $552,111 to political parties and individuals running for office. Most candidates received small campaign contributions, but there were six legislators who received over $10,000. Nevada State Assemblyman Bernie Anderson, a Democrat and long-standing member of the assembly, received the highest amount—$16,850.[51]

By many Nevadans' estimates, Reno lawyer Harvey Whittemore, though not elected to any public office, was the most powerful person at the legislature. His control was legendary: Teresa Price laughed, "one legislator—not my dad—said to me, 'if Harvey doesn't want it we don't do it.'" Whittemore worked for both the Nevada Resort Association and R. J. Reynolds and was often quoted in the papers affirming that smoking was essential to casinos' and the state's health. "Let's be frank," Whittemore (or Harvey, as he's known to nearly everyone in Nevada) said in one committee session. "By our own experience, we know that many of the visitors to our state are smokers. If there was this huge public out there that was suggesting that we want to visit a nonsmoking only facility, the three or four failed experiments of designating entire casinos as nonsmoking would have succeeded." Casinos were interested in the comfort and well-being of employees and guests, Whittemore went on, "but whether we like it or not, individuals who choose to work in the gaming industry know the circumstances under which they choose to work. They're working in an environment where we try to satisfy patrons' desires and that includes the ability to smoke when those patrons choose to do so."[52]

Teresa Price did not have much truck with that. "Look," she said. "I've been there for twenty-five years. People smoke because they can. 'I smoke because I'm in Vegas,' they tell me. [The message here is] 'Light up! Have a drink! Have a prostitute!'"

Despite all this, Nevada's small band of anti-smoking activists marched forward into the Carson Valley. They included the Washoe County Cancer Society, whose director had contracted throat cancer from, he speculated, years of dealing; individuals from the Department of Health; advocates such as Teresa, who drove up from Las Vegas; and a small handful of courageous legislators, including Teresa's father, Bob Price, who had agreed to introduce AB159.

What happened next was instructive. The Ways and Means Committee shepherded by Bernie Andersen, its chair, scrupulously avoided dangerous ground and declined to differ with Whittemore and the casino lobby. "The committee took no action," the newspapers reported next day, and AB159, like its predecessors, died in committee.

For smoke control activists, the strategy to crush them at the legislature, while in the short run successful, only increased their determination to take their struggle to the electorate where, we shall see, for the first time they began to win.

At the same time that Teresa and others were taking on the legislature, Tony Badillo in Las Vegas was drawing dealers into a court case against the tobacco industry. Tony, whom we met in chapter 8, was a passionate advocate for dealers and worried a lot about smoke. "Women deal up to the eighth month of pregnancy," he told us when we met at a downtown Las Vegas café.[53] "It can't be good for the babies. I think the secondhand smoke is dangerous, and the dealer doesn't have any right to complain because he will be terminated immediately.... One of my fellow workers asked a customer to move an ashtray slightly. The floorman got involved, and the dealer was terminated. The customers are very touchy."[54]

With no union to protect them, Nevada dealers' options were limited. Court cases involving casinos in Nevada invariably are expensive, long drawn-out affairs with not a lot of hope for success; nevertheless, Badillo, with nine other dealers, filed suit against seventeen big tobacco companies and organizations.[55] It was Tony's idea to sue the tobacco industry. "Leave the casinos out," he said, convinced casinos were too powerful to take on in a Nevada court.

The Badillo suit followed an earlier unsuccessful claim, *Palmer v. Del Webb's High Sierra.*[56] In 1992, Palmer, a pit boss with twenty years of experience, brought suit against the High Sierra, claiming that his coughing and breathing problems were an occupational disease. (Palmer did not smoke himself and was in fact an active recreationist and jogger.) The Nevada Supreme Court rejected the claim, writing that "an occupational disease must be incidental to employment in order to be compensable." (Breathing coal dust, for example, is incidental to the work of coal mining—smoke, while "common," is not a "natural incident" of bars or casinos.) The court went on to note, "The legislature, of course, is free to declare that any person who contracts some secondary smoke-related disease at work is eligible for occupational disease compensations. The courts, we believe, do not have this power."[57]

Eight years later, in *Badillo*, dealers argued that because smoke in the casino workplace is abundant, ever-present, and extremely dangerous, they were entitled to medical monitoring. "Constant exposure to secondhand smoke entitles casino dealers to regular checkups paid for by the tobacco industry," their attorney told the newspaper. "We're not asking for compensation," he went on. "[We] want a program set up by the University of Nevada Medical School to take care of these employees."[58] The tobacco industry raged at the idea of having to pay for "increased risk" as opposed to actual damage,[59] and rejoiced when District Judge Philip Pro declined to certify *Badillo* and three other lawsuits by smokers and casino workers as class actions.[60] "Courts continue to recognize that class actions are inappropriate in tobacco litigation because of the overwhelming number of individual issues," smiled William Ohlemeyer, vice president and associate general counsel for Philip Morris. "Medical monitoring class actions are simply no different."[61]

Tony Badillo, a salt of the earth kind of guy, sighed: "In the end we lost. I think it was all arranged between the judge and the industry."

Chris Pritsos is a quiet man with a mission. A biochemist and chairman of the Nutrition Department at the University of Nevada, Reno, Dr. Pritsos has dedicated the last decade of his life to tobacco-related research. He has served as president of the Nevada Prevention Coalition, a tobacco control advocacy group, and along with Teresa Price is a familiar face at the state legislature. A dealers' friend, he says, "All the workers we have [here in Nevada] are constantly exposed to environmental tobacco smoke. It's really not right. I think it's time we step to the plate and protect our workers."[62]

The results of Pritsos's five-year, $2.5 million dollar National Institutes of Health–funded study were in the process of being released when we met him in his University of Nevada, Reno office. Based on blood draws and urine samples from 125 casino floor employees, the results were stunning—a direct link between exposure to secondhand smoke and DNA damage.[63] Chris was quoted in press coverage that spread from Nevada across the country: "The more [workers] were exposed to environmental tobacco smoke, the more the DNA damage, and that's going to lead to a higher risk of heart disease and cancer down the road."[64]

We were familiar with the study from newspaper reports but wanted to get a sense of a Nevada tobacco study from the inside out. What was most on our minds—which at that point were filled with stories of Big Tobacco and Big Gaming's behind-the-scenes manipulations—was what it was like to be a secondhand smoke researcher in the state of Nevada where gaming takes any opposition very seriously. Had Chris been threatened? Was he nervous? There was that old Dead-in-the-Desert worry. Chris seemed very nice, and we were not sure he could successfully handle a death threat.

Pritsos laughed and said he hadn't "received any personal threats."[65] He had actually sought the casinos' cooperation. "We tried to talk with gaming people so we could get access to employees," he said, "but they wouldn't talk. They are aware of the study. I guess they felt if they didn't talk to us then they wouldn't have to officially deny us."

But who had received threats and who Pritsos honored were the study's 125 participants, some of whom, he said, were told that if the casino found out that they had participated in the study they would be terminated. Participants, who had to have been nonsmokers for five years and have worked in a secondhand-smoke environment for two years, were recruited from ads, television spots, and billboards. "Casino employees were really worried about their jobs," Chris said. "We had to think a lot about confidentiality. Some didn't even want to be seen walking out of our office." Chris's Las Vegas assistant Katherine Robinson added, "These people were absolutely fabulous. [They'd tell us] 'we know your study won't have an impact on us, but we want it to have an impact on future dealers.' They were interested in making a difference, making a better world."[66]

By all rights, this chapter should conclude with a victory with Teresa Price as its heroine. But it doesn't—not yet anyway, although it surely will in time. Teresa contacted a lawyer in 2006, but at the time of our interview her pro bono case appeared to be low on his agenda. On the casino floor, dealers are still eating smoke.

But the side of this story to put your money on if you are a betting person is the side on which little people like Teresa gather for health and a chance at clean air. In 2006 George W. Bush appointee, U.S. Surgeon General Richard H. Carmona, released a major scientific report concluding that the only way to protect nonsmokers from the dangerous chemicals in secondhand smoke is to eliminate smoking indoors and that even the most sophisticated ventilation systems cannot completely eliminate secondhand smoke exposure: only smoke-free environments afford full protection.[67] It was a blow to casinos' ventilation claims. In that same year, despite the gaming industry's well-financed campaign to obfuscate the question, 54 percent of Nevada voters approved the 2006 Nevada Clean Indoor Air Act, bypassing a legislature that appeared to be permanently bought on this issue. The act repealed preemption and strengthened the state's clean air law, and though it exempted casinos and "stand alone bars," nevertheless it was a major step forward. (In the following legislative session, in what Nevada researcher and newspaper columnist John Packham labeled the session's "most cynical piece of legislation," legislators attempted to undo the voters' will and dismantle the Clean Indoor Air Act. But in 2009 it was the pro-smoking bill that died in committee, another measure of the sea change that was occurring.)[68]

Also in that year—2009—the National Institute for Occupational Safety and Health (NIOSH) at long last released its study *Environmental and Biological Assessment of Environmental Tobacco Smoke Exposure Among Casino Dealers.* It was the study Teresa Price and others had requested in 2005 when she was still employed at Caesars Palace. Over 50 percent of dealers, the study reported, complained of symptoms related to air quality—irritated eyes, cough, stuffy nose, runny nose, and headache. Thirty-five percent had symptoms suggestive of work-related asthma. "We've been waiting a long time for this," Teresa told reporters.[69]

Finally, smoke-free casinos began appearing across the nation, and while the gaming industry rushed to attribute any decline in revenue to smoke regulation, it was clear that significant cracks were appearing in the tobacco and gaming industries' resolve to maintain casinos as the last bastion of smoking environments.

In many ways, there is nothing new about this tale of smoke. It is the story, a thousand times told, of corporate greed and the ability of big money to buy legislative influence, research, court dominance, and favorable media coverage. Still, there are many things to be learned from old stories. We have come away changed from our encounter with dealers like Teresa Price, compelled by the nature of their jobs to ingest massive amounts of tobacco smoke. There is a *cri de coeur* here as well. Is the pleasure of lighting up at the gaming table worth another person's life? If it isn't, Teresa suggests smokers tell it to casino management: "I smoke, but I don't want dealers dying."[70]

Part V

WOMEN IN MANAGEMENT

CROSSING OVER TO THE OTHER SIDE

I still flinch to think that I spent all those weeks under the surveillance of men (and later women) whose job it was to monitor my behavior for signs of sloth, theft, drug abuse, or worse. Not that managers and especially "assistant managers" in low wage settings...are exactly our class enemies....But everybody knows they have crossed over to the other side, which is, crudely put, corporate as opposed to human.

—Barbara Ehrenreich, *Nickel and Dimed*

Harrah's Entertainment, Inc., invites applicants who visit its employment webpage to consider a management position in the human resource department. "The Human Resource team at Harrah's," the webpage reads, "is passionate about taking care of our internal service culture which ensures that each Moment of Truth we have with each other meets or exceeds each other's expectations. You see, it's our job to ensure that we are doing more than just taking care of our employees; we are responsible for maintaining a culture where people want to take care of each other."[1]

The invitation frankly feels false, but its authors must believe that the opportunity to contribute to a workplace culture "where people take care of each other" will appeal to persons looking for careers in management and wanting at the same time to make a positive impact on the workers under them. Sharon Nesbit, a human resource manager in a nonunion Las Vegas casino, hoped to do just that. She was proud of creating programs that on the one hand developed workers' skills, theoretically preparing them for better jobs, and on the other, contributed to her casino's bottom line by reducing worker turnover. She hoped to have it both ways—satisfied employees and satisfied bosses and shareholders.

A second page on Harrah's website describes the ideal employee as "driven to win,"[2] and *Business Week Online* in a 2002 article "How to Win with Harrah's" echoes its tone, advising readers that "Harrah's...is driven quantitatively, so people who have been trained and think in terms of analytics do well here."[3] Both suggest that drive, a competitive spirit, and careful attention to profits will enable managers to thrive. No mention is made of a caring environment.

In this chapter we draw upon the narratives of five middle-and upper-management women to examine how they became managers, the nature of their work, and their work-related successes and disappointments. We ask if they as managers within global gaming corporations were able to create a "culture of caring," as the Harrah's website encourages, and in doing so contribute positively to the lives of workers (like the rank-and-file women of this book); and we ask what was the cost, if any, they paid for "crossing over." We begin with Barbara Bradford's story.[4]

Barbara Bradford

Barbara Bradford was vice president of gaming and assistant general manager of a nonunion Las Vegas casino, just one position below the property's top executive. That she worked in the same casino where she had started twenty-five years earlier made success even sweeter. "When I [first] got hired, I went through five interviews to get the job," she said, looking around her office. "I would never in a million years have envisioned that I would one day be sitting [here]."[5]

Barbara had worked in many casinos over the years, mostly outside Nevada. She had returned to Las Vegas two years earlier, giving up a general manager position in the Midwest in order to be within driving distance of her elderly mother. "It was a step down for me," she said, "but I wasn't getting much time to spend with [my mother so] I accepted the position." An attractive, high-energy woman who looked much younger than her fifty years, Barbara had been married twice and had never had children.[6] At the time of our interview, her mother had recently died and her second marriage was failing. "I can't say that it's going to last," she admitted sadly. Once again, work had become a top priority.

The casino had recruited Bradford when she was still an undergraduate.[7] "I started working five days after I turned twenty-one as a $14–a–shift check racker," she laughed. "It was nothing fancy—check rackers pick up chips for the roulette dealer." A year later she became a 21 dealer, and two years after that she moved to craps. "[My] company," she said, "was the first that I know of to send a woman to craps school…and I finished top of the class."[8] From craps she moved into lower management, first as a box supervisor ("I think I was the first female box supervisor in the state of Nevada," she proudly told us) and then as a pit boss, again, one of only a few women to do what many considered to be a man's job. A few years later, Barbara was promoted into upper management and left Las Vegas to become the executive manager of a successful Ohio casino.

Over the next seven years, this was Barbara's mode of operation—moving from one casino to another, always rising up the management hierarchy. Then making an abrupt career change, she left gaming altogether to become a tennis teaching professional. "I am the type of person that loves a challenge, and I don't mind working hard," she said, smiling at our surprise. "I used to hit the ball until my hands were bloody. I wanted to see what I could accomplish in the game—I wanted to be a professional." Always open to new challenges, Barbara looked for opportunities to prove herself as a woman. "I'm an extremely ambitious, competitive individual," she said. "I could use the term feminist. I believe every woman should have the opportunity to achieve whatever she damn well pleases and should be acknowledged for those accomplishments." She added, "[As] women growing up, I don't think we're taught how to deal with competitiveness." Becoming a tennis pro, she said, had taught her how to do this.

Seven years later, Bradford returned to the casino industry. "I never really had a strong desire to get back into casino operations," she said, "but I was always thinking, 'I wonder where I could have gone? [I] wonder what I could have done?'" When a Native American tribe in the Southwest asked her to open a new casino, Barbara decided to find out. "You know, the door just swung open," she told us, "and I said to myself, 'let's go take a shot and see what happens.'"

Over the next nine years, Barbara worked in several large casinos throughout the United States, always advancing. She liked the challenge. "It's very demanding," she said of her current vice president position, "but there's also lots of rewards....The biggest success that I have in this business is watching folks develop, learn, move forward, and achieve their goals. I believe my management style is such that I can provide benefits for [employees] and they can enjoy themselves in the workplace. What is not a good match with my management style are people who really don't care about the folks at work—[who don't] focus on their development."

The work was grueling. "In casino executive management, you need to understand a couple of things," Barbara said. "You may need to move to another property and maybe to another state. And you're mostly going to work fifty to sixty hours a week—and that represents a huge commitment." It was the bottom line, though, that ultimately determined a manager's success or failure, Barbara pointed out emphatically. That had become particularly apparent in the recent casino market downturn: "It's been a challenge," Bradford said. "There are folks [at the top], they're driving [us] very hard. 'What are you going to do to make money? What are you going to do to make money?' So we are obligated to perform."

Barbara offered some advice to women considering a casino management career. "The only thing that I would truly [suggest]," she said, "is to understand what's important to you and balance your life accordingly. It's a tough, tough challenge. As women, a lot of times we think we can do it all, but I don't know how successful we'll be so [you need to] truly focus on what's important to you."

A few days later, we tried to call Barbara at her office. A receptionist told us she no longer worked there.

Six years passed before we had a chance to talk with Bradford a second time. "We parted ways," she remarked about her quick departure from the casino. "It was a mutual decision…it was not a good fit." She finally said, "I didn't enjoy corporate America. Their expectations are not always realistic."[9]

Barbara's exit was not entirely surprising: lower-, middle-, and even upper-level casino managers have relatively little authority, are subject to enormous pressure to produce, and enjoy surprisingly little job security. They are subject to top corporate officers who wield the real power, and they must implement "corporate's" policies—for which they are held accountable should the policies fail to increase profits.[10] And it is power, not implementation, that is ultimately rewarded. At Harrah's Entertainment, Inc., for example, in 2006 the chairman/president/CEO was paid over $14 million[11] while, during the same year, casino general managers in the Reno/Sparks area earned a mean salary of $147,000.[12] While an upper-management position like Barbara's might appear impressive and is paid more than middle- and lower-management jobs (which pay in the range of $40,000 and $36,000, respectively),[13] in reality vice presidents like Barbara are much closer in income to cocktail waitresses than they are to corporate leaders.

Managers, even top managers like Barbara, have little job security. We encountered many descriptions of mass firings of supervisors, middle managers, and upper managers, "St. Valentine's Day massacres," as one woman in the Human Services focus group put it. It was not unknown during these periodic upheavals, she said, for the entire management staff of a specific department to be relieved of their duties in an effort to "downsize," "restructure," or "flatten the corporate structure."[14] When casinos change ownership, which is not uncommon, new managers often replace the old.

Robert Brown, the director of a Reno employee assistance program holding contracts with many casinos said that the number of management personnel seeking psychological services was increasing. "You see it in supervisors and in mid-level managers and up," he said. "The crisis and depression is related to [the] fear [of downsizing]."[15] In a recent example from his practice, he said, "there were six shift managers—and that's a big job. [The casino] had all six interview for their own jobs, but now instead of six jobs, there were four. If you lost, you were out. If you won, you were now one of four people doing the work of six. Then there were four interviewing for two jobs. If you survived, there was more work and the expectation you might be the next to go."

The radical restructuring of the world's economy under globalization has resulted in many changes for employees: decreased wages and benefits, increased job turnover, and more contract and contingency work are some of them.[16] Although these workplace changes are usually associated with rank-and-file workers, they are also felt by mid- and even upper management, and reflect the near hegemony of a neoliberal ideology with its emphasis on competition, individualism, self-reliance, and accountability.[17] These changing work conditions are reflected in the lives of the middle managers we interviewed.

Carol Hancock

"I'm funny," Carol Hancock warned at the beginning of her interview. She had once worked for a well-known comedian, she explained. She then proceeded to regale us with an impressive repertoire of stories, not all of them funny.[18]

Carol had worked twenty-one years in the same unorganized neighborhood casino in Las Vegas, starting on the showroom stage crew and working her way up to keno manager. She was fifty-four years old; tall, slim, and red-headed (Lucille Ball comes to mind); and blessed with boundless energy. "I never would have thought of working in a casino in my life," she said. She had hoped to have a public relations career in entertainment, and after college had started out in Hollywood promoting some big-name stars. A few years later, she had come to Las Vegas for a Labor Day weekend with her husband. "It was typical wonderful [Las Vegas] weather," she said. "Bright blue skies, white puffy clouds. [Driving] home, we had to turn on the car lights because the smog was so bad...so we made the decision to come! No jobs. No nothing. We sold our house [and] just came."

Once in Las Vegas, Hancock got a job hosting her own radio show and later sold real estate. "I made a lot of money until the mortgage rates went up to 23 and 24 percent," she said. "That was a killer." When her builder husband began covering his construction cost overruns with her commissions, their already faltering marriage came to a bitter and financially devastating end. "I just traded my equity in the house for full custody of my son" was how she explained it.

Now single and solely responsible for her son, Carol applied for a job on the stage crew of a Las Vegas casino. "I'd always done the lights, the sets, and the costumes when I [majored in theater in college]," she explained, "[so] I thought I could work at night and, because it was a man's wage, that it would pay a lot more money." Night shift gave her more time with her son, but the job presented some difficult challenges. "I would come in to work between 4:00 and 6:00 [in the afternoon]," she explained, "and I'd go home anywhere from 11:00

to 2:00 in the morning, depending on whether I worked the last show." That was on weeknights. On Friday and Saturday nights when there were five shows, she often didn't get off work until 3:00 or 4:00 in the morning. "I would sometimes have to leave my son in a twenty-four-hour place that was just awful. I hated it. It stunk," she said. "[But thankfully] I had a friend who would take him at night and get him ready for school in the morning. Then I'd pick him up after school before I went to work. I don't think I can ever repay her."

Carol's job on the stage crew eventually turned sour. One of only a handful of women, she was continually harassed by her male coworkers. "[Some] would say, 'There's never going to be any fucking woman here!' [T]hey used to tell me that!" she exclaimed. "I had one man on the crew say that he was going to put a gun to my head, and I believed him. And nothing was done about it because the manager was very ineffective."

Carol stayed on the stage crew for nineteen years. "I needed the job," she explained. "I was making $18 an hour, and for a woman, that was good—the secretaries around here top out at $12 or $14." In time Carol remarried, and when her son graduated from college, she finally felt secure enough economically to move out of the showroom and start climbing the casino career ladder.

She set her sights first on casino operations. "All I know is that to get anywhere in the casino business, you've got to be in operations," she told us. Her first move was a big step down: a part-time job promoting the new customer rewards card. "I went from $18 to $8 an hour," she said, "[but] all of a sudden, I began meeting the people upstairs, and this is what I needed." Carol eventually found her way into casino operations—the result of a massive staff reduction. "They had nineteen supervisors in the keno department, and it just wasn't working," she said. "So they made everyone reapply for a job but [now] there were only four [positions] available. I interviewed for [one] and they hired me." Over the next few years, more supervisors lost their jobs, and Carol was "promoted" again. "Since I began, we've had two [more] restructurings," she said, using management's sanitized term for staff layoffs and firings. "Now I am not only the sole supervisor, I'm also the manager!" Carol shared none of the Employee Assistance Program Director Robert Brown's alarm.[19] She thought the layoffs were an economic necessity and compared herself favorably to managers who complained about them: "When I came to operations," she said, "if managers were told they had to cut back, it was the end of the world. But with me, I've made an opportunity out of it."

At the time of her interview, Hancock had been managing the keno department for a little over a year and was responsible for more than thirty employees. Although she liked working with the mostly immigrant women under her, she was surprised by their lack of interest in career advancement. "They step back from it," she said, "and that's difficult for me to deal with." True to her promise, she had made opportunities for herself, promoting player tournaments and staying in contact with her best customers. She was proud that her keno department had been recently rated number one in Nevada. Still, Carol wanted more than keno and hoped something better would come along. But she refused to complain. "Life is way too short," she told us. "I'm out there squeezing lemons, looking for sugar."

How was it that Carol, who had proven herself to be courageous and spirited, raising a son and working in a male-dominated casino showroom, could become so utterly compliant? Her spirit, which theoretically should have served her well in casino management, enabling her to be autonomous, independent, and effective, over time, it appeared, had dropped away, and in its place had developed a well-disciplined acceptance of managerial culture. In middle managers' perception it is often compliance not autonomy that provides some measure of protection as professional management moves "from one of the most secure occupations to one of the least."[20] Consequently, Carol didn't complain when the nineteen supervisors in the keno department had to reapply for only four positions, and she didn't object when those positions were eliminated and she was promoted to manager—nor did she hesitate to ultimately depoliticize these layoffs or firings by referring to them as a "restructuring." "I'm way behind," she told us sadly, acutely aware that her late entry already had severely limited her career opportunities.[21] She didn't want to jeopardize them further.

Success on these terms, of course, comes at a price. Like Carol, most of us yearn for the opportunity to develop our talents and to prove ourselves to others. But success in the corporate world is often a zero-sum game, and those aspiring to a corporate career, according to Mander, "must be ready to climb over [their] own colleagues."[22] Carol knew this. Consequently, unlike the rank-and-file women who evaluated success in very different parameters—the creation of a just and humane work place achieved through collective action—she defined success in highly individualistic and competitive terms. As a manager, she was required to conform to corporate expectations *and* to rise above coworkers.

Sharon Nesbit

Unlike Barbara Bradford and Carol Hancock, who began at the bottom in local casinos, Sharon Nesbit arrived in the gaming world from outside, brought into

management because of her prior training and experience. She was an attractive, high-energy, twice-married grandmother of two and the vice president of
human resources in one of Las Vegas's neighborhood casinos.

With an undergraduate degree in education and master's and Ph.D. degrees
in human resource management, Nesbit was the most highly educated of the
management women we interviewed. She had worked for eighteen years in "personnel, internal audit, and the operational area" of several high-profile Midwest
insurance corporations. She especially enjoyed personnel administration and
described employee development and training as her "first love."[23]

In a surprise move, Sharon decided to quit insurance entirely and move to
Arizona so she could be closer to her new grandchild. Five years later, she re-
sumed her career in Las Vegas. There she found herself courted by one of the
city's large (nonunionized) casino corporations. "I received a telephone call from
one of its executives," she said, "asking me if I'd be interested in development
and training," and after some discussion she "decided to do it." As manager of
Personnel Services, she was in charge of employee-training programs, the first of
several human resource jobs she would hold in Las Vegas casinos over the next
twelve years.

In Sharon's view, Nevada casinos were way behind other industries in progressive management and leadership skills. "Until about 1990, everybody [in
Vegas] had their own little way of doing business," she said. "They hadn't yet
gotten to the point where they were looking at things from a big picture basis.
How do you not have 100 percent turnover in your companies? If employees are
so important, how do you retain them?" Nesbit impressed her bosses by simply
implementing employee training and development policies that were considered
routine outside the industry—"I could seem like a genius," she laughed. "It was
a great opportunity."

Sharon had recently developed eleven "worker colleges," some in-house
(such as management skills, which she herself designed) and others contracted
out (such as nutrition). The colleges, she hoped, would both serve the interests
of rank-and-file workers and contribute to the casino's bottom line by increasing worker satisfaction and decreasing turnover. Like Barbara Bradford, Sharon
believed in the service-profit chain—happy workers produce satisfied customers
who, in turn, produce larger profits.[24]

What did not create happy workers was a union contract, Nesbit claimed,
reminding us that she had worked in both union and nonunion Las Vegas casinos. "It's more difficult in a unionized environment," she said, "to have the flexibility to meet all the employees' needs. [Instead] . . . you have to [focus on] what
a specific [group of workers] who yell the loudest want." She also thought it was

difficult to recognize people who "accomplish things" in a union environment, "because it's the nature of union contract that everybody's [treated] the same." She continued, "It guarantees them a certain wage, [so] they know where they stand, but in terms of real motivation and real feeling about their self-worth, you can't [say] 'Joe Blow, you did a wonderful job at this, so here's what I'm going to do for you' because the union won't let you do that."

From Sharon's perspective, unions were good for one thing, protecting workers' seniority. This was the major reason, she thought, that Las Vegas's casinos had a stable workforce.[25] Still, unions in her view just didn't care about their workers: "They don't even know who they are until it comes time [for] arbitration," she argued.

Sharon Nesbit entered upper management with two objectives that she assumed were compatible—developing worker-friendly programs and serving the economic interests of the casino corporation. As it turned out, they weren't. The very people who hired her for her experience in worker training and development were frightened by the prospect of empowering workers with "worker colleges" and feared they might lead to a workers' union. With each new program, she complained, they became more ambivalent. "Sometimes the reality of it and talking about it are two different things," Sharon said. "But that's why they brought me here—to make it different.... When it started happening, it scared them half to death. Their perception was that it put more power into employees' hands and less into theirs [and this] made them very nervous." She concluded with some sadness, "So I can't say that I've progressed as rapidly as I intended."

Like Barbara Bradford, Sharon Nesbit hoped she could have it all—the authority and salary associated with being a vice president and the opportunity to make a meaningful contribution to employees' lives. Vice presidents of human resources in local casino operations do have authority relative to housekeepers and busboys, and their salaries (Sharon's was about $140,000) allow for an enormously different lifestyle from that of a nonunion housekeeper who earns $15,000 (assuming a $7.50/hour, forty-hour work week). But the gap between her salary and those at the top was even greater and an indicator of the limits of her power.[26]

There was considerable irony in Sharon Nesbit's professed dedication to "worker development" on the one hand and her rejection of unions on the other. The Culinary Training Academy, a product of labor-management collaboration, is by far the best example of worker training and development in Nevada, and to all appearances it serves the interests of both workers and management well, providing opportunities for job entry, job advancement, and English language training. Its reach extends far beyond Nesbit's worker colleges and suggests that programs won through collective bargaining significantly outperform management-financed "benevolent" programs.

Kate Rodriguez

Kate Rodriguez, a communications manager in a Las Vegas casino, was different from the other management women we interviewed. She was younger (only thirty-one years old); had launched her casino management career right out of college; and had been in the casino for only two years.[27] An attractive young woman with long dark brown hair and a bright smile, she had never married and was close to her family. Employee communications, public relations, and community affairs/donations were the principal responsibilities of her middle-management position.[28] Public relations was the most challenging—"heavy" was the word Kate used to describe it. "That means I'm the casino's spokesperson," she said. For Kate and other corporate spokespersons, that meant carrying corporate views to the press, including those on Darlene Jespersen's case, for example, or on worker issues like wages and high heel requirements.

Rodriguez enjoyed working for a global corporation. "It's just so much larger," she said. "I mean with [the corporation having so many] properties, you have a lot more resources. I personally like the corporate environment—the standardization—and [the fact that] it's very organized." The corporate-size rewards also pleased her. "There's a lot to say for [the] benefits [and] the pay," she said. "The company's been good to me." Her health insurance plan had started immediately (unlike, she said, rank-and-file workers' plans, which were awarded after a three-month probationary period), and sick leave and vacation benefits were generous, too (she received a two-week vacation after the first year, "but again that's only at the management level").

As a middle manager, Kate had started at $40,000 a year—two years later her salary had climbed to $55,000. "[It's] very good," she told us, "at least for [someone] my age in this industry." She added, "You work long hours for it, though." Kate had received a 5 percent annual merit raise her first year and a 7 percent raise her second. Her bonuses were $1,700 and $2,000 for the same periods. "Bonuses are only given to management," she explained, "and you have to be a certain grade. You [also] have to make budget and a profit, and your revenues have to be at certain levels."

Frequent turnover was also a part of management life. "In middle management and above," Kate said, "you have people come in for a few years. They don't necessarily leave the industry, they just go to another company. I've met people that have worked at four or five different casino companies—it's like, 'What can another company do better for me?'" Professional ambition was only a part of it, Kate explained. "The gaming industry, like most corporations, is a bottom line business. It's all about money, and there's a lot of pressure.... So for one or two years, you might have a great management team, [but] if things aren't working, there needs to be a change." We asked what happens if managers don't meet expectations. "I see it in my company," Kate said, "especially at the director and the vice president level—you either perform or you don't—and if you don't, it's a bottom line business. I'm not saying you're fired, but you're either transitioned to somewhere else or you're [moved] within the property. I see a lot of that kind of movement."

In the two years Kate had been in casino management, three marketing directors and four casino general managers had come and gone. "It's all in the numbers," she explained. "There's quarterly reviews—most Fortune 500 companies have them. They list the stock prices for publicly traded companies. That's our job—to make the stockholders happy. It's strictly numbers and how the property's doing. It's that simple." As a result, managers were younger; Kate's current boss was forty, and other managers in her department were still in their thirties. The time and energy demands of the job, she believed, were responsible.

Rodriguez's job was fast-paced and unpredictable; she worked long hours, "sometimes 10–12 hours a day," and often weekends. "I spend a lot of time putting out fires," she said. As for her personal life, "I have no life," she sighed. "I have no time for anything else. I'm not married and so I don't have a family. I don't date because I don't have time to date. When I do have some time, I watch television. The last thing I want to do is have a conversation with anyone because so much of my job is verbal communication."[29]

We asked what she would say to someone considering a job in casino management. "I would tell them that the job is generously rewarded if it is done well," she said. "It is demanding, but it is also exciting—unexpected things happen every day." The further one goes up the management ladder, the greater the pressure to perform," she added. [There's] "more prestige, money, independence, and responsibility," but it requires "total commitment." She ended by saying, "I don't plan to stay in casino management much longer. I would like someday to eventually marry and have a family."

Kate Rodriguez was happy with her career and seemed to accept without question that profit generation was a manager's top priority. She spoke for the casino—even when it meant (as it did) speaking out against employees; gave up personal relationships, including those with family; and accepted the norms of competition, constant insecurity, escalating demands and isolation from coworkers. To her, these were the costs of a successful career, and at least for the time being, she was willing to accept them.

Kate, like Carol Hancock and other up-and-coming new managers, knew she couldn't afford to lag behind. Even standing still could be dangerous. According to Robert Jackell, "only rising stars validate the ethos of the corporation and can claim and win the respect and perhaps the anticipatory fear of others."[30] In her struggle to get ahead, Kate did what she was told.

Kate, like Sharon Nesbit, *never* talked about other workers except in an abstract or disembodied way. It was as if she worked entirely alone. She never referred to coworkers as "family," as rank-and-file women often did, nor did she share in their collective energy to create a more humane workplace. Her own answer was to someday leave the casino, the only way she felt that she could maintain relationships with her family and perhaps one day have one of her own.

Michel Foucault argues that power is never hegemonic, that there is always the possibility of resisting it.[31] Unionized rank-and-file women and women such as Edna Harman and Darlene Jespersen who united with others in a particular struggle, found space to resist, and their courage and concern for each other were clearly evident in their stories. The same cannot be said for the management women. In contrast, they told stories of compliance and conformity and, ultimately, of frustration and disappointment.

Management women's stories reveal a great deal about neoliberalism and the global economy. Corporations' control over their managers has always been close to total, but it has increased with globalization. In casinos, this means policies that undermine the economic security not only of rank-and-file workers, but increasingly of managers as well. In today's global corporation, there are no "company men" or "company women." Instead, there is built-in obsolescence that requires management personnel to constantly reinvent themselves to meet the changing needs of the corporation.[32] If a management woman's skills are not what is needed to keep the corporation competitive, she will be replaced by someone whose skills are, testimony to the fact that the traditional model of employee-employer loyalty has given way to day-to-day contingency and expediency. "No matter how loyal [management personnel] may be to their companies," management theorists O'Toole and Lawler write, "their companies say they can't promise loyalty to them in return. Executives do not believe they are being cold-hearted; rather, they say they have no choice if they are to ensure the survival of the organization."[33]

"That's our job—to make [the stockholders] happy," Kate said. Policies and programs feed the casino's bottom line at workers' expense; lower wages, downsizing, reduced benefits, and firing veteran workers were the order of the day.

As social critic Jerry Mander reminds us, "The most basic rule of corporate operation is that it must show a profit over time. All other values are secondary—the welfare of the community, the happiness of workers, the health of the planet, and even general prosperity.... So human beings within the corporate structure, whatever their personal morals or feelings, are prevented from operating on their own standards. Like the assembly line worker who must operate at the speed of the machine, corporate employees are strapped onto the apparatus of the corporation and are forced to operate by its rules."[34]

We began this chapter with an invitation from Harrah's Human Resource Team. "It is our job," they wrote, "to ensure that we are doing more than just taking care of our employees; we are responsible for maintaining a culture where people want to take care of each other."[35] In the end, the promise was illusory. The management women all acknowledged on some level that they couldn't serve the interests of both the corporation and its workers. They had to make a choice, and in the last analysis, they chose the corporation. In Barbara Ehrenreich's words, "They...crossed over to the other side[,] which is, crudely put, corporate as opposed to human."[36] Their individual will to resist was no match against corporate power. As Mander has pointed out, it is a mistake to assume that the corporation is amenable to human control; in truth, it is essentially an "autonomous technical structure that behaves by a system of logic uniquely well-suited to its primary function: to make profit, to give birth and impetus to new products and technologies, to expand its reach and power, and to spread the consumer lifestyle around the globe."[37] To leave nothing to chance, corporate management by law is required to act primarily in the economic interests of its shareholders.[38] Is it so surprising that Carol and Kate in their desperate climb up the casino career ladder conformed to corporate expectations?

This is not to suggest that the management women should be absolved of responsibility for their behavior or that their compliance in the face of corporate power was inevitable. They did have choices, but there were costs associated with them. Thus, Carol, as keno manager, remained silent when her department was downsized, and Kate, as casino spokesperson, defended policies oppressive to workers. In this, the two women mirror a dilemma we all face daily—how to survive in a highly competitive and individualistic society without relinquishing deeply held values and principles. The rank-and-file workers provide an inspiring example. Their courageous acts of resistance suggest that it is through solidarity and community that we are most likely to succeed both personally and collectively.

CONCLUSION

"A Marvelous Victory"

The compassion of the oppressed for the oppressed is indispensable. It is the world's one hope.

—Bertolt Brecht, "The World's One Hope" (in Forché 1993)

Magdalena Ruiz, a lovely thirty-one-year old, met us in the library of a Reno family resource center where she recently had been hired as a teacher's aide. After ten years of casino hostessing, she was relieved to be out of the gaming industry and delighted with her new job. Work was not the only major change in Magdalena's life; just a few weeks earlier, she had walked out on an alcoholic and abusive husband. "Do I want my kids to live in hell, always in fear of when he drinks? No!" she said. "It's hard being a single mom.... You want your family to be in a healthy environment and to have all the good things. If I stayed with my husband, I would have good things... but when you die, you're not going to take none of that. You're going to take your happiness—not a car, not a house—you'll take your values."[1]

Originally from El Paso, Magdalena and her husband had moved to Reno in the late eighties and had quickly found work in a local casino, she as a maid and he as a waiter. Maid's work was hard: "I mean you go in there and they assign you—omigod—fifteen rooms in one day," Magdalena exclaimed. "Whoa! How am I gonna do that in eight hours? I felt [a lot of] pressure because I'd never done that before, and I was young. I would just go home so tired."

After a month, Magdalena quit to look for something better: "I thought, 'what am I doing here working as a maid? I graduated from high school!'" Job interviews intimidated her, but she decided to just be herself—"this is who I am and, if you want to give me an opportunity, I'll work hard." Eventually, she was hired as a casino restaurant hostess, a job she grew to love. "It's what I like to do," she said with pride. "When you really want to do something, you have to work [at] it. I feel that with any job...[you need] to be the best."

Over the years, Magdalena had become disillusioned with the gaming industry in Reno and especially resented the low pay and lack of job mobility. "I don't like that you don't go up," she said. "I don't see no promotion. My ex-husband has been working in a casino all his life. He's nowhere, he's still a waiter.... [I say to him] 'What you going to do when you get older? I mean you don't have any future there.'"

It was the day-to-day impact of the work on her young family, however, that finally persuaded Magdalena to leave. "It's like, you're too exhausted, too tired. You work in a casino and...you just want peace and quiet. And what about your kids? They've been out there with the babysitter—they've been out there in school. They need your affection. They need your care." The casino's 24/7 work schedule was a major part of the problem Magdalena thought: "Basically, you work weekends, so when are you going to see your kids? Monday? Tuesday? They go to school. They get home [and] you don't have time for them because you have to wash...clean your house, do your errands. Weekends they're by themselves."

Magdalena soon found temporary work on an assembly line at a local pillow factory. "You work Monday through Friday, like [on] school days," she said. "Holidays you don't work at all. And you have great insurance—they pay 95 percent." She began at $7.15 an hour and was up to $8.65 in only a few weeks. "In casinos, that doesn't happen," she said. "I would never go back and work in a casino. Never! I would go hungry instead."

Later Magdalena was hired at the family resource center where she was happy to find that a major part of her job involved supporting women just like herself. She appreciated the nine-to-five schedule. "When I get home I play with my kids and I [still] have time to clean," she said. "No matter if it's 9 o'clock at night, I clean the kitchen and have my house organized." And her weekends were free: "One day for me, washing, errands; one day for my kids—play, movies, whatever they want."

With the divorce, Magdalena's responsibilities had become even greater. "When I was young I had time to party," she said. "Now I have kids. It's time for them. When they get older, I can do my own things again, but right now, they need me. They need me to teach them good values, good morals, good principles, and if I don't teach that to my kids, it will be tough luck when they get older. We're going through a very, very hard situation because I'm divorcing. They don't take it well, and that's where I have to give them all my love and attention."

Magdalena was outraged that casinos did not contribute more to the well-being of Reno families and communities. "They make millions of dollars!" she said. "Casinos should get together and build [something] nice [for the community]...something here for our kids, for our teenagers.... There are water slides on McCarran but it's so expensive, $13 for one day—that's outrageous! If you have five children, how much would that be? I'm sorry, I'm tired of McDonalds. We could find something more for [the children]—an amusement park, a zoo." She would participate in the effort, too, she said.

Magdalena had a vision for the future: "I want to build a business here— something for the entire family," she said smiling. "I love to help people. That's my mission."

Magdalena Ruiz at thirty-one had come to two important realizations: first that the overload and exhaustion that accompanied casino work left her too drained to participate sufficiently in her children's lives and second that the gaming industry took "millions!" and gave, in her opinion, hardly anything back. Her choice, a reasonable one in nonunion Reno, was to leave casino work and try her luck elsewhere. It was far from a perfect solution—a wage of $8.65 is still less than half the living wage for a Washoe County, Nevada, family of three—but it affirmed her values as a working mother and gave her time with her children.[2]

Sociologist Joan Acker describes in her theory of gendered organizations, neoliberal corporations' claims of "non-responsibility" for employees' non-work life. Corporations, Acker maintains, increasingly feel they are entitled to "unencumbered workers," that is, employees who can function as if there is another person at home at all times to care for children, parents, and household and community responsibilities.[3] This line of reasoning, which particularly punishes poor women who have few resources and many "encumbrances," conveniently relieves corporations and the states they dominate of responsibility for adequate wages, benefits, and services—and underlines the "cultural chasm" that has opened up between corporate America and the lives of ordinary people.[4] "It's [all] corporate politics," as Edna Harman, the seventy-year-old pit boss, said. "I mean, they have no feeling—there's no thought—no caring for the employees. They're just a commodity. They're something that you throw away when you're through with them."

"Unencumbered" as a concept flies in the face of everything that the women workers we interviewed stood for. "Encumbrances," they would say—sons, daughters, mothers, fathers, grandmothers, grandfathers, partners, spouses, grandchildren, great grandchildren, uncles, aunts, cousins, neighbors, friends— are all the meaning in life, and the idea of separating them from work or work from them would be absurd. What characterized their lives was the integration of "public and private spheres," as theorists would put it, not separation.[5] Furthermore, the women's concept of "family" was expansive and not the dominant culture's narrow view; family well-being in their minds extended to all families, not just their own. The many references to coworkers as "family" and the descriptions, for example, of picket line life—"as we keep fighting, we became like a family [and] that was really, really special," Mirna Preciado said—bear witness to that.

The legacy that corporate policies of non-responsibility has left in Nevada, which for decades has acceded to corporate demands, is a harsh one in locales where labor is unorganized. For individual workers it has meant the low wages and thin benefit packages that force them to take second and third jobs, constant insecurity, the absence of ladders up, and the widespread practice of disregarding employees' family responsibilities in workplace scheduling. Hard-working parents often see dreams for a better life for their children collapse into a world of permanent poverty and separation from those they most love. "I can count with my fingers with one hand," waitress Consuela Hernan said, "how many times I was home for the holidays in the fourteen years that I have been working for the casino. That is a big loss—you kind of lose track of what it is to be a family."

At the community and state level, the damage from non-responsibility is equally high. The state's infrastructure and measures of its education system, health care, social services, and general quality of life languish at the bottom of nearly every register. The security of children—the generation into which the women workers poured so much of their energy—has been particularly compromised. Nevada ranks forty-third in child well-being, forty-seventh in per pupil school expenditures, and forty-eighth in education spending.[6] In health, Nevada in 2008 was forty-second nationally in overall indicators: 21 percent of the state's adult residents and 19 percent of its children had no health insurance,[7] and an estimated 40 percent of the state's hotel/gaming employees were without health benefits.[8] Gaming corporations in everyone's measure have dominated the state and legislature for decades, and it is arguable that the poor outcomes are a measure of the value they put on children and families: if gaming were determined to assemble the resources and political will to increase state expenditures for health, education, and services, it would happen.

Fortunately, as we have seen, corporate power, as fierce as it is, does not occupy the entire screen; it is neither as strong nor its workers as weak as we have been encouraged to believe. In Las Vegas, four decades of struggle by organized, determined, and compassionate women and men, fully encumbered with family and friends, have won for workers and their families middle-class wages, job security for the families' breadwinners, high-quality health coverage free to employees and their families, and opportunities to move up a career ladder. "You know, the union really [is] my life," said Hattie Canty, underscoring the relationship between job and family that corporations do their best to disregard. "It was my life when I was bringing up my kids. It was that bloodstream that kept the money coming in where I was able to pay the bills and some of my kids went to college."

The intangibles were important as well to both workers and their families: dignity, belief that dreams really might come true, community and friendships, an alternative to the hatred and separation that characterize so much of 21st century life, and genuine political power. Finally, there was the knowledge that these changes, although continually under attack, would not go away easily; having stood up before against corporate power, the women could stand up again.

Casino Women, as we wrote in chapter 1, is the story of women moving, and sometimes not moving, in the context of enormous corporate power. It is an exploration as well of the consequences of keeping silent and speaking out. "People pay for what they do," James Baldwin wrote in 1972, "and still more for what they have allowed themselves to become, and they pay for it, very simply, by the lives they lead."[9] In the lives of women who remained silent—like the dealers who kept their heads down at work and chose instead to pursue happiness individually or management women who cast their lot with the corporation—the cost seemed very high. In the lives they led, money flowed more easily, but so did sadness and despair.

As for the women who acted, we have learned a great deal from them. It may be useful to sum up the factors that seemed to stand at the heart of their activism and of the transformation they experienced. Poverty was the first. Nine children on a cardboard pallet in Mexico, raises of ten cents a year, working two and even three jobs were all remembered. And remembering their own experience, the women were consistently unwilling to turn away from suffering, another critical characteristic. They were also willing to see and feel beyond their own personal and family lives, to feel and do something about the pain of others, and to open themselves up to people from across the world, and in so doing contradict the suspicions, racism, xenophobia fed us on a regular basis.

Furthermore, women who acted had close experience with power and an embodied consciousness that the interests of those in power—police in El Salvador, landlords in Mississippi, Big Tobacco, Big Gaming—were not their own interests. They had a healthy suspicion of corporate power, including the knowledge that those in charge may speak one way and act another, and were outraged that profit generation in gaming corporations regularly trumped any concern for workers and families.

The women were also willing to act collectively and militantly, even when they were afraid. They knew what it was like to be in battle mode, and self-hatred rarely asserted itself. The women found joy in comradeship, in struggling and laughing together, in keeping on keeping on for a very long time, and knew at their core that workers, consigned to the bottom, may yet have a role in history.

"The compassion of the oppressed for the oppressed is indispensable," Bertolt Brecht writes. "It is the world's one hope." This book has led us to ask if it is possible in a grossly unequal world to close ourselves and our families off from the suffering of others and enjoy our own modest or substantial resources. Conceivably, those who did not act may have thought, "I cannot do anything, for if I do, I will be fired, and I cannot live at the level I desire without this job." Or perhaps they occupied themselves with the distractions so readily available in our world that blot out suffering.

But it appears that life is not so simple, that we are in touch with our neighbors, and that to ignore their suffering in some way fundamentally compromises our own well being and certainly our ability to be authentic. For if we remain silent when another is abused, we become in some terrible way complicit. Our relations with others take on a surface quality, and we are constrained from talking about what is real. Only in stepping forward can we be authentic and avoid becoming alienated from ourselves, others, and our work. And it is only in being authentic, in acting, that we can find genuine connection with each other. The relation between acting and love is not difficult to find in the women's stories. It spills out, an affirmation of the connections among us all that are so endangered in a world dominated by corporate values.

There is one final story. Although the tragic events of September 11, 2001, occurred a decade ago, in many ways they seem like yesterday. Las Vegans' experience of September 11th and its aftermath illustrates well the difference between corporate "non-responsibility" and union workers' engagement.

In the days immediately following the attack on the World Trade Center, approximately fifteen thousand Las Vegas casino workers were laid-off from their jobs. Added to the collective shock and sorrow that descended on the nation (the Union especially grieved its seventy brothers and sisters, all workers at the Trade Center's famed Windows on the World restaurant, who died in the attacks), there was the rumor that Las Vegas might be next. It emptied the city of tourists. "9/11 hit Las Vegas very hard," Pam Phillips, a Las Vegas food server and union activist, said. "In the nonunion hotels immediately people's hours were cut; [in union casinos, layoffs] started happening within a week.... All the hotels canceled their expansion plans.... All the construction workers got laid off, cab drivers immediately took a huge hit, and then there's just this ripple effect."[10]

The impact on casino workers was massive. Workers scrambled to apply for unemployment, trying to stay ahead of Nevada's draconian eviction laws that allow landlords to remove tenants after only five days of nonpayment of rent. Unemployment claims in Nevada are made by telephone, and according to Pam, "the whole system was immediately overwhelmed. I mean, people sat on the phone for hours and hours.... For days they couldn't get through. And the thing is that the longer that you don't get through, the farther that unemployment check recedes in front of you. I mean, you've got to get through to them to get any money."

The Union, acting where others seemed paralyzed, began immediately to organize a "Helping Hand Center," a rapid-response, one-stop center housed in a huge tent in the Culinary Union parking lot that could provide essential services to union and nonunion workers. The unemployment and welfare departments, the utility company, United Way, HUD, and other social service agencies all were invited to set up mobile units. "People didn't have to wait hours and days to communicate with [service providers]," said Geoconda Kline. "We have United Way [to] help people with rent assistance, Nevada Partners for training—we have a lot of things."

It was an enormous undertaking on very short notice. "Like in a week, we pulled this whole thing together," Pam said. "I can't believe we managed to do it. I mean, the day before, the tent was going up but it was going up very slowly, and I thought, 'Oh, my God. We're not going to make it.' But the next morning we got here at about 7 o'clock…and there were about fifty, sixty people in line, and they had been there since 4 o'clock." Over a thousand people showed up that first day and more than seven thousand received services during the center's three weeks of operation. Both union and nonunion workers were welcome. "We invite people on the TV," Geoconda said. "We invite people on the radio.…We told people, union or no union, come. We have a lot of workers from all different casinos where they [don't have a] union. And that was a good feeling."

Volunteering daily at the center were 150 union casino workers, along with union leaders and organizers such as Geoconda and Pam. They told people where to park, which table to go to for help, and how to apply for unemployment insurance. "That's the kind of sharing I think we have to ask for," said Geoconda. "It [is] great to see how people get together in helping each other."

Casinos continued to lay off workers. In nonunion casinos, workers "suddenly discovered that there is no such thing as seniority," Pam said. "I mean, in a situation like this…the juice becomes very evident. The boss's favorite does not get laid off [or] does not have to go to graveyard.…All kinds of things don't happen to the boss's favorite. And all kinds of things happen, too, if you haven't been popular. At a time like this, it's real obvious to people."

In the midst of the crisis, a pattern of corporate behavior began to emerge, and relatively quickly it became apparent that companies not only were nonresponsive to workers needs, they also were using 9/11 to justify the dismantling of contractual agreements with the union. They "put the squeeze on people," Pam said, asking the remaining maids to clean more rooms and waitresses to serve more tables. The union printed up coupons for workers to hand their supervisors—"I'm not refusing to work, but I am going to do just one job," or "I did two jobs. Do I get two paychecks?" Geoconda Kline explained, "You know these workers give their life to the company. You can see the majority of the departments, they're immigrants. And when [the casinos] see that, too, they're thinking these people don't know their rights, they don't know the language, they don't know nothing."

The union did everything it could to get people back to work, proposing a six-month interim agreement in which workers, normally guaranteed a forty-hour week, would work thirty-two hours. It was an agreement that required sacrifice on the part of the union and its members—they would waive an important protection guaranteed by contract to get workers back to work without undermining casino profits—but the casinos were not interested. "Why [do] we [always] ask workers for more?" Geoconda asked. "Why [do] we always have to sacrifice the working people? Why [don't] we ask sacrifice [from] the corporations?"

> I think casinos [are] making [workers] feel they don't care, because, you know, when they give that massive layoff, they're not thinking...that a lot of single mothers [are going to be on] the street [because]not everybody is eligible for unemployment.... The casinos are always thinking about the money. They're always thinking, 'How can we get more money from these people?' They don't see the people like human beings.

León Gieco, the great Argentinean singer-songwriter who, like Bruce Springsteen, fills stadiums, writes "Solo le Pido a Dios..."

> The only thing I ask of God
> is that he not let me be indifferent to the suffering,
> and that when death, that dusty time, comes
> that I not be alone and empty, having not given my everything.

In Latin America, "Solo le Pido a Dios" is sung as a call for justice and against war. What is not apparent on the page but leaps out in performance is the anthem's joy, for though the pronoun is "I," behind it is an implicit "we"—you and I and a thousand others together. In the end, that is what the casino women were saying—don't sit alone declining to act, for a committed life is so much more joyous than a life of self-protection and consumption, and connection with each other in struggle so much more rewarding than lives lived alone.

We close with Howard Zinn, who in the essay "The Optimism of Uncertainty" captures some of our hopes for this book. "What we choose to emphasize in this complex history will determine our lives," Zinn writes.

> If we see only the worst, it destroys our capacity to do something. If we remember those times and places—and there are so many—where people have behaved magnificently, it energizes us to act, and raises

at least the possibility of sending this spinning top of a world in a different direction. And if we do act, in however small a way, we don't have to wait for some grand utopian future. The future is an infinite succession of presents, and to live now as we think human beings should live, in defiance of all that is bad around us, is itself a marvelous victory."[11]

Notes

CHAPTER 1. "YOU HAVE TO DO IT FOR THE PEOPLE COMING"

1. "About Culinary Workers Union Local 226," Culinary Workers Union Local 226 website, http://www.culinaryunion226.org/about.asp. Data accessed September 17, 2010.

2. Interview with Mirna Preciado and Geoconda Arguella Kline, February 22, 2001, Las Vegas, NV. Transcript in the possession of the authors. All quotations from Mirna Preciado and Geoconda Kline are from this interview unless otherwise noted.

3. Freire, *Pedagogy of the Oppressed*, 1986.

4. "Committees," made up of 10–15 rank-and-file workers, are the building blocks of union organizing.

5. In total we talked with forty-six women casino workers in two- to four-hour, semi-structured interviews; conducted five focus groups (of human service workers, educators, Latino community members, health workers, and former casino workers) with a total of thirty-five participants; and interviewed seventy-five "key informants," including demographers, union officials, researchers, historians, geographers, economists, family members, advocates, etc. We have assigned pseudonyms to all the women we interviewed confidentially and to all the participants of the focus groups. In certain cases we have further protected them by changing identifying characteristics.

6. These women included Geoconda Kline, Mirna Preciado, Hattie Canty, Mary Burns, and Jeanette Hill (all Culinary Union officers and activists); Teresa Price (an advocate for stronger smoking regulations—see chapter 10), and Darlene Jespersen (who brought suit against Harrahs Entertainment—see chapter 6).

7. Thank you to Vicki Ruiz, *From Out of the Shadows*, 1998, for providing this description of qualitative researchers' task. See Blake, "Auguries of Innocence," 1971, 585.

8. See Perez, *The Decolonial Imaginary*, 1999; and Perez, "Queering the Borderlands," 2003, for more description of uncovering "hidden geographies."

9. John Sweeney quoted in Cooper, "Labor Deals a New Hand," 1997, 11.

10. Greenhouse, "Organized: Local 226," 2004.

11. Denton and Morris, *The Money and the Power*, 2001, 8.

12. Ben Affleck quotation in Kirn and Ressner, "Poker's New Face," 2004, 31. The state-wide revenue from gaming and the lodging, food, and beverages associated with it, was $25,257,000,000 in 2008 (gross gaming revenue alone was about $12,000,000,000). Figures from the University of Nevada, Las Vegas, Gaming Institute, http://gaming.unlv.edu/abstract/nvstate_revenues.html#2008. Data accessed March 14, 2010.

13. Puzo, *Inside Las Vegas*, 1976, 22.

14. Denton and Morris, *The Money and the Power*, 2001, 3, 391, 3–15.

15. "State of the States: The AGA Survey of Casino Entertainment," 2009. The Las Vegas Strip is the top U.S. casino market by annual revenue ($6.121 billion); Reno Sparks is the eleventh, with a 2008 annual revenue of about $780 million.

16. Rosenthal, Interview, 1997.

17. Rothman, *Neon Metropolis*, 2003, 22.

18. Marfels, "Concentration, Competition and Competitiveness," 1999, 59.

19. Dandurand and Pinney, "Structural Dynamics," 1999.

20. Bonacich and Appelbaum, *Behind the Label,* 2000); Hondagneu-Sotelo, *Domestica,* 2001; Louie, *Sweatshop Warriors,* 2001.

21. Geron, "The Local/Global Context," 1997.

22. Rawe et al., "Vegas Plays to the World," 2004.

23. Moehring, "Growth, Services, and the Political Economy," 2002, 79.

24. Kroll, Miller, and Serafin, "The World's Billionaires," 2009.

25. Moehring, "Growth, Services, and the Political Economy," 2002, 81–82.

26. Chandler, "Working Hard, Living Poor," 2001.

27. Denton and Morris, *The Money and the Power,* 2001, 8.

28. Ibid., 95.

29. Including California at 8.84 percent, New York at 7.1 percent, New Jersey at 9 percent, Pennsylvania at 9.99 percent, and Montana at 6.75 percent. See "State of the States," 2009.

30. Ibid. In its 2009 survey of casino entertainment, the American Gaming Association reports gaming taxes of 20 percent in Colorado, 15–50 percent in Illinois, 15–40 percent in Indiana, 19 percent in Michigan, and 21 percent in Missouri.

31. Sibelius, "Silence," 2001. While legislators have been fearful of taxing casinos, they are more courageous about imposing a high sales tax. Sales taxes of course are the most regressive among taxes, burdening those with low and modest incomes disproportionately, and Nevada's stands at 6.85 percent, the eighth highest in the nation. See "Fool's Gold," 2009.

32. Moehring, "Growth, Services, and the Political Economy," 2002, 84; McNichols and Johnson, "Recession Continues to Batter State Budgets," 2010.

33. Moehring, "Growth, Services, and the Political Economy," 2002, 84. In this argument Moehring references John Kenneth Galbraith, *Affluent Society,* 1958, 198–211.

CHAPTER 2. "THEY'RE TREATING US LIKE DONKEYS, REALLY"

1. Interview with Alicia Bermudez (not her real name), February 26, 2001, Reno, NV. Transcript in the possession of the authors. All quotations from Mrs. Bermudez are from this interview.

2. See chapters 4 and 5 for a full discussion of the Culinary Union.

3. Bernhardt, Dresser, and Hatton, "Moving Hotels to the High Road," 2003a.

4. Latino Community Leaders Focus Group, March 5, 1999, Reno, NV. Transcript in the possession of the authors.

5. Interview with Raquel Marquez (not her real name), April 27, 1999, Reno, NV. Transcript in the possession of the authors. All quotations from Mrs. Marquez are from this interview.

6. Interview with Valerie Miller (not her real name), May 21, 2001, Reno, NV. Transcript in the possession of the authors. All quotations from Mrs. Miller are from this interview.

7. Bernhardt, Dresser, and Hatton, "The Coffee Pot Wars," 2003b.

8. Ibid.

9. Milburn and Barrett, "Lumbosacral Loads in Bedmaking," 1999.

10. Krause, Scherzer, and Rugulies, "Physical Workload," 2005. See also Frumin et al., "Workload-Related Musculoskeletal Disorders," 2006; Krause, "Working Conditions," 1999; and "Creating Luxury, Enduring Pain," 2006.

11. Lee and Krause, "The Impact of a Worker Health Study," 2002.

12. Authors' interview with Diana Saren (not her real name), March 9, 2001. Transcript in the possession of the authors.

13. See Chandler, "Working Hard, Living Poor," 2001. Today it is estimated that a living wage for a two-person family (one adult and one child) in Washoe County, NV (Reno), is

$17.42; for a family of two adults and two children it is $28.44. See "Living Wage Calculator," http://www.livingwage.geog.psu.edu/counties/32031.

14. Authors' interview with Ana Ramirez (not her real name), May 8, 2004. Transcript in the possession of the authors.

15. Authors' interview with Magdalena Ruiz (not her real name), April 29, 1999, Reno, NV. Transcript in the possession of the authors. All quotations from Magdalena Ruiz are from this interview.

16. For more on this thesis, see Cobble, *Dishing It Out,* 1991.

17. Freire, *Pedagogy of the Oppressed,* 1986, 33.

CHAPTER 3. "KISS MY FOOT"

1. Interview with Heidi Abrahamson (not her real name), December 12, 1999, Reno, NV. Transcript in the possession of the authors. All quotations from Ms. Abrahamson are from this interview.

2. See chapter 10, "Big Tobacco Rides the Strip," for a longer discussion of casinos and smoke.

3. The phrase "libidinous beauties" is from Castleman, *Whale Hunt in the Desert,* 2004, 2.

4. Vogliotti, *The Girls of Nevada,* 1975.

5. Ibid., 179–180.

6. Bugsy Siegel rose from his status as a local gangster and leader with Meyer Lansky of New York's "Bugs-Meyer Gang" to being a major player and hit man in the East Coast Mafia. In 1945 he moved to Las Vegas where he established the Flamingo Hotel and Casino with financial backing from the mob. He was murdered on June 20, 1947.

7. Vogliotti, *The Girls of Nevada,* 1975, 180.

8. Ibid., 235–236. (In the 1950s and 1960s, Senator Estes Kefauver and Attorney General Robert Kennedy conducted major investigations into gambling's links with organized crime.)

9. Puzo, *Inside Las Vegas,* 1976, 176. Capitalization in the original.

10. Vogliotti, *The Girls of Nevada,* 1975, 239. Ed Reid and Ovid Demaris in *Green Felt Jungle,* a 1963 book in the muckraking tradition that was much scorned in Nevada, echoed Vogliotti: "The most lucrative job in Vegas is that of cocktail waitress in one of the hotel-casinos on the Strip....The most sought-after position is in the pit....Almost without exception, the girl in the pit is full of what Vegans call 'juice.'" See Reid and Demaris, *The Green Felt Jungle,* 1963, 111.

11. Hausbeck, "Who Puts the 'Sin' in 'Sin City' Stories?," 2002, 346.

12. See http://www.vegasmessageboard.com/forums/showthread.php?t=15098. Data accessed December 4, 2009.

13. See http://www.vegastripping.com/board/topic.php?topic=32. Data accessed December 4, 2009.

14. De Volo, "Service and Surveillance," 2003.

15. See Dunston, *Women of the Strip,* 2002.

16. A conversation with Kathleen Ramige (not her real name), a member of the Social Work Focus Group, December 2, 2001. Transcript in the possession of the authors.

17. Interview with Genette Louis (not her real name), November 2, 1999, Reno, NV. Transcript in the possession of the authors. All quotes from Genette Louis are from this interview.

18. Rios, *Casino Cocktail Waitresses,* 2003.

19. Ibid.

20. See Cobble, *Dishing It Out,* 1991, for an account of injury and its history in waitresses' lives.

21. Ibid.

22. Ibid.

23. *Las Vegas Review Journal.* Bulletin board entry in response to a job seeker asking how much cocktail waitresses make in Las Vegas. http://eforum.reviewjournal.com/lv/showthread.php?5=822.

24. Rios, *Casino Cocktail Waitresses,* 2003.

25. For a wonderful picture of older coffee shop waitresses, and especially their relationships with "regulars," see Taylor, *Counter Culture,* 2009.

26. Interview with Gloria Hanson (not her real name), May 11, 2000, Reno, NV. Transcript in the possession of the authors. All quotes from Gloria Hanson are from this interview.

27. Authors' interview with Tom Stoneburner, September 5, 2000. Transcript in the possession of the authors.

28. Rios, *Casino Cocktail Waitresses,* 2003.

29. Ibid.

30. Ibid.

31. Leong, "Mirage Waitresses Win Legal Victory," 2001.

32. Peterson, "Casino with Weight Policy Finds Boon," 2005.

33. Rios, *Casino Cocktail Waitresses,* 2003.

34. "MGM Cocktail Waitresses," in-house video produced by the Culinary Union. 1994. In the possession of the authors.

35. Interview with Kris Marroquin (not her real name), May 3, 2000, Reno, NV. Transcript in the possession of the authors. All quotes from Kris Marroquin are from this interview.

36. Strow, "Casino High Heel Policies Targeted," 2000.

37. See Chereb, "Waitresses Want to Give Shoe Rule the Boot," 2000; Gerrie, "Servers Rail Against High Heels," 2001; Strow, "Casino High Heel Policies Targeted," 2000; and Schoenmann, "These Feet Are Made for Walking," 2008.

CHAPTER 4. "I'LL ALWAYS LOVE THE UNION"

1. By far the best description of the migration of black Southerners to Nevada may be found in Annelise Orleck's *Storming Caesars Palace: How Black Mothers Fought Their Own War on Poverty,* 2005.

2. U.S. Census (2000): Nevada—Race and Hispanic Origin for Selected Large Cities and Other Places.

3. Interview with Hattie Canty, September 19, 2007, Las Vegas, NV. Transcript in authors' possession. Quotations from Hattie Canty unless otherwise cited are from this interview.

4. Interview with Mary Burns, September 19, 2007, Las Vegas, NV. Transcript in authors' possession. Quotations from Mary Burns are from this interview unless otherwise noted.

5. Essie Shelton Jacobs, interview by Claytee D. White, Las Vegas Women Oral History Project, University of Nevada, Las Vegas, 1997, 5.

6. Hattie Canty, interview by Claytee D. White, Las Vegas Women Oral History Project, University of Nevada, Las Vegas, 2000.

7. Viola Johnson, interview by Claytee D. White, Las Vegas Women Oral History Project, University of Nevada, Las Vegas, 1997, 17.

8. Jacobs interview, 1997, 7, 3.

9. Johnson interview, 1997, 17.

10. Canty interview by White, 1997.

11. See Freire, *Pedagogy of the Oppressed,* 1986.

12. Canty interview by White, 1997, 27.

13. Ibid., 39.

14. We decided early on to study women, partly because of long-standing commitments as feminists and partly because of our desire to unfold working women's experience in a globalizing world. We want to emphasize, however, that the women, and particularly the union women, though immensely proud of women's leadership, spoke with love and respect about the men alongside whom they worked. For that reason and others, this is but a half-history of the Culinary Union, and we look forward to the publication of a much-needed, fuller history.

15. Rothman, *Neon Metropolis,* 2003, 70.

16. Ibid., 70–71.

17. Ibid., 72.

18. Denton and Morris, *The Money and the Power,* 2001, 367.

19. Jacobs interview by White, 1997, 31–32.

20. Ruby Duncan (her real name), interview by authors, March 5, 2008, Reno, NV. Duncan, who hailed from Tallulah, Louisiana, Mary Burns's hometown, worked as a maid in the mid-1950s at the Stardust Casino until she was fired for informing a supervisor who was pressing her to work overtime that "we aren't in slavery times anymore." In the 1970s and '80s she led the Clark County Welfare Rights Organization. It was the African American women and families of the CCWRO who, with headliners such as Jane Fonda, Bernadette Devlin, Ralph Abernathy, George Wiley, and Julian Bond, closed down the Strip in 1971. They sat in at Caesars Palace carrying signs like "Nevada Gambles with Human Lives" and "Nevada Starves Children," protesting the state's purge of hundreds of families from the welfare rolls. Later, they went on to build a remarkable network of services on the city's west side: health clinics, old age homes, a library, and affordable housing. These activities propelled Ruby into legislative activity in Carson City and Washington, DC, along with Nevadan Maya Miller. See Annelise Orleck, *Storming Caesars Palace,* 2005.

21. Jacobs interview by White, 1997.

22. Canty interview by White, 1997, 4.

23. Brammer, "Sarah Hughes," 1974; and Orleck, *Storming Caesars Palace,* 2005.

24. Duncan interview by authors, March 5, 2008.

25. Orleck, *Storming Caesars Palace,* 2005. See also Claytee D. White, "'Eight Dollars a Day and Working in the Shade,'" 2003.

26. Duncan interview by authors, March 5, 2008.

27. Brammer, "Sarah Hughes," 1974.

28. Ibid.

29. Canty interview by White, 1997, 38.

30. Rothman, *Neon Metropolis,* 2003, 22.

31. Kraft, *Vegas at Odds,* 2010, 139–141.

32. Unidentified union leader quoted in Denton and Morris, *The Money and the Power,* 2001, 368.

33. A.D. Hopkins, n.d. "Al Bramlet, 1917–1977." "The Organizer. The First 100 Persons Who Shaped Southern Nevada. Part III. A City in Full." *Las Vegas Review-Journal.* Available at http://www.1st100.com/part3/bramlet.html. Data accessed August 22, 2010.

34. Kraft, *Vegas at Odds,* 2010, 147–148.

35. Ibid., 157.

36. Ibid., 156–158; "Las Vegas: An Unconventional History," 2008. *American Experience,* PBS. http://www.pbs.org/wgbh/amex/lasvegas/peopleevents/p_unions.html. Data accessed May 17, 2008.

37. For detailed accounts of the 1976 and 1984 strikes see Rothman, *Neon Metropolis,* 2003; and Kraft, *Vegas at Odds,* 2010.

38. Canty interview by White, 1997, 16.

39. Ibid., 8.

40. Ibid., 18.

41. Ibid., 26.

42. D. Taylor serves currently as secretary-treasurer of the Culinary Union; Glen Arnodo was the Union's political director from 1987 to 2005.

43. See analysis of the new union movement in Sherman and Voss, "'Organize or Die,'" 2000.

44. Canty interview by White, 1997, 17.

45. Mosle, "Letter from Las Vegas," 1996, 150.

46. Ibid.

47. Ibid.

48. Ibid., 18.

49. Ibid., 19.

50. Ibid., 39–40.

51. Ibid., 150.

52. For a careful analysis, see Alexander, "Rise to Power," 2002.

53. Ibid., 153.

54. Ibid., 167.

55. Canty interview by White, 1997, 43.

56. D. Taylor quoted in Benz, "Labor's Ace in the Hole," 2004, 537.

57. Alexander, "Rise to Power," 2002, 153.

58. The steady growth in Culinary's ranks began in 1989 "when 3,300 Mirage employees joined the union; later that year 2,100 workers at the Excalibur joined, in 1993 4,400 Treasure Island Luxor joined.... In just four years, the union increased its membership by 50 percent and, more importantly, unionized every new major hotel that opened in the city. Since then, Culinary's growth has continued at an equally impressive rate. From the opening of the Mirage until 2003 they gained 30,800 members for a total membership of 50,000." From Benz, "Labor's Ace in the Hole," 2004, 526.

59. Canty interview by White, 1997, 32.

CHAPTER 5. "HERE'S MY HEART"

1. John Sweeney, quoted in Cooper, "Labor Deals a New Hand," 1997, 11.

2. Benz, "Labor's Ace in the Hole," 2004.

3. Interview with Josefina Huerta (not her real name), September 18, 2000, Reno, NV. Transcript in the possession of the authors. All quotations from Josefina Huerta are from this interview.

4. The Reno union was Local 86 of Hotel Employees, Restaurant Employees (HERE) until 2000, when it was merged with Local 226 of UNITE-HERE.

5. Arriaza, "Grace Under Pressure," 1997, 6.

6. See Chandler and Jones, "You Have to Do It for the People Coming," 2003b, for a longer discussion of these themes.

7. Interview with Consuela Hernan (not her real name), May 6, 2000, Reno, NV. Transcript in the possession of the authors. All quotes from Consuela Hernan are from this interview.

8. Interview with Estela Contreras (not her real name), September 11, 2000, Reno, NV. Transcript in the possession of the authors. All quotations from Estela Contreras are from this interview.

9. Interview with Mary Burns, September 19, 2007, Las Vegas, NV. Transcript in the possession of the authors. All quotations from Mary Burns are from this interview unless otherwise noted.

10. *One Day Longer,* 1999.

11. Rothman, "Colony, Capital, and Casino," 2002, 83.

12. *One Day Longer,* 1999.

13. Ibid.

14. Ibid.

15. Annette Bernhardt, Laura Dresser, Erin Hatten, "Moving Hotels to the High Road," 2003a; Michael Bloom and Alison Campbell, "Success by Design," 2002.

16. "Something's Cooking," 2007.

17. Ibid.

18. 3 Square, which stands for three square meals a day, is a nonprofit initiative of MGM Mirage, Station Casinos, Harrah's Entertainment, and Boyd Gaming, in cooperation with the Culinary Training Academy. The organization is dedicated to eliminating hunger in the Las Vegas community and is the largest collaborative effort to help nonprofit organizations combat hunger among needy children, families, and seniors. http://www.theculinaryacademy.org/news4.php. Data accessed March 10, 2010.

19. Simpson, "Culinary Training Program Gets Financial Boost," 2003.

20. From the Culinary Training Academy website, http://www.theculinaryacademy.org/demand.htm.

21. Interview with Pilar Weiss, Las Vegas, NV, November 16, 2006. Transcript in the possession of the authors.

22. "Citizenship Project Does Brisk Business," 2006.

23. Ibid.

24. The position of the Culinary Workers Union is to strongly support immigration reform laws that will

- Restore the rule of law and enhance security at the nation's borders
- Create a sensible plan for the future flow of workers into the country
- Protect the rights of all workers, both U.S. and immigrant
- Create a pathway for undocumented immigrants already in the U.S. to earn legal status over a period of time. Accomplish this by developing a program that calls for a number of reasonable steps to be completed over a specified timeline
- After completing a program that leads to legal status, add a second level that allows immigrants who wish to become citizens a clear pathway to reach that goal
- Support legislation that helps communities foster citizenship programs, civic activities and reunites families separated under old laws. (From *The Culinary Worker* Fall 2006, p. 21)

25. "Immigrant Workers Freedom Ride," 2004.

26. Ibid.

27. Ibid.

28. Benz, "Labor's Ace in the Hole," 2004, 6.

29. Ibid.

30. Interview with Jeanette Hill, September 19, 2007, Las Vegas, NV. Transcript in the possession of the authors. All quotations from Jeanette Hill are from this interview.

31. Interview with Pilar Weiss, September 19, 2007, Las Vegas, NV. Transcript in the possession of the authors.

CHAPTER 6. DARLENE *JESPERSEN V. HARRAH'S ENTERTAINMENT, INC.*

1. Whitaker, Beverage Department "Personal Best" Program, 2000.

2. Ibid.

3. "It is imperative that the department supervisors utilize these photos as an 'appearance measurement' tool," the policy read, "and, on a daily basis, hold each employee

accountable to look his or her Personal Best." *Jespersen v. Harrah's Operating Company, Inc.*, 392 F 3d 1076 (9th Cir 2004), 7. Appellant's Opening Brief.

4. *Jespersen*, 392 F 3d at 6. Appellant's Opening Brief.

5. Ibid.

6. Darlene Jespersen, interview by authors, November 9, 2000, Reno, NV. All Darlene Jespersen quotations unless otherwise noted are from the interview.

7. Bartending historically has been a male profession. In 1890 less than 1 percent of bartenders were women, and bartenders unions went out of their way to keep the profession male, arguing that bar work would corrupt women. They also felt that women lowered standards by accepting inferior pay and that women could never become "professional mixologists," handle rowdy customers, or keep a good conversation going at the bar. For decades men continued to hold sway, but with the coming of Title VII of the Civil Rights Act, women won more and more bartending jobs, until in the late 1980s the majority of professional bartenders were women. At the same time, bartending became increasingly sexualized, and employers began to hire "bar babes" as much for their ability to please male customers as for their ability to mix drinks. Harrah's, however, did not participate in that particular trend. Harrah's bartenders, male and female, wore a unisex uniform—pants, vest, and shirt—and Darlene was clearly valued for her ability to mix drinks and interact with customers, not for bar babe attributes. For further information on the history of bartending, see Avery and Crain, "Branded," 2007; and Cobble, *Dishing It Out*, 1991.

8. *Jespersen*, 392 F 3d 1076 at 5. Appellant's Opening Brief.

9. *Jespersen*, 392 F 3d 1076 at 6. Appellant's Opening Brief.

10. Ibid., emphasis in the original.

11. *Jespersen*, 392 F 3d 1076 at 4. Appellant's Opening Brief.

12. The Winning Edge, http://www.the-winning-edge.com/about.html. Data accessed June 15, 2005. The current URL is http://www.tweconsultinggroup.com.

13. Ibid.

14. Ibid.

15. McCullough, Morton, and Schreiber, "People and Events," 2002.

16. Levine, "Culinary Union Says Program for Workers Is Intrusive," 2000.

17. Harrah's website at http://www.harrahs.com. Data accessed June 15, 2005.

18. Levinson, "Harrah's Knows What You Did Last Night," 2001.

19. Harrah's, "John Boushy, Senior Vice President and Chief Integration Officer," http://investor.harrahs.com/bios.cfm. Data accessed June 1, 2005. Satre described his and Boushy's "amazement" at what they discovered in their early "unsophisticated" customer surveys: "When we started to track it, we discovered many of our customers visited multiple properties.... We had customers who gamble in multiple locations. Our Atlantic City customers come to Las Vegas. Our Reno customers go to Lake Tahoe, and so on. Second, when we manually tracked these findings, we estimated twenty-five percent of our regular Atlantic City customers make an annual pilgrimage to Las Vegas. This planted a seed that there was an opportunity to create a loyalty marketing program to establish relationships with customers who bridge multiple gaming environments." In Shook, *Jackpot!*, 2003, 142.

20. Levinson, "Harrah's Knows What You Did Last Night," 2001. See also Shook, *Jackpot!*, 2003, for an extended account of Harrah's expanding technology-based efforts to develop customer loyalty.

21. Harrah's website at http://www.harrahs.com. Data accessed June 15, 2005.

22. Cooper, *The Last Honest Place in America*, 2004, 127.

23. Ibid., 129–130.

24. Levine, "Culinary Union Says Program for Workers Is Intrusive," 2000.

25. Ibid.

26. Quoted in Levinson, "Harrah's Knows What You Did Last Night," 2001.

27. Ibid.

28. Harrah's website at http://www.harrahs.com. Data accessed June 15, 2005.

29. Levine, "Culinary Union Says Program for Workers Is Intrusive," 2000.

30. "Policy at Harrah's Governs Appearance of Servers," 1999.

31. Ibid.

32. Ibid.

33. Ibid.

34. Harrah's, Reno. "Beverage Department 'Personal Best' Program—Image Transformation Employee Sign-Off," 2000. In the possession of the authors.

35. Christensen, "Rouge Rogue," 2001. See also "Facial Discrimination," 2000.

36. District Court decision as summarized in *Jespersen,* 392 F 3d at 8. Appellant's Opening Brief.

37. Ibid.

38. Lambda Legal Defense and Education Fund, http://www.lambdalegal.org. Data accessed June 21, 2005. See also Jennifer Pizer, "Facial Discrimination," 2007, 285–318. Pizer outlines Lambda Legal's reasoning in taking up the Jespersen case, writing that "restrictive, gender-based rules about personal appearance and deportment can pose particular burdens for anyone whose gender identity or expression varies from conventional stereotypes; lesbian, gay, bisexual, and transgender (LGBT) people are disproportionately burdened by such rules. Many LGBT people cannot readily conform to conventional gender stereotypes. For others, simply the process of "coming out" as LGBT or 'queer' gives rise to a deep critique of the artificially restrictive gender stereotypes that pervade our modern lives and shape corporate marketing campaigns. For many who come to understand themselves as naturally outside conventional gender norms, the unnatural wardrobes and artificial physical shapes of Mattel's Barbie and Ken dolls are not entirely benign" (287).

39. "Lambda Legal Appeals Federal Sex Discrimination Case on Behalf of Woman Fired from Harrah's Casino," 2003.

40. 42 U.S.C. 2000e-2(a)(1). You may read Title VII in its entirety at http://www.eeoc.gov/policy/vii.html. The relevant language reads in full:

UNLAWFUL EMPLOYMENT PRACTICES
SEC. 2000e-2. [Section 703]

(a) It shall be an unlawful employment practice for an employer
  (1) to fail or refuse to hire or to discharge any individual, or otherwise to discriminate against any individual with respect to his compensation, terms, conditions, or privileges of employment, because of such individual's race, color, religion, sex, or national origin; or
  (2) to limit, segregate, or classify his employees or applicants for employment in any way which would deprive or tend to deprive any individual of employment opportunities or otherwise adversely affect his status as an employee, because of such individual's race, color, religion, sex, or national origin.

(b) It shall be an unlawful employment practice for an employment agency to fail or refuse to refer for employment, or otherwise to discriminate against, any individual because of his race, color, religion, sex, or national origin, or to classify or refer for employment any individual on the basis of his race, color, religion, sex, or national origin.

(c) It shall be an unlawful employment practice for a labor organization
  (1) to exclude or to expel from its membership, or otherwise to discriminate against, any individual because of his race, color, religion, sex, or national origin;

    (2) to limit, segregate, or classify its membership or applicants for membership, or to classify or fail or refuse to refer for employment any individual, in any way which would deprive or tend to deprive any individual of employment opportunities, or would limit such employment opportunities or otherwise adversely affect his status as an employee or as an applicant for employment, because of such individual's race, color, religion, sex, or national origin; or

    (3) to cause or attempt to cause an employer to discriminate against an individual in violation of this section.

  (d) It shall be an unlawful employment practice for any employer, labor organization, or joint labor-management committee controlling apprenticeship or other training or retraining, including on-the-job training programs to discriminate against any individual because of his race, color, religion, sex, or national origin in admission to, or employment in, any program established to provide apprenticeship or other training.

  (e) Notwithstanding any other provision of this subchapter, (1) it shall not be an unlawful employment practice for an employer to hire and employ employees, for an employment agency to classify, or refer for employment any individual, for a labor organization to classify its membership or to classify or refer for employment any individual, or for an employer, labor organization, or joint labor-management committee controlling apprenticeship or other training or retraining programs to admit or employ any individual in any such program, on the basis of his religion, sex, or national origin in those certain instances where religion, sex, or national origin is a bona fide occupational qualification reasonably necessary to the normal operation of that particular business or enterprise, and (2) it shall not be an unlawful employment practice for a school, college, university, or other educational institution or institution of learning to hire and employ employees of a particular religion if such school, college, university, or other educational institution or institution of learning is, in whole or in substantial part, owned, supported, controlled, or managed by a particular religion or by a particular religious corporation, association, or society, or if the curriculum of such school, college, university, or other educational institution or institution of learning is directed toward the propagation of a particular religion.

41. Whisner, "Gender-Specific Clothing Regulation," 1982. See pages 80–83 for a discussion of the Haircut Cases.

42. Hart, *The Concept of Law,* 1979, 169.

43. *Carroll vs. Talman Federal Savings and Loan,* 604 F.2d 1028, 1033 (7th Cir. 1979).

44. *Carroll,* 604 F.2d 1028 at 1032.

45. *Carroll,* 604 F.2d 1028 at 1032–1033.

46. Whisner, "Gender-Specific Clothing Regulation," 1982, 119.

47. Ibid., 96–97.

48. *Carroll* 604 F.2d 1028.

49. *EEOC v. Sage Realty* 507 F. Supp. 599 (SDNY 1981).

50. Ibid.

51. *EEOC,* 507 F. Supp. 599 at 609.

52. Whisner, "Gender-Specific Clothing Regulation," 1982, 119.

53. *Frank v. United Airlines, Inc.,* 216 F.3d 845 (9th Cir. 2000).

54. *Price Waterhouse v. Hopkins,* 490 (U.S. 228 1989).

55. Ibid.

56. Ibid.

57. *Nichols v. Azteca Restaurant Enterprises, Inc.,* 256 F.3d 864 (9th Cir. 2001).

58. *Jespersen,* 392 F. 3d 1076. Brief of *Amici Curiae.*

59. *Jespersen,* 392 F 3d 1076 at 7. Appellant's Opening Brief.

60. *Jespersen,* 392 F 3d 1076. Brief of *Amici Curiae.* Of particular note is the Nevada ACLU's statement: "Thus, far from being a de minimis workplace requirement with no substantial impact on women's employment opportunities, being forced to wear makeup at work has a long-standing social and historical significance that is specifically sex-linked and is deeply offensive and disempowering to many women. While of course some women *like* wearing makeup and feel more comfortable with it on, the issue here is the significant harm and social message about women's roles in the workplace and society when an employer can *force* them—but not men—to wear it in order to keep their jobs."

61. *Jespersen,* 392 F.3d 1076 at 17457–17472. Opinion by Judge Tashima.

62. *Jespersen,* 392 F.3d 1076 at 17473–17479. Opinion by Judge Thomas.

63. Ibid.

64. Stoneburner quoted in Andrew Barbano, *Barbwire,* 2004. http://www.nevadalabor. com/barbwire/barb00/barb10-8-0. Data accessed May 17, 2005.

65. Newitz, "Wear It, Bitch," 2005.

66. Hannah Sheehan. n.d. http://www.esp.edu/burkas.htm. Data accessed May 16, 2005. The young women's responses reflected feminists' long-standing and diverse critiques/analyses of makeup. Of note among these are two book-length studies, Wolf, *Beauty Myth,* 1991, and Peiss, *Hope in a Jar,* 1998.

67. See Pizer, "Facial Discrimination," 2007, for an elucidating discussion of Lambda Legal's approach to the case.

68. *Jespersen,* 444F.3d 1104 (en banc).

69. Ibid.

70. Duke University Law School Dean Katherine Bartlett was the author of an early and seminal study of appearance law titled "Only Girls Wear Barrettes," 1994; see also Carbado, Fisk, and Gulati, "Making Makeup Matter," 2007.

71. See Carbado, Fisk, and Gulati, "Making Makeup Matter," 2007, for an excellent overview of the studies.

72. Avery and Crain, "Branded," 2007.

73. Ibid.

74. Pizer, "Facial Discrimination," 2007.

CHAPTER 7. LIBERATION THEOLOGY, PIT BOSS STYLE

1. Nelson-Pallmeyer, *School of the Assassins,* 1997. School of the Americas graduates have been implicated in terrorism, human rights abuses, violence, and atrocities throughout Central and South America.

2. Edna Harman interview, January 5, 2001, Reno, NV. (Not her real name.) Transcript in the possession of the authors. All Edna Harman quotations are from this interview unless otherwise noted.

3. Miller, *Inside the Glitter,* 2000, 24.

4. Noone, *The Same Fate as the Poor,* 1995, 7.

5. On December 2, 1980, members of the National Guard of El Salvador intercepted a van carrying four American churchwomen as they were leaving the international airport in San Salvador. Maryknoll Sisters Ita Ford and Maura Clark, Ursuline Sister Dorothy Kazel, and lay missioner Jean Donovan were taken to an isolated spot where they were shot dead at close range. In 1984 the soldiers were found guilty and sentenced to thirty years in prison. The Truth Commission noted that this was the first time in Salvadoran history that a judge found a member of the military guilty of assassination. In 1998 three of the

soldiers were released for good behavior. Two of the men remain in prison and have petitioned the government for pardons. The deaths of these women intensified a movement for social justice in Central America that continues today. From Maryknoll Sisters of St. Dominic, Inc., http://www.mklsisters.org.

6. Maya Miller was a Nevada activist who in the 1980s drove a truckload of medical supplies to Nicaragua.

7. Miller, *Inside the Glitter*, 2000, 25.

8. "A lot of work, not much money, right?"

9. Miller, *Inside the Glitter*, 2000, 24.

CHAPTER 8. DEALING

1. Interview with Jeanine Carter (not her real name), May 11, 2001. Transcript in the possession of the authors. All quotations from Jeanine Carter are from this interview.

2. University of Nevada Las Vegas Center for Gaming Research. "Gaming Revenue Report." Available at http://gaming.unlv.edu/abstract/nv_main.html. Data accessed March 3, 2010.

3. Rosenthal interview, 1997.

4. Gorman, "Dealers Reject Union," 2001.

5. Binkley, "In Drive to Unionize," 2001.

6. Interview with Alejandra Lomeli (not her real name), May 4, 2000, Reno, NV. Transcript in the possession of the authors. All quotations from Alejandro Lomeli are from this interview.

7. Interview with Remedios Cortez (not her real name), February 13, 2001, Reno, NV. Transcript in the possession of the authors. All quotations from Remedios Cortez are from this interview.

8. Interview with Cynthia Bowen (not her real name), May 11, 2000, Reno, NV. Transcript in the possession of the authors. All quotations from Cynthia Bowen are from this interview.

9. Enarson, "Emotion Workers on the Production Line," 1993, 227.

10. Interview with Connie Hogan (not her real name), May 22, 2000, Reno, NV. Transcript in the possession of the authors. All quotations from Connie Hogan are from this interview.

11. Interview with Jeanine Carter, 2001.

12. Interview with Grace Ling (not her real name), October 8, 1999, Reno, NV. Transcript in the possession of the authors. All quotations from Grace Ling are from this interview.

13. Benjamin, "Dealers' Illness Called Frequent," 2000.

14. Enarson, "Emotion Workers on the Production Line," 1993, 230.

15. Interview with Maxine Everett (not her real name), October 19, 1999, Reno, NV. Transcript in the possession of the authors. All quotations from Maxine Everett are from this interview.

16. Binkley, "In Drive to Unionize," 2001.

17. Butler, "Casino," 2004.

18. Interview with Tony Badillo, November 16, 2006, Las Vegas, NV. Transcript in the possession of the authors. All quotations from Tony Badillo are from this interview unless otherwise noted.

19. "About Us," International Union of Gaming Employees.

20. Ibid.

21. Whitford, "Losing the 'Auto' in United Auto Workers," 2007.

22. "Casino Dealers in Nevada Vote Union," 2007.

23. Stutz, "Casino Industry," 2007.

24. "Casino Dealer Organizing," 2009. "Perhaps the most outrageous example of these wholesale violations of workers' rights," wrote the AFL-CIO Executive Council in May 2009, "is Bally's Casino, a Harrah's property. Dealers at Bally's voted in favor of UAW representation by a margin of 628–255 in June 2007, but its corporate parent, Harrah's Entertainment, Inc., still refuses to bargain—even after the union has been certified by the NLRB and the company has lost multiple appeals. Meanwhile, Bally's has fired union activists, stripped workers of their seniority and stopped retirement fund contributions. The situation is similar in Las Vegas, where dealers at Caesars Palace, also owned by Harrah's, and Wynn Casino voted overwhelmingly to join the Transport Workers Union. While the employers go through the motions at the bargaining table, they effectively deny workers their right to a contract by stonewalling on issue after issue."

25. Thomas, "Don't Play Games," 2009. Available at http://www.seiu.org/2009/03/dont-play-games-with-atlantic-city-casino-dealers.php. See also http://FairDealForACDealers.org and the United Auto Workers' account of the formation of the Gaming Workers Council at http://www.uaw.org/solidarity/09/0609/uf07.php.

26. Interview with Maxine Everett (not her real name), October 19, 1999, Reno, NV. Transcript in the possession of the authors. All quotations from Maxine Everett are from this interview.

27. Cynthia Bowen, n.d., "A Day in the Life," personal essay. In the possession of the authors.

CHAPTER 9. STUCK

1. Aptheker, *Intimate Politics*, 2006, 6. This is Aptheker's reading of Zen teacher Bernard Glassman, *Bearing Witness*, 1999.

2. Cooper, *The Last Honest Place in America*, 2004, 09.

3. Aptheker, *Intimate Politics*, 2006, 540.

4. Jeanine Carter (not her real name), interview by authors, March 11, 2001, Reno, NV. All Jeanine Carter quotations are from this interview.

5. Lorde, "Uses of the Erotic," 1984.

6. Freire, *Pedagogy of the Oppressed*, 1986.

7. Remedios Cortez (not her real name), interview by authors, February 13, 2001. Transcript in the possession of the authors. All quotations from Cortez are from this interview.

8. Lorde, "Uses of the Erotic," 1984, 151.

9. Lather, *Getting Smart*, 1991, 63. Patty Lather, the feminist theorist, writes that "all critical inquiry is fundamentally dialogic and involves a mutually educative experience." She argues "for a more collaborative praxis-oriented and advocacy model that acts on the desire for people to gain self-understanding and self-determination both in research and in their daily lives."

10. Linda Elder (not her real name), interview by authors, October 5, 1999, Reno, NV. Transcript in the possession of the authors. All quotations from Linda Elder are from this interview.

CHAPTER 10. BIG TOBACCO RIDES THE STRIP

1. Interview with Teresa Price, November 16, 2006. Transcript in the possession of the authors. All quotations from Teresa Price are from this interview unless otherwise noted.

2. Interview with Remedios Cortez (not her real name), February 13, 2001, Reno, NV. Transcript in the possession of the authors. All quotations from Remedios Cortez are from this interview.

3. Interview with Maxine Everett (not her real name), October 19, 1999, Reno, NV. Transcript in the possession of the authors.

4. Interview with Grace Ling (not her real name), October 8, 1999, Reno, NV. Transcript in the possession of the authors.

5. Ibid.

6. Interview with Connie Hogan (not her real name), May 22, 2000, Reno, NV. Transcript in the possession of the authors.

7. Interview with Cynthia Bowen (not her real name), May 11, 2000, Reno, NV. Transcript in the possession of the authors.

8. Interview with Connie Hogan (not her real name), May 22, 2000, Reno, NV. Transcript in the possession of the authors.

9. Interview with Maxine Everett (not her real name), October 19, 1999, Reno, NV. Transcript in the possession of the authors.

10. U.S. Environmental Protection Agency, 1993.

11. Davis, "Exposure to Environmental Tobacco Smoke," 1998.

12. Ibid.

13. Statement of Michael P. Ericksen, SC.D., Office on Smoking and Health, National Center for Chronic Disease Prevention and Health Promotion, Centers for Disease Control and Prevention before the Committee on Environment and Public Works, U.S. Senate, April 1, 1998. http://epw.senate.gov/105th/eriksen.htm. Data accessed October 19, 2006.

14. Tout and Decker, "Health Hazard Evaluation Report," 1996. See also Curran, "For Casino Workers," 2004.

15. Davis, "Exposure to Environmental Tobacco Smoke," 1998.

16. "A Killer Lurking in the Room," 2001.

17. Davis, "Exposure to Environmental Tobacco Smoke," 1998. See also Eisner, Smith, and Blanc, "Bartenders' Respiratory Health," 1998.

18. Glantz, "Smoke in the Eye," 1999.

19. In November 1998, the attorneys general of forty-six states, including Nevada, signed a Master Settlement Agreement (MSA) with the five largest tobacco companies. The MSA, responding to states' Medicaid lawsuits against the tobacco industry for recovery of tobacco-related health-care costs, exempted the companies from private tort liability regarding harm caused by tobacco use. The companies in exchange agreed to limit certain tobacco marketing practices, as well as to pay the states, in perpetuity, annual payments to compensate them for the medical costs of caring for persons with smoking-related illnesses. The tobacco manufacturers agreed to pay a minimum of $206 billion over the first twenty-five years of the agreement. Nevada received about $374 million from the settlement. See http://www.ag.ca.gov/tobacco/msa.php. Data accessed October 2, 2010.

20. Kluger, Ashes to Ashes, 1996.

21. The Insider, 1999; Grisham, The Runaway Jury, 1996.

22. Tung and Glantz, "Swimming Upstream," 2008, 8.

23. Scoblete, "Sunbeams," 2006, 48.

24. Barbano, "Smoking or Non," 1999.

25. Babula, "Smoking Freedoms at Stake," 2001. The other states were Mississippi, North Carolina, Oklahoma, South Carolina, and Tennessee. See also Tung and Glantz, "Swimming Upstream," 2008.

26. Tung and Glantz, "Swimming Upstream," 2008, 8.

27. Babula, "Smoking Freedoms at Stake," 2001.

28. National Center for Chronic Disease Prevention and Health Promotion; Nevada Highlights. These are 2001 figures. Smoking rates have declined since 2000, and Nevada, instead of first in 2008 was fifteenth in the nation in level of smoking, at 21.2 percent. Tung and Glantz, "Swimming Upstream," 2008, 7.

29. "Second-Hand Smoke Study Expanded to Northern Nevada," 2002. Available at http://www.cigoutlet.net/news/second_hand_smoke_study_expanded _ to_northern_nevada. html.

30. Bynum, "Nevada Tops List of Smoking States," 2000.

31. Babula, "Smoking Freedoms at Stake," 2001.

32. "Second-Hand Smoke Study Expanded to Northern Nevada," 2002. This cost the state $253 per capita on smoking-attributable direct medical expenditures. See National Center for Chronic Disease Prevention and Health Promotion; Nevada Highlights.

33. "Survey Predicts Nevada Would Lose Big If Casino Smoking Were Prohibited," 1997.

34. Dobra, "Economic Impacts," 1996.

35. OSHA Communications Report, 1996a. Philip Morris Tobacco Papers. July 18. Bates No. 2061897534/7535. http://legacy.library.ucsf.edu/tid/gqw47d00. Data accessed October 27, 2006.

36. OSHA Communications Report, 1996b. Philip Morris Tobacco Papers, August 1. Bates No. 2061897515/7516. http://legacy.library.ucsf.edu/tid/cqw47d00. Data accessed October 27, 2006.

37. Dobra, "Economic Impacts," 1996, 11. "After five years, the cumulative loss in casino final demand would be $1.175 billion compared with the baseline scenario," Dobra concluded. "This amount is equal to 37 percent of the $3.209 billion of growth experienced by the sector in the baseline scenario."

38. Sorrells, OSHA Communications Report, 1996.

39. Interview with John Dobra, November 7, 2006, Reno, NV. Notes from the interview in the possession of the authors.

40. Tung and Glantz, "Swimming Upstream," 2008.

41. E-mail from Janice McDaniel, November 25, 1997. "Gaming Convention/Vegas." Philip Morris Tobacco Papers, Bates No. 2070292705A. http://legacy.library.ucsf.edu/tid/bjo16c00. Data accessed November 1, 2006

42. Letter from Robert W. Meyne to Frank J. Fahrenkopf Jr. March 6, 1996. Philip Morris Tobacco Papers, Bates No. 51446 2522. http://legacy.library.ucsf.edu/tid/fjo40d00/. Data accessed October 11, 2006.

43. "Potential Impact of Smoking Bans on the Gaming Industry—Draft." March 1996. Philip Morris Tobacco Papers, Bates No. 51446 2599. http://legacy.library.ucsf.edu/tid/fjo40d00/. Data accessed October 12, 2006.

44. Consolidated Safety Services, Inc. January 1, 1995. "Addressing Indoor Air Quality and Smoking Bans in the Gaming Industry." R. J. Reynolds Collection, Tobacco Papers, Bates Number 514462530/2533, p. 4. http://legacy.library.ucsf.edu/tid/bjo16c00. Data accessed August 29, 2006.

45. E-mail from Janice McDaniel, November 25, 1997. "Gaming Convention/Vegas." Philip Morris Tobacco Papers, Bates No. 2070292705A. http://legacy.library.ucsf.edu/tid/bjo16c00. Data accessed November 1, 2006.

46. Ibid.

47. Mandel and Glantz, "Hedging Their Bets," 2004, 272.

48. "Workplace Study Risks," 2006.

49. Babula, "Smoking Freedoms at Stake," 2001.

50. For an excellent study of the history of legislative efforts for tobacco control in Nevada see Tung and Glantz, "Swimming Upstream," 2008.

51. Ibid., 10–11. Others receiving over $10,000 were assemblypersons Richard Perkins-D ($16,300); Barbara Buckley-D ($15,700); Joseph Dini Jr.-D ($14,750); Lynn Hettrick-R ($11,500); and state senator Bill Raggio-R ($13,800).

52. Whaley, "Bill Would Mandate Nonsmoking Rules," 2001.

53. Interview with Tony Badillo, November 16, 2006, Las Vegas, NV. Transcript in the possession of the authors. All quotations from Tony Badillo are from this interview unless otherwise noted.

54. Macy, "Where There's Smoke There Are Profits," 1997b.

55. *Badillo v. American Tobacco Co.,* 202 F.R.D. 261 (D. Nev. July 2, 2001).

56. *Palmer v. Del Webb's High Sierra 838 P.2d 4355* (Nev. 1992).

57. Ibid.

58. Ryan, "Dealers Take Case against Tobacco to Supreme Court," 2000.

59. Ibid.

60. "Class-Action Denied in Four Tobacco Suits," 2001.

61. Ibid.

62. Tsuboi, "Smoke Free Casinos?," 2005.

63. Pritsos et al., "Secondhand Smoke and Nevada Casino Workers," 2006.

64. "Workplace Study Risks," 2006.

65. Interview with Chris Pritsos, October 9, 2006, Reno, NV. Transcript in the possession of the authors. All Pritsos quotes unless otherwise cited are from this interview.

66. Interview with Katherine Robinson, November 16, 2006, Las Vegas, NV. Transcript in the possession of the authors.

67. U.S. Department of Health and Human Services, 2006. *The Health Consequences of Involuntary Exposure to Tobacco Smoke: A Report of the Surgeon General.* For the full report see http://www.surgeongeneral.gov/library/secondhandsmoke/. Data accessed November 5, 2006.

68. Packham, "Senate Bill 372," 2009.

69. For the study, 124 casino dealers at Bally's, Caesars Palace, and Paris Las Vegas wore portable pumps measuring the level of tobacco smoke in the air while they were working, and 114 additional dealers gave urine samples before and after shifts. See Achutan et al., "Environmental and Biological Assessment," 2009. See also Benston, "Study Arms Smoking Foes," 2009a; and "Smoking Study Capped Caesars Dealer's Long, Lonely Fight," 2009b.

70. More information about smoking in Nevada and about smoking in casinos may be found at the website of Americans for Non-Smokers Rights, http://www.nosmoke.org.

CHAPTER 11. CROSSING OVER TO THE OTHER SIDE

1. "Careers/Human Resources." Harrah's Entertainment, Inc., website. Available at http://www.harrahs.com/harrahs-corporate/careers-department-overview. Data accessed June 29, 2007.

2. "Careers." Harrah's Entertainment, Inc., website. Available at http://www.harrahs.com/harrahs-corporate/careers-home.html. Data accessed June 29, 2007.

3. Wilmott and Hailey, "How to Win with Harrah's," 2002. Harrah's "IT commitment" (see Shook, *Jackpot!,* 2003) is what Marc Cooper in *The Last Honest Place in America* describes as "the science of decision-making prediction." He writes, "The newest trend in casino technology [is] computer programs that go far beyond just achieving how much a client has gambled.... [They take] information not only from the casino floor, but also from the front desk, hotel restaurants, and from the players club cards and instantaneously merge and integrate it into an intimately detailed individual profile. The same software tracks hold—or win—percentages on every table and machine, the popularity of different types and brands of slots, and allows casino management to 'see,' in real time, from a single monitoring computer which machines slot players are frequenting or shunning. From the central computer, casino managers can track up-to-the-second playing and betting patterns of an individual player and can immediately dispatch 'hosts' to rush over and offer them comps, rewards, and freebies" (2004, 130–131).

4. To protect their identity, we have used pseudonyms for all management women. In some cases, interview venues have been omitted and biographical information (including the title of their management positions and their casino's location) has been changed.

5. Barbara Bradford (not her real name), first interview, May 24, 2001. Transcript in the possession of the authors. All Barbara Bradford quotations are from her first or second interview. See note 9.

6. Three out of five of the study's management women did not have children, which raises the question of the impact of gender on women's management careers. Rothman and Davis (2002, 7) point out that it is women who make up the base of Las Vegas's job pyramid. They include 15,000 servers/waitresses and 10,000 room cleaners/maids, the two largest job categories in southern Nevada. At the upper levels, according to Karen Weber in her 1996 study of gender distribution in Las Vegas casino management, women hold 23.7 percent of senior executive management appointments and only 1.9 percent of top executive positions (1998, 432). Weber's findings echo the observations of focus group members who reported that women were disproportionately represented in human resources and middle management but that their upward mobility overall was limited. Hard work, communication and interpersonal skills, job knowledge, and personality were all perceived as important for career advancement among the management women in her study. Weber points out the importance of mentorship of top management women to balance the influence of "old boys" networks. The statistics for her study were derived from an analysis of Opton's 1997 *Casino Business Directory*. See Weber, "Women's Career Progression," 1998 and Opton, *Casino Business Directory*, 1997. Following Weber's example, we used the *Casino City's 2006 Gaming Business Directory* to look at gender distribution in casino management at six of Reno's high-end casinos (Atlantis, Eldorado, Harrah's, John Ascuaga's Nugget, Peppermill, and Silver Legacy) and found that out of the 32 percent of women in management overall, 10.4 percent were at the top upper-management level (general manager, assistant general manager, and vice president). At the Nevada properties of three corporate giants—Boyd Gaming Corporation, Harrah's Entertainment, Inc., and MGM Mirage—the percentage of women in management was essentially the same (36 percent, 34 percent, and 34 percent, respectively). MGM had the highest number of women in top upper management, twenty-one total, all vice presidents of specific casino operations; Harrah's was next with sixteen women; and Boyd Gaming was last with only three women (one general manager and two vice presidents). Of the three properties, Harrah's had the largest number of women in top upper-management positions, with two general managers, one president, one casino manager, and one assistant general manager. (See "USA Casinos and Cardrooms—Nevada" in the *Casino City's Gaming Business Directory* 2006, 83–153.) Additionally, women often have to delay their careers because of family responsibilities and the need to take time off to care for children or elderly parents (four of our management women either cared for children or parents). Others are forced to have little contact with their families (one management woman fit this profile). The two upper-management women in our study told us that management women with family responsibilities were greatly disadvantaged in getting ahead; Barbara Bradford could think of only one woman in upper management in her casino who had children.

7. Barbara Bradford's first casino job was in the same casino where she held a top management position during this interview.

8. Up until then, women dealers were not allowed to deal craps. Bending over a craps table, casino management claimed, damaged women's reproductive organs.

9. Second interview of Barbara Bradford conducted on the telephone by one author, August 22, 2007.

10. Robert Jackall, *Moral Mazes*, 1988, 20) describes the modern corporation as having a hierarchical authority structure in which "details are pushed down and credit is

pulled up," stating that it is typical to have both centralized and decentralized authority. In his words: "Power is concentrated at the top in the person of the chief executive officer (CEO) and is simultaneously decentralized; that is, responsibility for decisions and profits is pushed as far down the organizational line as possible" (17).

11. This included base salary, stock and option awards, nonincentive plan compensation, and "all other compensation." See Harrah's Annual Report—Form 10K (2007, 39), filed March 10, 2007, for year ending December 31, 2006. Our own investigation of the 2006 annual financial reports of three casino corporations—Boyd Gaming, Harrah's Entertainment, and MGM Mirage—provided additional evidence of the salaries paid to top executives of successful casino corporations. The total compensation (including base salary, stock rewards, bonus, option awards, nonincentive plan compensation, and other compensation) paid to the chairman/CEO and president/COO of Boyd Gaming in 2006, a corporation with revenues of $2,192.6 million for that year, was $7,683,242 and $2,997,392, respectively. The sole woman among the company's executive officers—a vice chairman/ senior vice president—was compensated $1,443,054 that year. Harrah's Entertainment, Inc., whose 2006 revenue was $9,679.9 million, paid its chairman/president/CEO, as was previously noted, $14,239,845 and its COO, $6,899,520. Its senior vice president and brand manager, the only woman among its executive officers, received $1,459,860. Lastly, at MGM Mirage, a corporation with 2006 revenue of $7,275.9 million, the chairman/ CEO was compensated $15,687,121 and its president/CFO/treasurer, $10,320,515. These figures come from each company's 2007 proxy statement of 2006 earnings. Available at http://www.sec.gov/Archives/edgar/data. Data accessed October 9, 2007.

12. As reported by the Nevada Department of Employment Training and Rehabilitation (DETR). Overall, the annual mean management salary in Nevada casinos in 2008 was $80,382. In the Las Vegas/Paradise area for the same time period, top executives were paid on average $133,810 and general and operations managers $137,465 in the Reno/Sparks area, one of the only management positions in which the Reno/Sparks area ranked higher. Much lower salaries were paid to middle managers, and they too varied across areas. In 2008, gaming managers, for example, were reported to have mean salaries of $68,049 in Las Vegas and $57,363 in Reno/Sparks. In contrast, financial managers earned on average $71,776 in Las Vegas and $80,633 in Reno/Sparks, another position in which mean salaries were reported higher in Reno/Sparks area. (See Occupational Wages, Nevada Workforce Informer, Nevada Department of Employment, Training, and Rehabilitation (DETR) Research and Analysis Bureau website, http://www.nevada workforce.com/. Data accessed August 4, 2008.) These numbers reveal that there are some income differences in management positions in Nevada's two urban locations, with Las Vegas corporate executives and upper managers usually earning slightly higher salaries. They also reflect differences between middle- and upper-management salaries in general. However, there are even greater differences between the salaries of middle and upper managers and those of lower managers. For example, gaming supervisors, a lower-management position, were reported to have annual salaries in both the Las Vegas/ Paradise area and Reno/Sparks area of around $36,000. Compare this with a dealer's earnings in a high-end casino in Las Vegas, where, according to Marc Cooper, a dealer can make as much as $225 a shift in tips. (See Cooper, *The Last Honest Place in America*, 2004, 108.) Earning even $175 a shift for fifty weeks would result in an annual salary of $88,000. Although lower-management supervisors on average are paid higher wages than dealers, they don't earn tips, so their overall earnings are lower. Moreover, as one dealer told us, the corporate demands on supervisors are greater than those on many of the rank-and-file workers. Therefore, it was not surprising to hear veteran dealer, Remedios Cortez, say "Nobody wants to be a supervisor because [dealers] make twice as much money as what [supervisors] make without the headache." She reported that turnover among

supervisors was so high casinos were having difficulty filling the positions. Still, managers do better than most workers. According to economist Paul Osterman: "In 2003, just under 6.5 million Americans worked as managers, and they earned an average annual salary of $83,400, while the average for all workers was $36,520. The unemployment rate for managers that year was 2.9 percent, less than half the overall employment rate of 6 percent. Clearly, managers are a privileged group." See Osterman, "The Changing Employment Circumstances," 2006, 193.

13. The middle-management salary estimate is based on the annual salary of one of the study's middle managers the first year on the job. This is in the same range as gaming managers' salaries, noted above, listed on the Nevada Workforce Informer website at around $60,000 in 2008 in both Las Vegas and Reno. The estimate for a lower-management salary is based on Nevada gaming supervisors' 2008 mean annual salary. See Nevada Workforce Informer at Nevada Department of Employment, Training, and Rehabilitation (DETR). Available at http://www.nevadaworkforce.com/. Data accessed January 18, 2009.

14. Jerry Mander writes about the euphemistic language used by global corporations to justify employee downsizing, including "flattening the corporate structure" for eliminating middle-management jobs; "efficiency" for replacing rank-and-file workers with machines; and "competitiveness" for lowering wages to match low-wage foreign competitors (1996a, 10). These cost-saving measures are also described by Cooper, *The Last Honest Place in America*, 2004; Eadington, "Preface," 1999; and Rothman, "Colony, Capital, and Casino," 2002.

15. Interview with Robert Brown (not his real name), July 2000, Reno, NV. Notes in the possession of the authors.

16. Global capitalism has also been referred to as the New Economy and neoliberal or postindustrial capitalism. For a comprehensive description of the nature of work under global capitalism, see Lawler III and O'Toole, *America at Work*, 2006; and O'Toole and Lawler III, *The New American Workplace*, 2006. For more political analyses, see Mander and Goldsmith, *The Case Against the Global Economy*, 1996; Sassen, *Globalization and Its Discontents*, 1998; Sassen, "The Excesses of Globalisation," 2001; Sassen, "Global Cities and Survival Circuits," 2002; and DeVault, *People at Work*, 2008.

17. Lawler III and O'Toole, *America at Work*, 2006; O'Toole and Lawler III, *The New American Workplace*, 2006; Mander and Goldsmith, *The Case Against the Global Economy*, 1996; and Sassen, *Globalization and Its Discontents*, 1998; Sassen, "The Excesses of Globalisation," 2001; Sassen, "Global Cities and Survival Circuits," 2002.

18. Interview with Carol Hancock (not her real name), May 14, 2001, Reno, NV. Transcript in the possession of the authors. All Carol Hancock quotations are from this interview.

19. The EPA director's story is presented earlier in the chapter.

20. Kunda and Ailon-Souday, "Managers, Markets, and Ideologies," 2005, 210, quoted in Osterman, "The Changing Employment Circumstances of Managers," 2006, 193.

21. Unlike Barbara Bradford, Carol Hancock was a mother, and this had delayed her career.

22. Mander, "The Rules of Corporate Behavior," 1996b, 316.

23. Interview with Sharon Nesbit (not her real name), May 14, 2001. Transcript in the possession of the authors. All quotations from Sharon Nesbit are from this interview.

24. This highly touted management principle first appeared in a 1994 *Harvard Business Review* in an article written by five members of the Harvard Business School, including Gary Loveman, the current CEO of Harrah's Entertainment, Inc. (See Heskett et al., "Putting the Service-Profit Chain to Work," 1994.) It is based on the premise that "profits and growth are stimulated primarily by customer loyalty. Loyalty is the direct result of customer satisfaction. Satisfaction is largely influenced by the value of the service provided

to customers. Value is created by satisfied, loyal, and productive employees." Quoted in Shook, *Jackpot!*, 2003, 174.

25. Sharon Nesbit, comparing job vacancies in Las Vegas to Reno, told us that for each of the large casinos in Las Vegas there were ten or fewer job vacancies at any given time, whereas in Reno, it was not unusual for one hundred or more positions to be open at a single casino.

26. See note 11.

27. The other women's ages ranged from forty-eight to fifty-four. Barbara Bradford also attended college but, unlike Kate Rodriguez, didn't graduate and worked her way up to the management level.

28. Interview with Kate Rodriguez (not her real name), March 30, 2001. Transcript in the possession of the authors. All quotations from Kate Rodriguez are from this interview.

29. Corporations based on neoliberal economics, as DeVault (*People at Work,* 2008) and Acker ("Hierarchies, Jobs, Bodies," 1990) have pointed out, treat workers as though they are unencumbered by any extraneous needs or limitations. They argue that this disproportionately disadvantages women workers, who are often also wives and mothers.

30. Jackall, *Moral Mazes,* 1988, 44.

31. The full quote is: "In relations of power, there is necessarily the possibility of resistance, for if there were no possibility of resistance—of violent resistance, of escape, of ruse, of strategies that reverse the situation—there would be no relations of power" (Foucault, *Politics, Philosophy, Culture,* 1988, 12), quoted in Foote and Frank ("Foucault and Therapy," 1999, 173). bell hooks also reminds us that marginalization can foster resistance and thereby challenge power by providing "a space for radical openness which allows the creation of a counter-hegemonic politics" (hooks, *Yearning Race, Gender, and Cultural Politics,* 1990, quoted in DeVault, *People at Work,* 2008, 136–137, as summarized by Rose, *Feminism and Geography,* 1993, 156).

32. O'Toole and Lawler III described it as "creative destruction," a concept found in the writings of Mikhail Bakunin and Friedrich Nietzsche and popularized by economist Joseph Schumpeter who used the term to describe the process of transformation that accompanies radical innovation (2006, 5).

33. Ibid.

34. Mander, "The Rules of Corporate Behavior," 1996b, 314.

35. Harrah's Entertainment, Inc., website, Career—Human Resources. Available at http://www.harrahs.com/harrahs-corporate/careers-department-overview. Data accessed June 29, 2007.

36. See Ehrenreich, *Nickel and Dimed,* 2001, 22.

37. See Mander, "The Rules of Corporate Behavior," 1996b, 310.

38. Ibid. As Mander has pointed out, corporate law designates corporations as *fictitious persons,* with the right to buy and sell property and to sue for injuries, slander, and libel, and their freedom of speech is protected under the Constitution's First Amendment. The recent Supreme Court decision—*Citizens United v. Federal Election Commission,* No. 08–205—lifting restrictions on corporations' contributions to political campaigns was argued on the basis of the First Amendment.

CHAPTER 12. CONCLUSION

1. Authors' interview with Magdalena Ruiz (not her real name), April 29, 1999, Reno, NV. Transcript in the possession of the authors. All quotations from Magdalena Ruiz are from this interview.

2. See "Living Wage Calculator." Available at http://www.livingwage.geog.psu.edu/. Data accessed February 10, 2010.

3. See Acker, "Gender, Capitalism and Globalization," 2004, 17–41. Acker introduced the term "non-responsibility" to describe global capitalism's increasing separation of work and family and how this schism disadvantages women workers in particular because, even though they now comprise a majority of the workforce, they still assume most of the care of children and the elderly.

4. Frank Rich explores this divide in "Hollywood's Brilliant Coda," 2009.

5. DuBois and Ruiz, *Unequal Sisters,* 1990, xiii.

6. *Fool's Gold,* 2009.

7. See "Access and the Uninsured," 2006; see also *Fool's Gold,* 2009.

8. *Fool's Gold,* 2009. This in effect leaves the state to foot the bill for medical care in the form of increased support for public hospitals and emergency room services, a kind of subsidy, in Nevada economist Jeff Waddoups' calculation, for businesses, including very wealthy gaming corporations, who decline to provide employees health benefits at reasonable cost. Waddoups, "Public Subsidies of Low-Wage Employment," 2006.

9. Baldwin, *No Name in the Street,* 1972, 55.

10. Interview with Pam Phillips (not her real name), November 8, 2001, Las Vegas, NV. Transcript in the possession of the authors. All Pam Phillips quotes are from this interview.

11. Zinn, "The Optimism of Uncertainty," 2006, 270.

"A Killer Lurking in the Room: Serious Health Effects of Passive Smoking." 2001. ABC News Internet Ventures, 5 July. Available at http://kiiss.org/home/articles/article_lurking.html. Data accessed October 11, 2006.

"About Culinary Workers Union Local 226." Culinary Workers Union Local 226 website. Available at http://www.culinaryunion226.org/about.asp. Data accessed September 17, 2010.

"About Us." International Union of Gaming Employees. Available at http://www.iuge.net/about_us/about.htm. Data accessed July 10, 2005.

"Access and the Uninsured." 2006. Great Basin Primary Care Association. Available at http://www.gbpca.org/uninsured/. Data accessed June 13, 2009.

Achutan, Chandran, Christine West, Charles Mueller, Yvonne Boudreau, et al. 2009. "Environmental and Biological Assessment of Environmental Tobacco Smoke Exposure among Casino Dealers." Atlanta, GA: Department of Health and Human Services, Centers for Disease Control and Prevention. *Health Hazard Evaluation Report,* HETA 2005–0076; 2005–0201-3080.

Acker, Joan. 1990. "Hierarchies, Jobs, Bodies: A Theory of Gendered Organizations." *Gender and Society* 4:139–158.

———. 2004. "Gender, Capitalism and Globalization." *Critical Sociology* 30(1): 17–41.

———. 2006. *Class Questions: Feminist Answers.* Lanham, MD: Rowman and Littlefield.

Alexander, Courtney. 2002. "Rise to Power: The Recent History of the Culinary Union in Las Vegas." In *The Grit beneath the Glitter: Tales from the Real Las Vegas,* edited by Hal K. Rothman and Mike Davis, 145–175. Berkeley: University of California Press.

Americans for Non-Smokers Rights website. Available at http://www.nosmoke.org.

America's Health Rankings. 2005. United Health Foundation. Available at http://www.unitedhealthfoundation.org/shr2005. Data accessed August 30, 2006.

"Annual Gaming Revenue." University of Nevada, Las Vegas Center for Gaming Research. Available at http://gaming.unlv.edu/abstract/nvstate_revenues.html. Data accessed September 27, 2010.

Appelbaum, Eileen, Annette Bernhardt, and Richard J. Murnane. 2003a. "Low-Wage America: An Overview." In *Low Wage America: How Employers Are Reshaping Opportunity in the Workplace,* edited by Eileen Appelbaum, Annette Bernhardt, and Richard J. Murnane, 1–29. New York: Russell Sage Foundation.

———, eds. 2003b. *Low Wage America: How Employers Are Reshaping Opportunity in the Workplace.* New York: Russell Sage Foundation.

Aptheker, Bettina. 2006. *Intimate Politics: How I Grew Up Red, Fought for Free Speech, and Became a Feminist Rebel.* Emeryville, CA: Seal Press.

Arriaza, Gilberto. 1997. "Grace Under Pressure: Immigration Families and the Nation-State." *Social Justice* 24:6–15.

Avery, Dianne, and Marion Crain. 2007. "Branded: Corporate Image, Sexual Stereotyping, and the New Face of Capitalism." *Duke Journal of Gender, Law and Policy* 14(13): 13–123.

Babula, Joelle. 2001. "Smoking Freedoms at Stake." *Las Vegas Review-Journal,*
    21 March. Available at http://www.reviewjournal.com/lvrj_home/2001/
    Mar/15637012.html. Data accessed July 10, 2007.
Badillo v. American Tobacco Co., 202 F.R.D. 261 (D. Nev. July 2, 2001).
Baker, Arlene Holt. 2009. "A Woman's Place Is in Her Union." In *The Shriver Report: A
    Woman's Nation Changes Everything.* A Report by Maria Shriver and the Center
    for American Progress, 236–237. Washington, DC: Center for American Prog-
    ress.
Baldwin, James. 1972. *No Name in the Street.* New York: Dial Press.
Barbano, Andrew. 1999. "Smoking or Non." *Nevada Labor.* Available at http://www.
    nevadalabor.com/barbwire/barb07/barb3-2-90.html. Data accessed July 10,
    2007.
Barbwire website. Available at http://www.nevadalor.com/barbwire.
Barnet, Richard, and John Cavanagh. 1994. *Global Dreams: Imperial Corporations and
    the New World Order.* New York: Simon and Schuster.
Bartlett, Katharine T. 1994. "Only Girls Wear Barrettes: Dress and Appearance
    Standards, Community Norms, and Workplace Equality." *Michigan Law
    Review* 92:2541.
"Bellagio, Mirage Poker Rooms Going Smokeless." *Gambling Magazine.* Available at
    http://gamblingmagazine.com/articles/27/27–1233.htm. Data accessed August 22,
    2006.
Benjamin, Caren. 2000. "Dealers' Illness Called Frequent." *Las Vegas Review Journal,*
    9 January. Available at http://www.reviewjournal.com/lvrj_home/2000/Jan-09-
    Sun-2000/news/12574069.html. Data accessed February 20, 2010.
Benston, Liz. 2009a. "Study Arms Smoking Foes." *Las Vegas Sun,* 7 May. Available at
    http://www.lasvegassun.com/news/2009/may/07/study-arms-smoking-foes.
    Data accessed June 15, 2009.
——. 2009b. "Smoking Study Capped Caesars Dealer's Long, Lonely Fight." *Las Vegas
    Sun,* 12 May. Available at http://www.lasvegassun.com/news/2009/may/12/
    longtime-dealer-feels-vindicated-smoke-study/. Data accessed June 15, 2009.
Benz, Dorothee. 2004. "Labor's Ace in the Hole: Casino Organizing in Las Vegas." *New
    Political Science* 36:525–550.
Bergeron, Suzanne. 2001. "Political Economy Discourses of Globalization and Femi-
    nist Politics." *Signs: Journal of Women in Culture and Society* 26(4): 983–1007.
Bernhardt, Annette, Heather Boushey, Laura Dresser, and Chris Tilly, eds. 2008. *The
    Gloves-Off Economy: Workplace Standards at the Bottom of America's Labor Mar-
    ket.* Champaign, IL: Labor and Employment Relations Association Series.
Bernhardt, Annette, Laura Dresser, and Erin Hatten. 2003a. "Moving Hotels to the
    High Road: Strategies that Help Workers and Firms Succeed." Madison, WI:
    Center on Wisconsin Strategy (COWS). Available at http://www.cows.org/pdf/
    rp-hotel-03.pdf. Data accessed July 27, 2007.
——. 2003b. "The Coffee Pot Wars: Unions and Firm Restructuring in the Hotel
    Industry." In *Low Wage America: How Employers Are Reshaping Opportunity in
    the Workplace,* edited by Eileen Appelbaum, Annette Bernhardt, and Richard J.
    Murnane, 33–76. New York: Russell Sage Foundation.
Binkley, Christina. 2001. "In Drive to Unionize, Casino Dealers Defy a Longtime Las Vegas
    Tradition." *Wall Street Journal,* 6 March. Available at http://www.iuge.net/news/2001/
    in_drive_to_unionize_casino_dealers_defy.htm. Data accessed September 17, 2006.
Blake, William. 1971. "Auguries of Innocence." In *Poems of William Blake,* edited by
    W. H. Stevenson. London: Longman Group Limited.
Blau, Joel. 1999. *Illusions of Prosperity: America's Working Families in an Age of Eco-
    nomic Insecurity.* New York: Oxford University Press.

Blevins, Audie, and Katerine Jensen. 1998. "Gambling as a Community Development Quick Fix." *The Annals of the American Academy of Political and Social Science,* 556:109–123.

Bloom, Michael, and Alison, Campbell. 2002. "Success by Design: What Works in Workforce Development." Conference Board of Canada Report #380-02. Ottawa, Canada: The Conference Board of Canada.

Bonacich, Edna, and Richard P. Appelbaum. 2000. *Behind the Label: Inequality in the Los Angeles Apparel Industry.* Berkeley: University of California Press.

Boushey, Heather. 2009. "The New Breadwinners." In *The Shriver Report: A Woman's Nation Changes Everything.* A Report by Maria Shriver and the Center for American Progress, edited by Heather Boushey and Ann O'Leary, 31–67. Washington, DC: Center for American Progress.

Boushey, Heather, and Ann O'Leary. 2009a. "Executive Summary." In *The Shriver Report: A Woman's Nation Changes Everything.* A Report by Maria Shriver and the Center for American Progress, edited by Heather Boushey and Ann O'Leary, 17–27. Washington, DC: Center for American Progress.

———, eds. 2009b. *The Shriver Report: A Woman's Nation Changes Everything.* A Report by Maria Shriver and the Center for American Progress. Washington, DC: Center for American Progress.

Brammer, Janet. 1974. "Sarah Hughes, Agent, Loves People and Job." *Las Vegas Sun,* 13 January.

Brecher, Jeremy, Tim Costello, and Brendon Smith. 2000. *Globalization from Below: The Power of Solidarity.* Cambridge, MA: South End Press.

Brecht, Bertolt. 1993. "The World's One Hope." In *Almost Forgetting: Twentieth–Century Poetry of Witness,* edited by Carolyn Forché, 219. New York: W. W. Norton.

Brownell, Judi. 1998. "Striking a Balance: The Future of Work and Family Issues in the Hospitality Industry." *Marriage & Family Review* 28(1/2): 109–123.

Burbank, Jeff. 2000. *License to Steal: Nevada's Gaming Control System in the Megaresort Age.* Reno: University of Nevada Press.

Butler, Gregory. 2004. "Casino." *LaborNet.* Available at http://www.labornet.org/news/1004/casinos.htm. Data accessed July 11, 2005.

Bynum, Russ. 2000. "Nevada Tops List of Smoking States." *Associated Press,* 2 November. Available at http://www.mindfully.org/Health/Nevada-Top-Smoking-State.htm. Data accessed August 30, 2006.

Canty, Hattie, interview by Claytee D. White. 2000. Las Vegas Women Oral History Project, University of Nevada, Las Vegas.

Cappelli, Peter. 2006. "Changing Career Paths and Their Implications." In *America at Work: Choices and Challenges,* edited by Edward E. Lawler, III and James O'Toole, 211–226. New York: Palgrave Macmillan.

Carbado, Devon, Catherin Fisk, and Mitu Gulati. 2007. "Making Makeup Matter." *Duke Journal Gender of Law & Policy* 14(1): 1–16.

"Careers/Human Resources." Harrah's Entertainment, Inc., website. Available at http://www.harrahs.com/harrahs-corporate/careers-department-overview. Data accessed June 29, 2007.

Carroll vs. Talman Federal Savings and Loan Ass'n, 604 F.2d 1028, 1033 (7th Cir. 1979).

Casino. 1995. Martin Scorsese, director. Universal Pictures. Film.

Casino City's Gaming Business Directory: Casinos, Cardrooms, Horse Tracks, Dog Tracks, Cruise Ships, and Property Owners. 2006. Newton, MA: Carson City Press.

"Casino Dealer Organizing." 2009. AFL-CIO Executive Council Statement, May 5. AFL-CIO. Available at http://www.aflcio.org/aboutus/thisistheaflcio/ecouncil/. Data accessed June 23, 2009.

"Casino Dealers in Nevada Vote Union." 2007. *Unbossed.com*. May 22. Available at http://www.unbossed.com/index.php?itemid-1527. Data accessed June 23, 2009.

Castaneda, Carlos. 1972. *Journey to Ixtlan*. New York: Washington Square Press.

Castleman, Deke. 2004. *Whale Hunt in the Desert: The Secret Las Vegas of Superhost Steve Cyr*. Las Vegas: Huntington Press.

Chambon, Adrienne S., Allan Irving, and Laura Epstein, eds. 1999. *Reading Foucault for Social Work*. New York: Columbia University Press.

Chandler, Susan. 2001. "Working Hard, Living Poor: A Living Wage Study for Nevada." Las Vegas: Progressive Leadership Alliance of Nevada (PLAN).

Chandler, Susan, and Jill B. Jones. 2003a. "Because a Better World is Possible: Women Casino Workers, Union Activism, and the Creation of a Just Work Place." *Journal of Sociology and Social Welfare* 30(4): 57–78.

——. 2003b. "You Have to Do It for the People Coming: Union Organizing and the Transformation of Immigrant Women Workers." *Affilia: Journal of Women and Social Work* 18(3): 254–271.

——. 2006. "Now I Can't Wait for Tomorrow: Immigrant Latina Leaders in Unionized Nevada Casinos." *Border-Lines: Journal of the Latino Research Center* 1(1): 70–88.

Chang, Grace. 2000. *Disposable Domestics: Immigrant Women Workers in the Global Economy*. Cambridge: South End Press.

Chereb, Sandra. 2000. "Waitresses Want to Give Shoe Rule the Boot," *Nevada Appeal*, May 16. Available at http://www.lasvegassun.com/casino-cocktail-waitresses-want-to-give-shoe-rule. Data accessed September 20, 2008.

Christensen, Jon. 1995. "Learning from Las Vegas." *High Country News* 27(6): 14–15.

——. 2001. "Rouge Rogue," *Mother Jones*, March/April. Available at http://mother-jones.com/politics/2001/02/rouge-rogue. Data accessed June 24, 2004.

"Citizenship Project Does Brisk Business." 2006. *The Culinary Worker*. Culinary Workers Newsletter. Las Vegas: Culinary Union.

"Class-Action Denied in Four Tobacco Suits." 2001. Fox News. 30 August. Available at http://www.foxnews.com/story/0,2933,28850,00.html. Data accessed October 1, 2010.

Cobble, Dorothy Sue. 1991. *Dishing It Out: Waitresses and their Unions in the Twentieth Century*. Urbana: University of Illinois Press.

——. 2004. *The Other Women's Movement: Workplace Justice and Social Rights in Modern America*. Princeton, NJ: Princeton University Press.

Collins, Jane L. 2003. *Threads: Gender, Labor, and Power in the Global Apparel Industry*. Chicago: University of Chicago Press.

Consolidated Safety Services, Inc. January 1, 1995. "Addressing Indoor Air Quality and Smoking Bans in the Gaming Industry." R. J. Reynolds Collection, Tobacco Papers, Bates Number 514462530/2533, 4. Available at http://legacy.library.ucsf.edu/tid/bjo16c00. Data accessed August 29, 2006.

Cooper, Marc. 1997. "Labor Deals a New Hand." *The Nation*, March 24:11–16.

——. 2004. *The Last Honest Place in America: Paradise and Perdition in the New Las Vegas*. New York: Nation Books.

Craig, Elizabeth F., and Douglas T. Hall. 2006. "Bringing Careers Back in the Changing Landscape of Careers in American Corporations Today." In *America at Work: Choices and Challenges*, edited by Edward E. Lawler, III and James O'Toole, 131–152. New York: Palgrave Macmillan.

Cravey, Altha J. 1998. *Women and Work in Mexico's Maquiladoras*. London: Rowman & Littlefield.

"Creating Luxury, Enduring Pain: How Hotel Work is Hurting Housekeepers." 2006. Detroit, MI: UNITE HERE.

Culinary Training Academy website. Available at http://www.theculinaryacademy.org/demand.htm.

Curran, John. 2004. "For Casino Workers, Study Accents Hazards of Secondhand Smoke." *Las Vegas Sun,* 29 October. Available at http://www.lasvegassun.com/news/2004/oct/29/for-casino-workers-study-accents-hazard-of-secondh/. Data accessed September 20, 2008.

Dandurand, Lawrence, and J. Kent Pinney. 1999. "Structural Dynamics in the Las Vegas Casino Gaming Market." In *The Business of Gaming: Economic and Management Issues,* edited by William R. Eadington and Judy A. Cornelius, 45–62. Reno, NV: Institute for the Study of Gambling and Commercial Gaming.

Davis, Ronald M. 1998. "Exposure to Environmental Tobacco Smoke." *Journal of the American Medical Association* 280:1947–1949. Editorial.

Denton, Sally, and Roger Morris. 2001. *The Money and the Power: The Making of Las Vegas and Its Hold on America, 1947–2000.* New York: Alfred A. Knopf.

DeVault, Marjorie L., ed. 2008. *People at Work: Life, Power, and Social Inclusion in the New Economy.* New York: New York University Press.

De Volo, Lorraine Bayard. 2003. "Service and Surveillance: Infrapolitics at Work among Casino Cocktail Waitresses." *Social Politics* 10:346–376.

Diamond, Irene and Lee Quinby, eds. 1988. *Feminism & Foucault: Reflections on Resistance.* Boston: Northeastern University Press.

Dirlik, Arif. 1994. *After the Revolution: Waking to Global Capitalism.* Hanover, NH: University Press of New England.

Dobra, John L. 1996. "Economic Impacts of the Proposed OSHA Smoking Ban on the State of Nevada." Philip Morris Tobacco Papers. Available at http://tobaccodocuments.org/pm/2072360688–0711.html. Data accessed June 10, 2007.

DuBois, Ellen Carol, and Vicki L. Ruiz, eds. 1990. *Unequal Sisters: A Multicultural Reader in U.S. Women's History.* New York: Routledge.

Dunston, Darlene. 2002. *Women of the Strip: A Gendered History of Las Vegas.* University of Hawaii, unpublished masters thesis.

Eadington, William R. 1999. "Preface." In *The Business of Gaming: Economic and Management Issues,* edited by William R. Eadington and Judy A. Cornelius, xv–xx. Reno, NV: Institute for the Study of Gambling and Commercial Gaming.

Eadington, William R., and Judy A. Cornelius, eds. 1999. *The Business of Gaming: Economic and Management Issues.* Reno, NV: Institute for the Study of Gambling and Commercial Gaming.

Earley, Pete. 2000. *Super Casino: Inside the "New" Las Vegas.* New York: Bantam Books.

Early, Steve. 2009. *Embedded with Organized Labor: Journalistic Reflections on the Class War at Home.* New York: Monthly Review Press.

"Economists: Casinos Could Bear Tax Increase." 2007. *Reno Gazette Journal,* 15 October, 3A.

EEOC v. Sage Realty, 507 F. Supp. 599 (SDNY 1981).

Ehrenreich, Barbara. 2001. *Nickel and Dimed: On (Not) Getting by in America.* New York: Metropolitan Books.

Ehrenreich, Barbara, and Arlie Russell Hochschild, eds. 2002. *Global Woman: Nannies, Maids, and Sex Workers in the New Economy.* New York: Metropolitan Books.

Eisner, Mark D., Alexander K. Smith, and Paul D. Blanc. 1998. "Bartenders' Respiratory Health after Establishment of Smoke-Free Bars and Taverns." *Journal of the American Medical Society* 280:1909–1914.

Enarson, Elaine. 1993. "Emotion Workers on the Production Line: The Feminizing of Casino Card Dealing." *NWSA Journal* 5(2): 218–232.

Erem, Suzan. 2001. *Labor Pains: Inside America's New Union Movement.* New York: Monthly Review Press.

Ericksen, Michael P. 1998. Office on Smoking and Health, National Center for Chronic Disease Prevention and Health Promotion, Centers for Disease Control and Prevention. Before the Committee on Environment and Public Works, US Senate, April 1. Available at http://epw.senate.bov/105th/eriksen.htm. Data accessed October 19, 2006.

"Facial Discrimination: Bartender Darlene Jespersen, Fired for Not Wearing Makeup, Accuses a Reno Casino of Gender Bias." 2000. *People* 54(25). Available at http://www. people.com/people/archive/article/0.20133197.00.html. Data accessed June 24, 2004.

Fernandez-Kelly, Maria Patricia. 1983. *For We Are Sold, I and My People: Women and Industry in Mexico's Frontier.* Albany: State University of New York Press.

Figart, Deborah, Ellen Mutari, and Marilyn Power. 2002. *Living Wages, Equal Wages: Gender and Labor Market Policies in the United States.* New York: Pantheon.

Figueroa, Hector. 1998. "Back to the Forefront: Union Organizing of Immigrant Workers in the Nineties." In *Not Your Father's Union Movement: Inside the AFL-CIO,* edited by Jo-Ann Mort, 87–98. New York: Verso.

Fitzsimons, Patrick. 1999a. "Managerialism and Education." Available at http://www. ffst.hr/ENCYCLOPAEDIA/managerialism.htm. Data accessed June 1, 2008.

——. 1999b. "Michel Foucault: Regimes of Punishment and the Quest of Liberty." *International Journal of the Sociology of Law* 30(4): 379–399.

Fool's Gold. The Silver State's Tax Structure: Inadequate and Inequitable. 2009. Las Vegas, NV: Progressive Leadership Alliance of Nevada (PLAN).

Foote, Catherine E., and Arthur W. Frank. 1999. "Foucault and Therapy: The Disciplining of Grief." In *Reading Foucault for Social Work,* edited by Adrienne S. Chambon, Allan Irving, and Laura Epstein, 157–187. Chicago: University of Chicago Press.

Forché, Carolyn. 1993. *Almost Forgetting: Twentieth-Century Poetry of Witness.* New York: W. W. Norton.

Foucault, Michel. 1980. *Power/Knowledge: Selected Interviews and Other Writings, 1972–1977,* edited by Colin Gordon. New York: Pantheon.

——. 1988. *Politics, Philosophy, Culture: Interviews and Other Writings, 1977–1984,* edited by L. D. Kritzman. New York: Routledge.

Frank v. United Airlines, Inc., 216 F.3d 845 (9th Cir. 2000).

Freeman, Carla. 2001. "Is Local:Global as Feminism:Masculine? Rethinking the Gender of Globalization." *Signs: Journal of Women in Culture and Society* 26(4): 1007–1038.

Freire, Paulo. 1986. *Pedagogy of the Oppressed.* Translated by Myra Bergman Ramos. New York: Continuum.

Fromm, Erich. 1965. *Marx's Concept of Man.* New York: Frederick Ungar Publishing.

Frumin, Eric, Joan Moriarty, Pamela Vossenas, John Halpin, et al. 2006. "Workload-Related Musculoskeletal Disorders Among Hotel Housekeepers: Employer Records Reveal a Growing National Problem." Detroit, MI: UNITE HERE.

Galbraith, John Kenneth. 1958. *Affluent Society.* New York: Mentor Books.

Galeano, Eduardo. 1995. *The Book of Embraces.* New York: W. W. Norton.

"Gaming Convention/Vegas." November 25, 1997. Philip Morris Tobacco Papers, Bates No. 2070292705A. Available at http://legacy.library.ucsf.edu/tid/bjo16c00. Data accessed November 1, 2006.

"Gaming Revenue Report." 2008. University of Nevada, Las Vegas Center for Gaming Research. Available at http://gaming.unlv.edu/abstract/nv main.html. Data accessed March 3, 2010.

Geron, Kim. 1997. "The Local/Global Context of the L.A. Hotel-Tourism Industry." *Social Justice* 24:85–102.

Gerrie, Sharon. 2001. "Servers Rail Against High Heels." *Las Vegas Review-Journal,* 16 June. Available at http://www.reviewjournal.com/lvrj_home/2001/Jun-16-Sat-2001/business/16337479.html. Data accessed September 4, 2006.

Glantz, Stanton. 1999. "Smoke in the Eye." Interview. *Frontline,* PBS. Available at http://www.pbs.org/wgbh/pages/frontline/smoke. Data accessed October 3, 2006.

Glassman, Bernard. 1999. *Bearing Witness.* New York: Random House.

Goodwin, Joanne L. 2002. "She Works Hard for Her Money: A Reassessment of Las Vegas Women Workers." In *The Grit beneath the Glitter: Tales from the Real Las Vegas,* edited by Hal K. Rothman and Mike Davis, 243–259. Berkeley: University of California Press.

Gorman, Tom. 2001. "Dealers Reject Union at Most Las Vegas Casinos." *Los Angeles Times,* 26 February. Available at http://articles.latimes.com/2001/feb/23/news/mn-29183. Data accessed February 20, 2010.

Greenhouse, Steven. 2004. "Organized: Local 226, 'The Culinary' Makes Las Vegas the Land of the Living Wage." *New York Times,* 3 January. Available at http://www.nytimes.com/2004/06/03/us/organized-local-226-the-culinary-makes-las-vegas-the-land-of-the-living-wage. Data accessed September 20, 2010.

Grisham, John. 1996. *The Runaway Jury.* New York: Doubleday.

Harding, Sandra, ed. 1987. *Feminism and Methodology: Social Science Issues.* Bloomington: Indiana University Press.

Hardt, Michael, and Antonio Negri. 2000. *Empire.* Cambridge: Harvard University Press.

———. 2004. *Multitude: War and Democracy in the Age of Empire.* New York: The Penguin Press.

———. 2009. *Commonwealth.* Cambridge: Harvard University Press.

Harrah's Entertainment, Inc., website. Available at http://www.harrahs.com.

Harrah's, Reno. 2000. "Beverage Department 'Personal Best' Program—Image Transformation Employee Sign-Off." In authors' possession.

Harrah's 2007 Annual Report—Form 10K. Available at http://www.sec.gov/Archives/edgar/data/858339/000119312508043934/d10k.htm. Data accessed October 9, 2007.

Hart, Herbert Lionel Adolphus. 1979. *The Concept of Law.* New York: Oxford University Press.

Harvey, David. 2005. *A Brief History of Neoliberalism.* New York: Oxford University Press.

Hausbeck, Kathryn. 2002. "Who Puts the 'Sin' in 'Sin City' Stories? Girls of Grit and Glitter in the City of Women." In *The Grit beneath the Glitter: Tales from the Real Las Vegas,* edited by Hal K. Rothman and Mike Davis, 335–346. Berkeley: University of California Press.

"The Health Consequences of Involuntary Exposure to Tobacco Smoke: A Report of the Surgeon General." 2006. U.S. Department of Health and Human Services. Available at http://www.surgeongeneral.gov/library/secondhandsmoke/fact sheets/factsheet5.html. Data accessed November 5, 2006.

Heskett, James L., Thomas O. Jones, Gary W. Loveman, W. Earl Sasser, Jr., et al. 1994. "Putting the Service-Profit Chain to Work." *Harvard Business Review,* March/April 64:164–174.

Hidalgo, Jason. 2010. "Nevada No. 1 for Distressed Properties in '09." *Reno Gazette Journal,* 14 January, 5A-6A.

Hondagneu-Sotelo, Pierrette. 1994. *Gendered Transitions: Mexican Experiences of Immigration.* Berkeley: University of California Press.

———. 2001. *Domestica: Immigrant Workers Cleaning and Caring in the Shadows of Affluence.* Berkeley: University of California Press.

hooks, bell. 1990. *Yearning Race, Gender, and Cultural Politics.* Boston: South End Press.

Hopkins, A.D. n.d. "Al Bramlet, 1917–1977. The Organizer. The First 100 Persons Who Shaped Southern Nevada." Part III. "A City in Full." *Las Vegas Review-Journal.* Available at http://www.1st100.com/part3/bramlet.html. Data accessed June 22, 2005.

Hulse, James W. 1986. *Forty Years in the Wilderness: Impressions of Nevada.* Reno: University of Nevada Press.

"Immigrant Workers Freedom Ride." 2004. Produced by The Culinary Union. Video, in authors' possession.

Insider (The). 1999. Directed by Michael Mann. Touchstone Pictures. Film.

Jackall, Robert. 1988. *Moral Mazes: The World of Corporate Managers.* New York: Oxford University Press.

Jacobs, Essie Shelton, interview by Claytee D. White. 1997. Las Vegas Women Oral History Project, University of Nevada, Las Vegas.

Jaggar, Alison M. 1983. *Feminist Politics and Human Nature.* Totowa, NJ: Rowman & Allanheld.

Jespersen v. Harrah's Operating Company, Inc., 280 F. Supp. 2nd 1189, 1192–1119. (D. Nev. 2002).

Jespersen v. Harrah's Operating Company, Inc., 392 F 3d 1076 (9th Cir 2004). Appellant's Opening Brief.

Jespersen v. Harrah's Operating Company, Inc., 392 F 3d 1076 (9th Cir 2004). Brief of amicus curiae.

Jespersen v. Harrah's Operating Co., Inc., 392 F.3d 1076 (9th Cir. 2004), 17457–17472. Opinion by Judge Tashima.

Jespersen v. Harrah's Operating Co., Inc., 392 F.3d 1076 (9th Cir. 2004), 17473–17479. Opinion by Judge Thomas.

Jespersen v. Harrah's Operating Company, Inc., 444F.3d 1104 (9th Cir 2006) (en banc).

Jespersen v. Harrah's Operating Company, Inc., 444F.3d 1104, 1117–18 (9th Cir. 2006). Opinion by Judge Kozinski.

"John Boushy, Senior Vice President and Chief Integration Officer." Available at http://investor.harrahs.com/bios.cfm. Data accessed June 1, 2005.

Johnson, Viola, interview by Claytee D. White. 1997. Las Vegas Women Oral History Project, University of Nevada, Las Vegas.

Jones, Jill B. 2008. "Economic Globalization and the Transmigration of Women Workers." *Social Work and Human Welfare in a Changeable Community—Proceedings of 21st International Social Work Conference.* Cairo, Egypt: Helwan University Press.

Jones, Jill B., and Susan Chandler. 2001. "Connecting Personal Biography and Social History: Women Casino Workers and the Global Economy." *Journal of Sociology and Social Welfare* 28:173–193.

———. 2007. "Surveillance and Regulation in a Globalized Work Site: Casinos and the Control of Women's Bodies." *Affilia: Journal of Women and Social Work* 22(2): 150–162.

Judd, Dennis R., and Susan S. Fainstein, eds. 1999. *The Tourist City.* New Haven, CT: Yale University Press.

"Judge Rejects Linking Lawsuits, Class Action Status Denied for Claims in Four Tobacco Cases." 2001. *Winston-Salem Journal.* 6 July. Journal Staff and Wire Report. Available at http://www.journalnow.com/wsj/business/MGB69PUA TOC.html. Data accessed July 17, 2006.

Jurik, Nancy. 2004. *Bootstrap Dreams: U.S. Microenterprise Development in an Era of Welfare Reform.* Ithaca, NY: Cornell University Press.

Kazis, Richard, and Marc S. Miller, eds. 2001. *Low-Wage Workers in the New Economy.* Washington, DC: The Urban Institute Press.

Kilby, Jim, Jim Fox, and Anthony F. Lucas. 2005. *Casino Operations Management.* 2nd edition. Hoboken, NJ: John Wiley & Sons.

Kingfisher, Catherine, ed. 2002. *Western Welfare in Decline: Globalization and Women's Poverty.* Philadelphia: University of Pennsylvania Press.

Kirn, Walter, and Jeffrey Ressner. 2004. "Poker's New Face." *Time Magazine,* 26 July. Available at http://www.time.com/time/magazine/artcle/0,9171,994714,00.hrml. Data accessed December 2, 2005.

Kluger, Richard. 1996. *Ashes to Ashes: America's Hundred-Year Cigarette War, the Public Health, and the Unabashed Triumph of Philip Morris.* New York: Alfred A. Knopf.

Korten, David. 1995. *When Corporations Rule the World.* San Francisco: Sierra Club Books.

Kossek, Ellen Ernst. 2006. "Work and Family in America: Growing Tensions between Employment Policy and a Transformed Workforce." In *America at Work: Choices and Challenges,* edited by Edward E. Lawler, III and James O'Toole, 53–72. New York: Palgrave Macmillan.

Kraft, James P. 2010. *Vegas at Odds: Labor Conflict in a Leisure Economy, 1960–1985.* Baltimore, MD: The Johns Hopkins University Press.

Krause, Niklas (with Pamela Lee, Pamela Thompson, Reiner Rugulies, and Robin Baker). 1999. "Working Conditions and Health of San Francisco Hotel Room Cleaners." Unpublished study. School of Public Health at the University of California, Berkeley.

Krause, Niklas, Teresa Scherzer, and Reiner Rugulies. 2005. "Physical Workload, Work Intensification, and Prevalence of Pain in Low Wage Workers: Results from a Participatory Research Project with Hotel Room Cleaners in Las Vegas." *American Journal of Industrial Medicine* 48:326–337.

Kroll, Luisa, Matthew Miller, and Tatiana Serafin, eds. 2009. "The World's Billionaires." *Forbes Magazine,* 11 March. Available at http://www.forbes.com/fdc/welcome_ mjx.shtml. Data accessed March 1, 2010.

Kunda, Gideon, and Galit Ailon-Souday. 2005. "Managers, Markets, and Ideologies: Design and Devotion Revisited." In *The Oxford Handbook of Work and Organization,* edited by Stephen Ackroyd, Rosemary Batt, Paul Thompson, and Pamela Tolber, 200–219. New York: Oxford University Press.

"Lambda Legal Appeals Federal Sex Discrimination Case on Behalf of Woman Fired from Harrah's Casino." 2003. Lambda Legal Defense and Education Fund. Available at http://www.lambdalegal.org/cgi-bin/iowa/news/press.html/. Data accessed June 21, 2005.

Lambda Legal Defense and Education Fund website. Available at http://www.lambda legal.org.

Lamphere, Louise, Alex Stepick, and Guillermo Grenier, eds. 1994. *Newcomers in the Workplace: Immigrants and the Restructuring of the U.S. Economy.* Philadelphia: Temple University Press.

Land, Barbara, and Myrick Land. 1999. *A Short History of Las Vegas.* Reno: University of Nevada Press.

"Las Vegas: An Unconventional History." 2008. *American Experience,* PBS. Available at http://www.pbs.org/wgbh/amex/lasvegas/. Data accessed May 10, 2009.

Las Vegas Review Journal. Bulletin board entry in response to a job seeker, how much do cocktail waitresses make in Las Vegas. Available at http://eforum.reviewjournal.cojm/lv/showthread.php?5=822. Data accessed December 4, 2009.

"Latest IRS Data Reveal Fundamental Mismatches in the States; Most Unequal States Either Don't Have a Personal Income Tax or Have One in Need of Improvement," April, 2006. Institute of Taxation and Economic Policy. Available at http://www.ctj.org/itep/iteppub.htm. Data accessed July 7, 2007.

Lather, Patti. 1991. *Getting Smart: Feminist Research and Pedagogy with/in the Postmodern.* New York: Routledge.

Lawler, Edward E., III, and James O'Toole, eds. 2006. *America at Work: Choices and Challenges.* New York: Palgrave Macmillan.

Lee, Pam Tau, and Niklas Krause. 2002. "The Impact of a Worker Health Study on Working Conditions." *Journal of Public Health Policy* 23(3): 268–285.

Leong, Grace. 2001. "Mirage Waitresses Win Legal Victory in Discrimination Case." *Las Vegas Sun,* 19 April. Available at http://www.lasvegassun.com/sunbin/stories/test/2001/apr. Data accessed May 17, 2005.

Letter from Robert W. Meyne to Frank J. Fahrenkopf, Jr. March 6, 1996. Philip Morris Tobacco Papers, Bates No. 52446 2522. Available at hhtp://legacy.library.ucsf.edu/tid/fjo40d00/. Data accessed November 1, 2006.

Levine, Phil. 2000. "Culinary Union Says Program for Workers Is Intrusive." *Las Vegas Sun,* 11 May. Available at http://www.lasvegassun.com/news/2000/may/11/harrahs-sets-appearance-standards/. Data accessed October 2, 2010.

Levinson, Meridith. 2001. "Harrah's Knows What You Did Last Night," *CIO,* 6 June. Available at http://www.cio.com.au/article/44514/harrah_knows_what_did_last_night. Data accessed February 18, 2009.

"Life at Harrah's." Harrah's Entertainment, Inc. website. Available at http://www.harrahs.com/harrahs-corporate/careers-life at harrahs/html. Data accessed June 13, 2009.

Lincoln, Yvonna S., and Egon G. Guba. 1985. *Naturalistic Inquiry.* Newbury Park, CA: Sage Publication.

Logsdon, Richard, Todd Scott Moffett, and Tina D. Eliopulos, eds. 2003. *In the Shadow of the Strip: Las Vegas Stories.* Reno: University of Nevada Press.

Lorde, Audre. 1978. "A Litany for Survival." *The Black Unicorn: Poems.* New York: W. W. Norton.

——. 1984. "Uses of the Erotic: The Erotic as Power." *Sister Outsider: Essays and Speeches.* Freedom, CA: Crossing Press, 147–153.

Louie, Miram Ching Yoon. 2001. *Sweatshop Warriors: Immigrant Women Workers Take on the Global Factory.* Cambridge, MA: South End Press.

Macy, Robert. 1997a. "Tobacco Deal Will Exempt Casinos." *AP Online,* 3 August. Available at http://www.aparchive.com/. Data accessed July 8, 1998.

——. 1997b. "Where There's Smoke There Are Profits, Casino Operators Say." *Los Angeles Times,* 30 November. Available at http://articles.latimes.com/1997/nov/30/business/. Data accessed January 3, 1998.

Mandel, Lev L., and Stanton Glantz. 2004. "Hedging Their Bets: Tobacco and Gambling Industries Work Against Smoke-Free Policies." *Tobacco Control* 13(3): 272.

Mander, Jerry. 1996a. "Facing the Rising Tide." In *The Case Against the Global Economy and for a Turn Toward the Local,* edited by Jerry Mander and Edward Goldsmith, 3–19. San Francisco: Sierra Club Books.

——. 1996b. "The Rules of Corporate Behavior." In *The Case Against the Global Economy and for a Turn Toward the Local,* edited by Jerry Mander and Edward Goldsmith, 309–322. San Francisco: Sierra Club Books.

Mander, Jerry, and Edward Goldsmith, eds. 1996. *The Case Against the Global Economy and for a Turn Toward the Local.* San Francisco: Sierra Club Books.

Marfels, Christian. 1999. "Concentration, Competition and Competitiveness in the Casino Gaming Industry." In *The Business of Gaming: Economic and Management Issues,* edited by William R. Eadington and Judy A. Cornelius, 29–44. Reno: University of Nevada, Reno Institute for the Study of Gambling and Commercial Gaming.

McCullough, David, David Morton, and Liev Schreiber. 2002. "People and Events: America's Beauty Culture. Miss America." *American Experience,* PBS. Available at http://www.pbs.org/wgbh/amex/missamerica/peopleevents/e_beauty.html. Data accessed May 31, 2008.

McDaniel, Janice. 1997. "Gaming Convention/Vegas," Philip Morris Tobacco Papers, Bates No. 2070292705A. Available at http://legacy.library.ucsf.edu/tid/bjo16c00. Data accessed November 1, 2006.

McNichols, Elizabeth, and Nicholas Johnson. 2010. "Recession Continues to Batter State Budgets: State Responses Could Slow Recovery." Center for Budget and Policy Priorities. Available at http://www.cbpp.org/cms/index.cfm?fa=view&id=711. Data accessed March 5, 2010.

"Measuring up 2000—State Profiles." 2000. National Center for Public Policy and Higher Education. San Diego, CA.

"MGM Cocktail Waitresses." 1994. Produced by The Culinary Union. In-house video.

Milburn, Peter D., and Rod S. Barrett. 1999. "Lumbosacral Loads in Bedmaking." *Applied Ergonomics* 30:263–273.

Milkman, Ruth. 2006. *L.A. Story: Immigrant Workers and the Future of the U.S. Labor Movement.* New York: Russell Sage Foundation.

Milkman, Ruth, and Kim Voss, eds. 2004. *Rebuilding Labor: Organizing and Organizers in the New Union Movement.* Ithaca, NY: Cornell University Press.

Miller, Kit. 2000. *Inside the Glitter: Lives of Casino Workers.* Carson City, NV: Great Basin Publishing.

Mills, C. Wright. 1959. *The Sociological Imagination.* New York: Oxford University Press.

Mishel, Lawrence, Jared Bernstein, and Heidi Shierholz. 2009. *The State of Working America 2008/2009.* Ithaca, NY: Cornell University Press.

Mitchell, Merwin C., and Yvonne Stedham. 1999. "A Profile of Pro-Union Casino Workers in Northern Nevada." In *The Business of Gaming: Economic and Management Issues,* edited by William R. Eadington and Judy A. Cornelius, 205–214. Reno: University of Nevada, Reno Institute for the Study of Gambling and Commercial Gaming.

Mittelman, James H. 2000. *The Globalization Syndrome: Transformation and Resistance.* Princeton, NJ: Princeton University Press.

Moberg, David. 2001. "Organization Man." *The Nation* 273(3): 23–29.

Moehring, Eugene. 2002. "Growth, Services, and the Political Economy of Gambling in Las Vegas, 1970–2000." In *The Grit beneath the Glitter: Tales from the Real Las Vegas,* edited by Hal K. Rothman and Mike Davis, 73–98. Berkeley: University of California Press.

Moehring, Eugene, and Michael S. Green. 2005. *Las Vegas: A Centennial History.* Reno: University of Nevada Press.

Mort, Jo-Ann, ed. 1998. *Not Your Father's Union Movement: Inside the AFL-CIO.* New York: Verso.

Mosle, Sara. 1996. "Letter from Las Vegas: How the Maids Fought Back." *New Yorker,* 16 February/4 March, 148–157.

Naples, Nancy A., and Manisha Desai, eds. 2002. *Women's Activism and Globalization: Linking Local Struggles and Transnational Politics.* New York: Routledge.

Narvarro, Vincente, ed. 2007. *Neoliberalism, Globalization and Inequity: Consequence for Health and Quality of Life.* Amityville, NY: Baywood Publishing Company.

National Center for Chronic Disease Prevention and Health Promotion; Nevada Highlights. Available at http://www.cdc.gov/tobacco/statehi/html_2002/nevada.htm. Data accessed August 30, 2006.

Nelson-Pallmeyer, Jack. 1997. *School of the Assassins: Guns, Greed, and Globalization.* Maryknoll, NY: Orbis Books.

"Nevada Study Links Casino Smoke, DNA Damage." 2006. *CBS News,* 16 May. Available at http://www.cbsnews.com/stories/2006/05/16/ap/health/mainD8H KHNCG0.shtml. Data accessed July 31, 2008.

"Nevada Tops in Smoking." *Gambling Magazine.* Available at http://gamblingmaga zine.com/articles/40/40–272.htm. Data accessed August 26, 2006.

Newitz, Analee. 2005. "Wear It, Bitch." *Alternet.org,* 12 January. Available at http:// www.alternet.org/story/20963/. Data accessed May 31, 2008.

Nichols v. Azteca Restaurant Enterprises, Inc., 256 F.3d 864 (9th Cir. 2001).

Noone, Judith. 1995. *The Same Fate as the Poor.* Maryknoll, NY: Orbis Books.

Occupational Wages. Nevada Workforce Informer. DETR Research and Analysis Bureau website. Available at http://www.nevadaworkforce.com/. Data accessed August 4, 2008.

O'Connor, Alice. 2001. *Poverty Knowledge: Social Science, Social Policy, and the Poor in Twentieth-Century U.S. History.* Princeton, NJ: Princeton University Press.

O'Leary, Ann, and Karen Kornbluh. 2009. "Family Friendly for All Families." In *The Shriver Report: A Woman's Nation Changes Everything.* A Report by Maria Shriver and the Center for American Progress, edited by Heather Boushey and Ann O'Leary, 75–109. Washington, DC: Center for American Progress.

One Day Longer: The Story of the Frontier Strike. 1999. Los Angeles: A Bal-Maiden Films Production. Documentary.

Ong, Aihwa. 1999. *Flexible Citizenship: The Cultural Logics of Transnationality.* Durham, NC: Duke University Press.

Ong, Paul, Edna Bonachich, and Lucie Cheng, eds. 1994. *The New Asian Immigration in Los Angeles and Global Restructuring.* Philadelphia: University of Pennsylvania Press.

Opton, Michael, ed. 1997. *Casino Business Directory.* (North American Edition). Reno: Nevada Gaming Publishing.

Orleck, Annelise. 2005. *Storming Caesars Palace: How Black Mothers Fought Their Own War on Poverty.* Boston: Beacon Press.

OSHA Communications Report. 1996a. Philip Morris, July 18. Bates No. 2061897534/7535. Available at http://legacy.library.ucsf.edu/tid/gqw47d00. Data accessed October 27, 2006.

OSHA Communications Report. 1996b. Philip Morris. August 1. Bates No. 2061897534/7516. Available at http://legacy.library.ucsf.edu/tid/gqw47d00. Data accessed October 27, 2006.

Osterman, Paul. 2006. "The Changing Employment Circumstances of Managers." In *America at Work: Choices and Challenges,* edited by Edward E. Lawler, III and James O'Toole, 211–226. New York: Palgrave Macmillan.

O'Toole, James, and Edward E. Lawler, III. 2006. *The New American Workplace.* New York: Palgrave Macmillan.

Packham, John. 2009. "Senate Bill 372 Guts Statewide Smoking Ban." *Reno Gazette-Journal,* 31 March, 1B, 3B.

———. 2010. "The 'Tobacco Sweep' and Other Assaults on Public Health." *Reno Gazette-Journal,* 16 February, 3B.

Palmer v. Del Webb's High Sierra 838 P.2d 4355.

Parrenas, Rhacel Salazar. 2001a. *Servants of Globalization: Women, Migration, and Domestic Work.* Stanford, CA: Stanford University Press.

———. 2001b. "Transgressing the Nation-State: The Partial Citizenship and 'Imagined (Global) Community' of Migrant Filipina Domestic Workers." *Signs: Journal of Women in Culture and Society* 26(4): 1129–1154.

Peiss, Kathy Lee. 1998. *Hope in a Jar: The Making of America's Beauty Culture.* New York: Metropolitan Books.

Perez, Emma. 1999. *The Decolonial Imaginary.* Bloomington: Indiana University Press.

———. 2003. "Queering the Borderlands: The Challenges of Excavating the Invisible and Unheard." *A Journal of Women's Studies* 24:122–131.

Peterson, Iver. 2005. "Casino with Weight Policy Finds Boon in Controversy." *New York Times,* 14 March, A20.

Pizer, Jennifer. 2006. "Analysis of the Humpty Dumpty Decision." *Barbwire,* 14 April. Available at http://www.nevadalabor.com/barbwire/barb06/docs/barb4–16–06pizer. Data accessed June 2, 2007.

———. 2007. "Facial Discrimination: Darlene Jespersen's Fight Against the Barbie-fication of Bartenders." *Duke Journal of Gender, Law and Policy* 14(13): 285–318.

"Policy at Harrah's Governs Appearance of Servers." 1999. *Gambling Magazine.* Available at http://www.gamblingmagazine.com/articles/26/26–408.htm. Data accessed June 3, 2005.

"Potential Impact of Smoking Bans on the Gaming Industry—Draft." 1996. Philip Morris Tobacco Papers, Bates No. 51446 2599. Available at http://legacy.library.ucsf.edu/tid/bjo16c00. Data accessed October 12, 2006.

"Preemptive State Smoke-Free Indoor Air Laws—United States, 1999–2004." *Morbidity and Mortality Weekly* Report Centers for Disease Control and Prevention, March 18, 2005, 54/10, 250–253. Available at http://www.cdc.gov/MMWR/preview/mmwrhtml/mm5410a4.htm. Data accessed April 12, 2007.

Price Waterhouse v. Hopkins, 490 (U.S. 228 1989).

Pritsos, Chris A., Gary Cutter, Sachiko St Jeor, Judith Ashley, et al. 2006. "Secondhand Smoke and Nevada Casino Workers: Exposure and Health Risks." 13th International Conference on Gambling & Risk-Taking. Reno: University of Nevada, Reno Institute for the Study of Gambling and Commercial Gaming.

Puzo, Mario. 1976. *Inside Las Vegas.* New York: Grosset & Dunlap.

Raento, Pauliina, and Kate A. Berry. 1999. "Geography's Spin at the Wheel of American Gambling." *Geographical Review* 89:590–95.

Rawe, Julie, Neil Gough, Carmen Lee, Austin Ramzy, et al. 2004. "Vegas Plays to the World." *Time Magazine,* 26 July. Available at http://www.time.com/time/magazine/article/0.917,994715,00. Data accessed August 2005.

Reid, Ed, and Ovid Demaris. 1963. *The Green Felt Jungle.* New York: Trident Press.

Rich, Frank. 2009. "Hollywood's Brilliant Coda to America's Dark Year." *New York Times,* 12 December. Available at http://www.nytimes.com/2009/12/13/opinion/13rich.html. Data accessed December 13, 2009.

Riessman, Catherine K. 1987. "When Gender Is Not Enough: Women Interviewing Women." *Gender & Society* 1:172–207.

Rios, Valerie L. Corson. 2003. *Casino Cocktail Waitresses: How Has This Profession Impacted Their Lives?* Master's project, Reno: University of Nevada, Reno.

Rose, Gillian. 1993. *Feminism and Geography: The Limits of Geographical Knowledge.* Minneapolis: University of Minnesota Press.

Rosenthal, Frank "Lefty." 1997. Interview. "Easy Money." *Frontline,* PBS. Available at http://www.pbs.org/wgbh/pages/frontline/shows/gamble/interviews/lefty.html. Data accessed August 13, 2006.

Rothman, Hal K. 2002. "Colony, Capital, and Casino; Money in the Real Las Vegas." In *The Grit beneath the Glitter: Tales from the Real Las Vegas,* edited by Hal K. Rothman and Mike Davis, 307–374. Berkeley: University of California Press.

———. 2003. *Neon Metropolis: How Las Vegas Started the Twenty-First Century.* New York: Routledge.

Rothman, Hal K., and Mike Davis, eds. 2002. "Introduction: The Many Faces of Las Vegas." In *The Grit beneath the Glitter: Tales from the Real Las Vegas.* Berkeley: University of California Press.

Rothman, Hal K., and Mike Davis, eds. 2002. *The Grit beneath the Glitter: Tales from the Real Las Vegas.* Berkeley: University of California Press.

Roy, Arundhati. 2001. *Power Politics.* Cambridge, MA: South End Press.

Rubin, Lillian B. 1976. *Worlds of Pain: Life in the Working-Class Family.* New York: Basic Books.

Ruiz, Vicki L. 1998. *From Out of the Shadows: Mexican Women in Twentieth-Century America.* New York: Oxford University Press.

Ryan, Cy. 2000. "Dealers Take Case against Tobacco to Supreme Court." *Las Vegas Sun,* 15 September. Available at http://www.lasvegassun.com/news/2000/sep/15/deal ers-take-case-against-tobacco-to-supreme-court/. Data accessed August 26, 2006.

Sallaz, Jeffrey J. 2002. "The House Rules: Autonomy and Interests Among Service Workers in the Contemporary Casino Industry." *Work and Occupations* 29:394–427.

Salzinger, Leslie. 2003. *Genders in Production: Making Workers in Mexico's Global Factories.* Berkeley: University of California Press.

Sassen, Saskia. 1998. *Globalization and Its Discontents.* New York: The New Press.

———. 2001. "The Excesses of Globalisation and the Feminisation of Survival." *Parallax* 7:100–110.

———. 2002. "Global Cities and Survival Circuits." In *Global Woman: Nannies, Maids, and Sex Workers in the New Economy,* edited by Barbara Ehrenreich and Arlie Russell Hochschild, 254–274. New York: Metropolitan Books.

———. 2004. "Local Actors in Global Politics." *Current Sociology* 52(4): 649–670.

———. 2005. "Regulating Immigration in a Global Age: A New Policy Landscape." *Parallax* 11(1): 35–45.

Schmitt, John, and Kris Warner. 2009. *The Changing Face of Labor 1983–2008.* Washington DC: Center for Economic and Policy Research.

Schoenmann, Joe. 2008. "These Feet Are Made for Walking." *Las Vegas Weekly,* 10 August, 6.

Scoblete, Frank. 2006. "Sunbeams." *The Sun* 372:48.

"Second-Hand Smoke Study Expanded to Northern Nevada." 2002. Available at http://www.sigoutlet.net/news/second_hand_smoke_study_expanded_to_northern_Nevada.html. Data accessed July 21, 2006.

Selmi, Michael. 2007. "The Many Faces of Darlene Jesperson." *Duke Journal of Gender Law & Policy* 14:465. Available at http://papers.ssrn.com/sol3/cf_ dev/AbsBy Auth.cfm?per id=183322. Data accessed March 12, 2010.

Sennett, Robert, and Jonathan Cobb. 1973. *Hidden Injuries of Class.* New York: Vintage Books.

Shailor, Barbara. 1998. "A New Internationalism: Advancing Workers' Rights in the Global Economy." In *Not Your Father's Union Movement: Inside the AFL-CIO*, edited by Jo-Ann Mort, 145–156. New York: Verso.

Sheehan, Hannah. n.d. "Into the Burkas We Go!" Available at http://www.esp.edu/burkas.htm. Data accessed May 16, 2005.

Sheehan, Jack E., ed. 1997. *The Players: The Men who Made Las Vegas*. Reno: University of Nevada Press.

Shepperson, Wilbur S., ed. 1989. *East of Eden, West of Zion*. Reno: University of Nevada Press.

Sherman, Rachel, and Kim Voss. 2000. "'Organize or Die': Labor's New Tactics and Immigrant Workers." In *Organizing Immigrants: The Challenge for Unions in Contemporary California*, edited by Ruth Milkman, 81–108. Ithaca, NY: Cornell University Press.

Shklar, Judith N. 1991. *American Citizenship: The Quest for Inclusion*. Cambridge, MA: Harvard University Press.

Shook, Robert L. 2003. *Jackpot! Harrah's Winning Secrets for Customer Loyalty*. Hoboken, NJ: John Wiley & Sons.

Sibelius, Steve. 2001. "Silence." *Las Vegas Review Journal*, 15 April. Available at http://www.reviewjournal.com/cgi-bin/printable.cgi?/lvrj_home/2001/Apr-15-Sun-2001/opinion/15871453.html. Data accessed March 2, 2010.

Simpson, Jeff. 2003. "Culinary Training Program Gets Financial Boost from Federal Government." *Las Vegas Review-Journal*, 21 October. Available at http://www.reviewjournal.com/lvrj_home/2003/Oct-21-Tue-2003/business/224. Data accessed September 28, 2007.

Smith, Catherine P. 1995. "Athena at the Manuscript Club: John Cage and Mary Carr Moore." *The Musical Quarterly* 79:351–367.

Smith, Dorothy E. 1987. "Women's Perspective as a Radical Critique of Sociology." In *Feminism and Methodology: Social Science Issues*, edited by Sandra Harding, 84–96. Bloomington: Indiana University Press.

Smith, Linda Tuhiwai. 1999. *Decolonizing Methodologies: Research and Indigenous Peoples*. New York: Zed Books Ltd.

Smith, Vicki. 2001. *Crossing the Great Divide: Worker Risk and Opportunity in the New Economy*. Ithaca, NY: Cornell University Press.

"Something Cooking." 2007. *Las Vegas Review Journal*, 11 July. Available at http://www.lvrj.com/business/8427907.html. Data accessed September 28, 2007.

Sorrells, J. 1996. OSHA Communications Report 12/20/1996. Philip Morris. 20 December. Bates No. 2078123205/3206. Available at http://legacy.library.ucsf.edu/tid/wyu75c00. Data accessed October 27, 2006.

"State of the States: The AGA Survey of Casino Entertainment." 2009. Washington, DC: American Gaming Association.

"Statewide Nevada Gaming Win, All Nonrestricted Locations." 2009. University of Nevada, Las Vegas Center for Gaming Research. Available at http://gaming.unlv.edu/abstract/nv_main.html. Data accessed March 3, 2010.

Stedham, Yvonne, and Merwin C. Mitchell. 1999. "Voluntary Turnover Among Nonsupervisory Casino Employees." In *The Business of Gaming: Economic and Management Issues*, edited by William R. Eadington and Judy A. Cornelius, 255–276. Reno: University of Nevada, Reno Institute for the Study of Gambling and Commercial Gaming.

Steger, Manfried B. 2002. *Globalism: The New Market Ideology*. Lanham, MD: Rowman and Littlefield.

Stewart, James B. 1998. *Follow the Story: How to Write Successful Nonfiction.* New York: Simon & Schuster Paperbacks.

Stinchfield, Randy, and Ken C. Winters. 1998. "Gambling and Problem Gambling among Youth." *The Annals of the American Academy of Political and Social Science* 556:172–185.

Strow, David. 2000. "Casino High Heel Policies Targeted." *Las Vegas Sun,* 11 February. Available at http://www.lasvegassun.com/news/2000/feb/11/. Data accessed June 12, 2005.

Stutz, Howard. 2007. "Casino Industry: Dealers at Wynn Resort Ratify Union." *Las Vegas Review-Journal.* Available at http://www.lvrj.com/business/7491402.html. Data accessed June 23, 2009.

"Survey Predicts Nevada Would Lose Big If Casino Smoking Were Prohibited." 1997. *Las Vegas Review-Journal,* 7 July. Available at http://legacy.library.ucsf.edu:8080/tid/shr45d00. Data accessed November 1, 2006.

Taylor, Candacy A. 2009. *Counter Culture: The American Coffee Shop Waitress.* Ithaca, NY: Cornell University Press.

Terkel, Studs. 1972. *Working: People Talk About What They Do All Day and How They Feel About What They Do.* New York: Pantheon Books.

——. 2003. *Religion and Ethics Newsweekly.* Interview, PBS, 19 December. Available at http://www.pbs.org/wnet/religionandethics/week716/exclusive.html. Data accessed March 14, 2010.

Thomas, Clive, and Ronald Hrebenar. 1999. "Interest Groups in the States." In *Politics in American States,* 5th edition, edited by Virginia Gray, Herbert Jacob, and Robert Albritton, 399. Glenview, IL: Scott, Foresman.

Thomas, Kate. 2009. "Don't Play Games with Atlantic City Casino Dealers." *Service Employees International Union,* 24 March. Available at http://www.seiu.org/2009/03/dont-play-games-with-atlantic-city-casino-dealers.php. Data accessed June 23, 2009.

Tiano, Susan. 1994. *Patriarchy on the Line: Labor, Gender, and Ideology in the Mexican Maquila Industry.* Philadelphia: Temple University Press.

Tout, Douglas, and John Decker. 1996. "Health Hazard Evaluation Report 95–0375-2590." Bally's Park Place Casino Hotel, Atlantic City, New Jersey.

Tsuboi, Kara, 2005. "Smoke Free Casinos?" *KOLO News,* 25 March. Available at http://www.kolotv.com/news/headlines/1396287.html. Data accessed July 31, 2008.

Tung, Gregory, and Stanton Glantz. 2008. "Swimming Upstream: Tobacco Policy Making in Nevada." San Francisco, CA: Center for Tobacco Control Research and Education, School of Medicine, University of California, San Francisco.

Turner, Byron S. 1991. "The Discourse of Diet." In *The Body: Social Process and Cultural Theory,* edited by Mike Featherstone, Mike Hepworth, and Bryan S. Turner, 157–169. London: Sage Publications.

"USA Casinos and Cardrooms—Nevada." 2006. *Casino City's Gaming Business Directory: Casinos, Cardrooms, Horse Tracks, Dog Tracks, Cruise Ships, and Property Owners.* Newton, MA: Casino City Press.

U.S. Census Bureau: Nevada. 2000. "Race and Hispanic Origin for Selected Large Cities and Other Places." U.S. Census. Washington, DC. Available at http://www.census.gov/population/www/documentation/twps0076/twps0076.html. Data accessed June 16, 2006.

U.S. Department of Health and Human Services. 2006. *The Health Consequences of Involuntary Exposure to Tobacco Smoke: A Report of the Surgeon General.* Full report available at http://www.surgeongeneral.gov/library/secondhandsmoke/. Data accessed November 5, 2006.

U.S. Environmental Protection Agency. 1993. "EPA Designates Passive Smoking a "Class A" or Known Human Carcinogen." EPA press release, January 7, 1993. Available at http://www.epa.gov/history/topics/smoke/01.htm. Data accessed October 2, 2010.

Vegas Message Board. Available at http://www.vegasmessageboard.com/forums/showthread.php?t=15098. Data accessed December 4, 2009.

Vogliotti, Gabriel. 1975. *The Girls of Nevada*. New Jersey: Citadel Press.

Waddoups, C. Jeffrey. 2000. "Unions and Wages in Nevada's Hotel-Casino Industry." *Journal of Labor Research* 21(2): 345–361.

——. 2001. "Unionism and Poverty-Level Wages in the Service Sector: The Case of Nevada's Hotel-Casino Industry." *Applied Economics Letters* 8(3): 162–167.

——. 2006. "Public Subsidies of Low-Wage Employment: The Case of Uncompensated Health Care." *Journal of Economic Issues* 40(3): 813–824.

Ward, Kathryn, ed. 1990. *Women Workers and Global Restructuring*. Ithaca, NY: Cornell University Press.

Weber, Karen. 1998. "Women's Career Progression in the Las Vegas Casino Industry: Facilitators and Constraints." *Journal of Hospitality & Tourist Research* 22(4): 431–449.

Welcome to the Culinary Workers Union, Local 226, Las Vegas, Nevada. Las Vegas: Culinary Workers Union Publication.

Whaley, Sean. 2001. "Bill Would Mandate Nonsmoking Rules in Casinos." *Las Vegas Review-Journal*, 2 March. Available at http://www.lvrj.com/cgi-bin/printable.cgi?lvrj_home/20. Data accessed August 29, 2006.

"What's the Status of Your State's Workplaces?" 2006. American Cancer Society. Available at http://www.cancer.org/docroot/NWS/content/NWS_1_1x_Smoking_or_Non smoking_Whats_the_Status_of_Your_States_Workplaces.asp. Data accessed October 11, 2006.

Whisner, Mary. 1982. "Gender-Specific Clothing Regulation: A Study in Patriarchy." *Harvard Women's Law Journal* 5:73–119.

Whitaker, Chuck. 2000. Beverage Department "Personal Best" Program. Letter to Food and Beverage Employees. (February). In the authors' possession.

White, Claytee D. 2003. "'Eight Dollars a Day and Working in the Shade': An Oral History of African American Migrant Women in the Las Vegas Gaming Industry." In *African American Women Confront the West, 1600–2000*, edited by Quintard Taylor and Shirley Ann Wilson Moore, 276–289. Norman: University of Oklahoma Press.

Whitford, David. 2007. "Losing the 'Auto' in United Auto Workers." *Fortune*, 12 September. Available at http://money.cnn.com/2007/09/11/news/uaw_casinos.for tune/index.htm. Data accessed June 23, 2009.

Williams, Amie. 2002. "Looking into a Dry Lake: Uncovering the Women's View of Las Vegas." In *The Grit beneath the Glitter: Tales from the Real Las Vegas*, edited by Hal K. Rothman and Mike Davis, 291–305. Berkeley: University of California Press.

Wilmott, Tim, and Susan Hailey. 2002. "How to Win with Harrah's." *Business Week Online*, May 2. Available at http://www.businessweek.com/bsschools/content/may2002. Data accessed June 10, 2007.

Winning Edge (The) website. Available at http://www.tweconsultinggroup.com.

Wolf, Naomi. 1991. *Beauty Myth: How Images of Beauty Are Used against Women*. New York: W. Morrow.

"Workplace Study Risks: Smoke Imperils Casino Staffs." 2006. *Las Vegas Review Journal,* 16 May. Available at http://www.reviewjournal.com/lvrj_home/2006/May-16-Tue-2006/business/7423494.html. Data accessed October 1, 2010.

Yates, Michael D. 2008. "The Injuries of Class." *Monthly Review* 58(8): 1–10.

Zinn, Howard. 2006. "The Optimism of Uncertainty." *A Power Governments Cannot Suppress.* San Francisco: City Lights Books.

Zuberi, Dan. 2006. *Differences That Matter: Social Policy and the Working Poor in the United States and Canada.* Ithaca, NY: Cornell University Press.

Index

Abrahamson, Heidi (cocktail waitress, pseudonym), 29–31, 36, 38, 39
Acker, Joan, 172–73, 199n3
Activism, among workers, 71, 133–34, 174
Addiction problems, among workers
  cocktail waitresses, 29, 38
  dealers, 97, 99, 121–22, 136
Adelson, Sheldon, 5, 9, 10
Affleck, Ben, 8
AFL-CIO, 121
African-American women, 47–60
  civil rights movement and, 49–50, 51, 53, 55–56, 68, 75
  individuals' stories, 47–50
  union organizational efforts, 50–60
Alexander, Courtney, 58, 59
Alliance for Workers Rights, 43, 93, 94
  Jespersen and, 88–89
American Civil Liberties Union (ACLU), 88, 93, 189n60
American Gaming Association, 147
Anderson, Bernie, 149, 150
Aptheker, Bettina, 125, 126, 129
Arnodo, Glen, 56, 74, 184n42
Arnold, Jim, 56, 59–60
Arriaza, Gilberto, 66
Atlantic City, NJ, 40
Avery, Diane, 95

Badillo, Tony, 120, 150–51
Badillo v. American Tobacco Co., 151
Baldwin, James, 174
Barbano, Andrew, 94, 143
Bartenders, 40, 81–82, 186n7
Bermudez, Alicia (housekeeper, pseudonym), 15–18, 25, 26, 66
Binion, Benny, 5, 60
Blake, William, 5
Borgata Babes, 40
Borgata Casino, Atlantic City, NJ, 40
Boushy, John, 84, 85, 186n19
Bowen, Cynthia (dealer, pseudonym), 114–15, 116, 123–24, 139
Boyd Gaming Corporation, 185n18, 195n6, 196n11

Bradford, Barbara (manager, pseudonym), 158–60
Bramlet, Al, 50–55
"Branded: Corporate Image, Sexual Stereotyping, and the New Face of Capitalism" (Avery and Crain), 95
Branding, at Harrah's, 83–86, 186n19
Brecht, Bertold, 174
Brown, Robert, 160
Burns, Mary
  background, 47–49, 51
  on Bramlet, 51–52
  Frontier Casino strike and, 68–70
Burpee, Sterling, 71
Butler, Gregory, 120

California, University of, San Francisco Medical School, 140, 142, 145
California Women's Law Center, 93
Canty, Hattie
  background, 6, 79–80
  Culinary Training Academy and, 72
  Culinary Union and, 55–60, 173
  Frontier Casino strike and, 68
  on Sarah Hughes, 52, 53
Carmona, Richard H., 152
Carroll, Mary, 91
Carroll v. Talman Federal Savings and Loan Association, 91
Carter, Jeanine (dealer, pseudonym), 109, 118, 126–30, 136
Citizens Concerned about Central America, 101–2
Citizenship Project, 71, 72–73
Civil rights movement, influence on labor movement, 49–50, 55–56
Clark, Maura, 101, 189n5
Clark County Welfare Rights Organization (CCWRO), 52, 183n20
Clients and guests, of casinos
  casino tracking of, 194n3
  cocktail waitresses and, 38–40
  loyalty and profits, 197n24
Cobble, Dorothy, 37

Cocktail waitresses, 29–43
    health and safety issues, 30, 35–37, 38, 43
    individuals' stories, 29–31, 35–36, 38–39,
        41–43
    nature of work of, 30–34, 37
    pay and benefit issues, 37–38
    relationships with casino guests, 38–40
    unions and power of, 36, 37–38, 41–43
Coleman, Rachel, 53
Concept of Law, The (Hart), 90
Conscientization, 3
Consolidated Safety Services, Inc., 147
Contreras, Estela (food server, pseudonym),
    27, 67
Cooper, Marc, 5, 84, 125, 194n3
Corporate gaming, 7–11, 53, 61
    control at casinos, 10–11
    nature of dealer's work and, 112–17
    political power and, 10–11, 55, 69, 94, 95,
        133, 140, 150–51, 169, 173, 174
Corporate Gaming Act
    Culinary Union after passage of, 53–60
    organized crime and, 8, 53
Cortez, Remedios (dealer, pseudonym), 114,
    130–34, 136, 138, 139, 196n12
Crain, Marion, 95
Culinary Training Academy (CTA), 71–72,
    165, 185n18
Culinary Union
    African-American women and, 47–60
    card check/card check neutrality and, 56,
        59, 74
    cocktail waitresses and, 37, 39
    Frontier Casino strike and, 54, 60, 68–70
    housekeepers and, 21
    immigrant women and, 61–68
    leadership of, 1–2, 18
    membership in, 59, 61, 184n58
    organizing campaigns in Nevada, 16–17
    partnership with casinos, 59, 71–73,
        165–66
    political power and, 2, 3, 5, 7, 42, 54, 75,
        184n57
    positions on immigration laws, 185n24
    projects of, 70–73
    September 11, 2001 and, 175–77

Davis, Mike, 195n6
Dealers, 109–36
    health issues and secondhand smoke,
        117–19, 122, 137–40, 150–53
    individuals' stories, 109, 111–16, 117–19,
        121–24, 126–36, 137–40, 150–53
    management's surveillance and control of,
        109–11, 135

    nature of work of, 115–17, 123–24, 125–26
    unions and, 110, 113, 119–21, 133, 191n24
Demaris, Ovid, 181n10
Denton, Sally, 8, 10
Dobra, John, 145–46, 193n37
Donovan, Jean, 101, 189n5
Dougherty, Joe, 69
Dreitzer, Daniele, 144
Duncan, Ruby, 52–53, 183n20

EEOC v. Sage Realty Company, 91–92
Egan, Pam, 71
Ehrenreich, Barbara, 169
El Salvador, 101, 189n5
Elardi, John, 68–70
Elardi, Margaret, 2, 60, 68–70
Elardi, Tom, 68–70
Elder, Linda (dealer, pseudonym), 134–36
Enarson, Elaine, 115
Environmental and Biological Assessment of
    Environmental Tobacco Smoke Exposure
    Among Casino Dealers (NIOSH study),
    153, 194n69
Environmental Protection Agency (EPA), 141
Environmental tobacco smoke (ETS). See
    Secondhand smoke (SHS)
Everett, Maxine (dealer, pseudonym), 119,
    121–23, 138, 139
Excaliber, 184n58
Eye in the sky surveillance, 10, 110, 115

Fahrenkopf, Frank, Jr., 147
Families, effect of casino work on, 170–74
Feldman, Alan, 118
Fine, Randy, 84–85
Fitzgerald's Casino, 2
FOCUS program, for dealers, 115, 116, 117
Ford, Ita, 101, 189n5
Foucault, Michel, 35, 168, 198n31
Frank v. United Airlines, Inc., 92
Freire, Paolo, 3, 28, 130
Frontier Casino, 1–2, 48
    strike against, 2–3, 54, 60

Gaming executives, 10, 32, 35, 85, 159, 168,
    195n10, 196nn11,12
Gaming Workers Council, 121
Gender issues
    casinos and "non-responsibility" for non-
        work life, 172–73, 199n3
    management and, 158, 195n6
    unions and, 21
Gender Public Advocacy Coalition, 93
Getting Smart (Lather), 191n9
Gieco, León, 177

Girls of Nevada, The (Vigliotti), 31–33
Glantz, Stanton, 142, 145
Globalization, 9, 19, 62, 161, 168, 197n14,
    197nn16,17, 199n3
Golden Nugget, Inc., 59
Good Morning America, 89
Green Felt Jungle, The (Reid and Demaris),
    181n10

Hancock, Carol (manager, pseudonym),
    161–63, 169
Hansen, Gloria (cocktail waitress, pseud-
    onym), 38–39
Harman, Edna, 97–106, 116, 118, 172
    background, 97–101
    liberation theology and, 6, 97,
        101–6, 133–34
Harrah's Entertainment, Inc., 9, 185n18
    employment advertisements, 157–58, 169,
        195n6, 196n11
    salaries, 160
    See also *Jespersen v. Harrah's Entertain-
        ment, Inc*
Hart, H. L. A., 90
Hasselman, Margaret, 91–92
Hausbeck, Kate, 33–34
Henry, Wanda, 41, 43
Hernan, Consuela (waitress, pseudonym), 65,
    66–67, 173
Hicks, Patrick, 95
Hill, Jeanette, 74–75
Hogan, Connie (dealer, pseudonym), 115, 116,
    117–19, 139
hooks, bell, 198n32
Hopkins, Ann, 92, 93
Hornbuckle, Bill, 110
Horseshoe Casino, 60
Horsford, Steven, 71, 75
Hospital Coalition for Indoor Air Quality
    (HCIAQ), 148
Hotel Employees, Restaurant Employees
    (HERE), 65, 184n4
Housekeepers, 15–28
    Canty on, 58
    health and safety issues, 15–16, 21, 23–24
    individuals' stories, 15–18, 20–22, 24,
        25–27, 28
    lack of respect for work of, 25–26
    mutual support among, 27–28
    nature of work of, 22–23
    pay and benefit issues, 24–25
    unions and, 21
Huerta, Josefina (activist, pseudonym),
    62–66, 67
Hughes, Heidi, 69

Hughes, Howard, 5, 8, 53, 54, 61, 69
Hughes, Sarah, 52–53

Immigrant women
    Harman's liberation theology work and,
        102–6
    housekeeping and, 16, 19–20, 27
Immigrant women, unions and, 61–68
    Citizenship Project and, 71, 72–73
    collective actions of, 67–68
    individuals' stories, 62–67
Immigrant Workers Freedom Ride, 73–74
Inside Las Vegas (Puzo), 32
International Union of Gaming Employees
    (IUGE), 120
Intimate Politics (Aptheker), 125, 126

Jackell, Robert, 168, 195n10
Jacobs, Essie, 47–48, 52
Jespersen, Darlene. See *Jespersen v. Harrah's
    Entertainment, Inc.*
Jespersen v. Harrah's Entertainment, Inc., 6,
    79–96
    Darlene Jespersen's background and work
        ethic, 80–82
    Personal Best Initiative, make up, and Jes-
        person's firing, 79–80, 82–88, 185n3
    rulings and reactions, 93–96
    Title VII and case law, 89–93, 187n40
Joffrion, Lydia, 70
Johnson, Viola, 49
Jones, Jan, 89

Kazel, Dorothy, 101, 189n5
Kefauver, Estes, 32, 181n8
Kennedy, Robert, 32, 181n8
Kiss My Foot, 43, 182nn36,37
Kline, Geoconda Arguella
    Culinary Union and, 1–5, 66, 67, 176–77
    Freedom Ride and, 73
    Frontier Casino strike and, 68, 69
Kozinski, Alex, 95

Lambda Legal Defense and Education Fund,
    89–90, 93, 94, 187n38
Language classes, at Culinary Training Acad-
    emy, 72, 165–66
Las Vegas, Nevada, 5–8, 11. *See also* Mafia/
    mob, in Las Vegas
Las Vegas Sands, 10
Last Honest Place in America, The (Cooper), 5,
    84, 125, 194n3
Lather, Patty, 191n9
Legal Aid Society—Employment Law Center,
    93

Lewis, John, 73–74
Liberation theology, Edna Harman and, 6, 97, 101–6, 133–34
Ling, Grace (dealer, pseudonym), 118, 139
Little, Michele, 86
Living wage, 172, 180n26, 190n13
Lomeli, Alejandra (dealer, pseudonym), 111–14, 119
Lorde, Audre, 129, 133
Louis, Genette (cocktail waitress, pseudonym), 35–36, 38
Loveman, Gary, 84, 85, 197n24

Macau, 9, 10
Mafia/mob, in Las Vegas, 6, 8, 50–55, 61, 119, 120, 181n6
Management, 157–69
   casino profits and, 162, 164, 168–69, 198nn32,38
   gender issues, 158, 195n6
   individuals' stories, 158–60, 161–68
   insecurity and, 160–61
   nature of work, 159–60, 167, 168–69
   salaries, 160, 165, 166, 196nn11,12, 197n13
Mander, Jerry, 163, 169, 197n14, 198n38
Marden, Reimi, 83
Marina Casino, 55
Marquez, Raquel (housekeeper, pseudonym), 20, 26, 27, 66
Marroquin, Kris (cocktail waitress, pseud-onym), 37, 41–43
Martinez, Asela, 73
Martinez, Kricket, 88
Maryknoll sisters, 97, 101–3, 189n5
Master Settlement Agreement (MSA), tobacco and, 142, 192n19
Maxey, Robert, 60
Maxim, 55, 57
McCallaghan, Mike, 54
Meyne, Rob, 142, 147
MGM Mirage, 9, 59, 60, 184n58, 185n18, 195n6, 196n11
Miller, Maya, 102
Miller, Valerie (housekeeper, pseudonym), 21–22, 28, 67
Moehring, Eugene, 10
Money and the Power, The (Denton and Morris), 10
Morris, Robert, 8, 10
Mystery shopper surveillance, 110, 135

National Employment Lawyers Association, 93
National Institute of Occupational Safety and Health (NIOSH), 138, 153, 194n69

National Institutes of Health tobacco study, 151–52
National Labor Relations Board, 56
Neal, Joe, 10
Nelson-Pallmeyer, Jack, 97
Neoliberalism, global capitalism, and post-industrial capitalism, 9, 161, 168, 172, 197n16, 198n29
Nesbit, Sharon (manager, pseudonym), 157, 163–66
Nevada
   corporate gaming in, 7–11
   smokers and, 143–44, 148–50
   tax policies in, 10–11, 188nn29–31
   welfare of children in, 173
Nevada, University of, in Reno, 140, 145, 146, 151
Nevada Casino Dealers Association, 120–21
Nevada Clean Indoor Air Act, 152–53
Nevada Resort Association, 32, 54, 154
Newtiz, Annalee, 94
Nichols v. Azteca Restaurant, 92–93
"Non-responsibility," corporate policy of, 172–73, 199n3
Northwest Women's Law Center, 93

Oalmer v. Del Webb's High Sierra, 150–51
Ohlemeyer, William, 151
Oppression of workers, 28, 116, 130, 133, 169, 174
"The Optimism of Uncertainty" (Zinn), 177–78
Organized crime
   Bramlet and, 52–55
   Corporate Gaming Act's effect on, 8, 53
   dealers and unions, 119–20
   investigation of, 181n8
   See also Mafia/mob, in Las Vegas
OSHA Communications Group, 142, 144, 145, 147
Osterman, Paul, 196–97n12

Packham, John, 153
Pedagogy of the Oppressed (Freire), 3
People Pledged to Excellence (PPE) program, for dealers, 115, 117, 123
Perkins, Charlie, 119
Philip Morris, 144, 145–46, 147–48, 151
Phillips, Pam, 175–76
Pit bosses. See Harman, Edna
Pizer, Jennifer, 90, 93, 94, 95–96, 187n38
Political power
   casino corporations and, 10–11, 55, 69, 94, 95, 133, 140, 150–51, 169, 173, 174

casino executives and, 10–11, 160,
    195nn6,10, 196n11
casino managers/supervisors and, 42, 65,
    165
casino workers and, 2, 3, 19, 22, 27, 42, 62,
    73, 75, 119, 130, 165
Culinary Union and, 2, 3, 5, 7, 42, 54, 75,
    184n57
relations of, 20, 26, 34–45, 91, 126, 129, 130,
    132–33, 168, 174
Preciado, Mirna
Culinary Union and, 1–5, 6, 7, 66, 67, 172–73
Freedom Ride and, 73
Frontier Casino strike and, 68–70
Price, Bob, 137, 150
Price, Teresa, 6, 137–40, 143, 149, 152, 153
Price Waterhouse v. Hopkins, 92, 93
Pritsos, Chris, 151–52
Pro, Philip, 151
Puzo, Mario, 8, 32

Ramige, Kathleen (cocktail waitress, pseud-
    onym), 35
Ramirez, Ana (housekeeper, pseudonym), 25
Reid, Ed, 181n10
Reno, Nevada, 5–6, 9
Resistance, against workplace policies, 7, 27,
    96, 130, 134, 138–69
REVPAC (Revenue Per Available Customer),
    84
Robinson, Katherine, 152
Rodriguez, Kate (manager, pseudonym),
    166–68, 169
Romero, Archbishop Oscar, 101
Rosenthal, Frank "Lefty," 8, 110, 120
Rothman, Hal, 51, 53, 69, 195n6
Ruffin, Phil, 70
Ruiz, Magdelana (housekeeper, pseud-
    onym), 170–71

Sage Realty Company, 91–92
Saren, Diana (housekeeper, pseudonym), 24
Satre, Phil, 84, 186n19
Schmoutey, Ben, 55, 59
School of Assassins (Nelson-Pallmeyer), 97
School of the Americas, 97, 102, 105
Schroeder, Mary, 95
Scoblete, Frank, 143
Secondhand smoke (SHS)
individuals' stories, 117–19, 122,
    137–40, 150–53
legal cases, 150–53
scientific studies of effects of,
    140–42, 151–53

supposed cost of smoking ban, 144–46,
    193n37
tobacco and gaming industry cooperation,
    140, 142–50
Seess, George, 71, 72
SEIU, 121
September 11, 2001, casinos and Culinary
    Union's responses to, 175–77
Sexual advances
cocktail waitresses and, 30–34
dealers and, 122
Sibelius, Steve, 11
Siegel, Benjamin "Bugsy," 5, 32, 33, 120, 181n6
"Solo le Pido a Dios" (Gieco), 177
Spilotro, Tony, 55
Station Casinos, 185n18
Stoneburner, Tom "Stoney," 39, 88, 94
Summa Corporation, 54, 69
Surveillance, of workers
eye in the sky, 10, 110, 115
mystery shopper, 110, 135
surveillance in general, 109, 110, 117, 123, 124

Talman Federal Savings and Loan, 91
Tax policies, in Nevada, 10–11, 188nn29–31
Taylor, D., 51, 56, 59, 69, 73, 74, 184n42
Thomas, Bernice, 72
Thomas, Sidney, 93–94
Thompson, Gary, 85
3 Square program, 72, 185n18
Title VII of the Civil Rights Act of 1964,
    Jespersen and, 89–93, 187n40
Tobacco companies. See Secondhand
    smoke (SHS)
Transformation, of workers, 6, 7, 27, 40, 62,
    70, 174
Transmigration, of workers, 9
Transport Workers Union of America (TWU),
    121
Treasure Island Luxor, 184n58
Tricky, Minnijean Brown, 74
Tynan, Roxana, 57, 58

Unions. See specific unions
United Airlines, 92
United Auto Workers (UAW), 121
UNITE-HERE, 120, 121, 184n4
"Uses of the Erotic, The" (Lorde), 129, 133

Ventilation systems, as proposed secondhand
    smoke solution, 146–48, 152
VESOL (Vocational English for Speakers of
    Other Languages), 72
Vogliotti, Gabriel, 31–33

Waddoup, Jeff, 199n8
Weber, Karen, 195n6
Weiss, Pilar, 73, 74–76
Whisner, Mary, 91
Whitaker, Chuck (manager, pseudonym), 79–80, 87
Whittemore, Harvey, 149, 150
Wiegand, Jeff, 142
Williams, Don, 10

WINet (Harrah's winner's information network), 84
Winn, Marilyn, 86
Winning Edge, The, 83, 86
Wynn, Steve, 5, 9, 10, 40, 59, 121
Wynn Resorts, 9

Zahn, Paula, 89
Zinn, Howard, 177–78